D1195525

THE GOVERNMENT
OF BUSINESS

Philip Allan textbooks in Business Studies

Consulting editors:

CHARLES BAKER
Professor of Business Studies and Director of
Durham University Business School

BRYAN CARSBERG
Professor of Accounting, University of Manchester

RAYMOND THOMAS
Professor of Business Administration,
University of Bath

THE GOVERNMENT OF BUSINESS

R. E. THOMAS

University of Bath

Philip Allan

021440

First published 1976 by
PHILIP ALLAN PUBLISHERS LIMITED
RED LION COTTAGE
MARKET PLACE
DEDDINGTON
OXFORD OX5 4SE

0 86003 501 8 (hardback)
0 86003 601 4 (paperback)

Typeset by Parchment (Oxford) Ltd
Printed in Great Britain by The Camelot Press Limited,
Southampton

CONTENTS

PREFACE

Business enterprises, whatever their ownership, are vital elements in modern society. Their activities affect both the daily lives of most of us and the economic — and therefore the social and political — progress of the community. They are in a continual state of evolution as they adapt to all manner of changes in their environment.

How they fit into the pattern of government in so complex a society as ours is therefore of interest not only to those whose immediate concern is their management but for all who seek a better understanding of their contribution to the progress of society. The range of possible readers to whom this book might be addressed is therefore wide.

First there are those men and women who are setting out to prepare for careers in business or government for whom an introduction to the main forms of business enterprise, their interaction with government and other institutions, and the assumptions as to their objectives are of direct concern. These range from undergraduates pursuing courses in business studies, economics, or management sciences to those who have already embarked on a career but who are now undertaking further studies of management issues.

Second there are those who, while not students as such, are concerned by the problems of interaction between firms and governments as the latter embark on increasingly interventionist policies. These are seen along with pressures for greater employee participation and consumer or environmental protection as adding to an increasingly complex, if not hostile, environment. Perhaps greater understanding of the 'system' may help them to assume a less defensive role.

Lastly there are those who are concerned at the unresolved issues concerning both the private and public sectors that increasingly sterile political argument does so little to resolve.

Whether as an introduction to business or economic organisation, or as a background to policy studies, the approach outlined in Chapter 1 draws upon the economic, legal, behavioural and political framework. In all but the last there is a substantial literature to which the references cited give a partial introduction. The evolution of the intervention of government is then discussed in Chapter 2 after which the main types of enterprise are reviewed. Government intervention is considered afresh in Chapter 8 after which general issues of accountability shared by all enterprises are reviewed in Chapter 9. The main conclusions are then brought together in Chapter 10. Study questions are appended to each chapter.

The present text is the first of two, the second being concerned with policy studies (*Business Policy*, 1977).

My thanks must go first to all those who, whether as students or managers, trades unionists or civil servants, have both stimulated me to write this book and contributed to the approach that I have adopted both here and in my teaching. Second, my thanks go to my wife, Cathleen, for patient support and constructive criticism as the text has evolved.

Raymond E. Thomas

ACKNOWLEDGEMENT

Tables 3.1, 3.2, 3.3, 3.4, 3.5, 4.1, 4.2, and 5.1 are reproduced by permission of the Controller of Her Majesty's Stationery Office.

1
THE CHANGING CONTEXT OF ENTERPRISE MANAGEMENT

1.1 Scope and Purpose

At a time of increasing turbulence in the economic scene, whether due to political uncertainties, technological changes, threats to supplies of resources or changing social values, it is appropriate to examine the forms of enterprise through which we operate the greater part of our commercial and industrial activities. This study seeks to introduce the reader not only to the forms of enterprise as conventionally portrayed and therefore the assumptions upon which they are thought to work, but also to the challenges posed for managers, governments and society as a whole.

Every year thousands of men and women enter business enterprises for the first time. Thousands more accept new responsibilities in roles that are conventionally described as managerial. The overwhelming majority are, and will remain, employees even though they may attain the highest level of roles in such enterprises. A minority aim to be self-employed and a minority of these may emerge as independent employers. Even these are likely to rely on the devices of partnerships and companies. All have to work within the constraints of both the economic system and the political framework; they have to adapt to and negotiate with those with the power to offer funds, with organised labour and with suppliers and consumers through the market place. In a Western society the combination of private capital, dispersed decision-taking on the use of resources and the right to free collective bargaining are all interacting within a framework of law and overall policy that is the responsibility of elected governments. Ever since the start of the 'Industrial Revolution' there has been what Van Der Haas has called a 'negotiated environment'[1]. Individuals and groups have negotiated both with each other and with government which, in turn, has regulated the environment within which all operate in each country.

But there are significant changes occurring in that environment that have to be understood and explored in any study of the enterprise. A key feature of Western societies hitherto has been the dispersal of economic initiative to enterprises that organised resources for specific purposes. Those in charge have been free to decide whether to continue to operate or not, and if so, in what direction.

Any study of the management of enterprises in the context of a mixed economy is concerned with power to take and implement decisions where there is inevitably interaction with other interests — trade unions, consumers, governments, other firms and various social pressure groups. There are at least four ways in which such a study might be approached.

The first, that of Industrial Economics, places a major emphasis on the role of markets, therefore on the type of competition, and with it, on the relation of size of firm to market influence. While such a basis of power cannot be ignored in this study, what is relevant is the degree to which enterprises seek to regulate competition through alternative arrangements culminating in mergers and governmental intervention.

The second, derived from management literature, relies mainly on the internal management problems that arise, on the possible managerial diseconomies to scale and the organisational and behavioural implications of both larger units and bureaucratisation. These are drawn upon but mainly in terms of the degree of turbulence in the environment with which the enterprise has to contend[2].

The third is to study ownership and control in parallel with the issues of size and growth either as Sargant Florence has done[3] or as part of the development of a theory for the growth of firms, such as that offered by Penrose[4], and the search for some new reconciliation of the observed behaviour of decision takers with the theories of the firm developed in economics[5]. The present study is concerned, inter alia, with the apparent divergence of established doctrine and observed practice but draws upon the fourth approach even more.

This is concerned with the analysis of the structure and decisions of enterprises in the economic-cum-political situation in which they have to survive. Studies such as those of Edwards and Townshend[6] and Channon[7] linked to the emerging interest in questions of strategy and objectives provide the context for the approach that follows. The stress is on the existing forms of business ownership and their regulation by government in the United Kingdom at a time of substantial challenge to, and change in, the role and standing of the enterprise in society. The enterprise or firm is taken as the key decision unit of the three identified by Sargant Florence[8] as the 'establishment', the 'firm' and the 'industry'.

The 'establishment' or 'plant' is the physical place of work or base of operations of a group of people performing interconnected tasks. It may be the same unit as the firm, as is so often the case with small businesses. However, many plants may be owned and controlled by a single firm.

The 'firm' is the governing organisation. Its precise legal identity may be no indication of whether it is truly independent, as firms own other firms. Therefore some extension of Sargant Florence's definition is required to identify the truly independent firm. Liebenstein has suggested three tests[9]. It must have the final decision on the use of profits, the choice of the principal activities through decisions on investment, and the appointment of key management personnel, thereby influencing the structure and style of the enterprise.

The 'industry' has been defined by Sargant Florence[10] as 'any kind of transactions (e.g. production) usually specialised in by a number of plants that do not usually perform any other kind of transaction.' Firms may operate in more than one industry though nationalised concerns may be confined by statute in this respect. While there is an intention to introduce 'sector planning' as part of national economic planning it is necessary to do this by planning agreements with companies, not industries.

The firm then is central to this study. But as an institution it is undergoing a radical challenge to the legitimacy of managerial decisions. Whereas in the past it could be accepted as a private institution — as very small firms still are — in which the founder or his successor appeared to base his authority to commence operations on the ownership of capital plus what may be termed an entrepreneurial role, this is no longer the case with larger concerns. Having started as small firms, many enterprises have grown into large bureaucratic organisations directed by professional managers subject to the checks of those who influence the supply of capital which comes increasingly via institutions that are similarly directed. Firms have been confronted by a widening range of countervailing pressures, first from employees through trade unions, now from consumer, environmental and minority groups and above all from government. The range of interests to be taken into account, if not demanding a share in the decisions of the enterprise, is widening.

Taking the mixed economy of the United Kingdom as our base, the first step in the power-sharing trend occurred when the separation of ownership and control began to appear. The subsequent spread of the demand for some control over their work situation, if not the policy of the enterprise, by employees has given rise to the demands not only for worker-representation through consultation and then joint decision-taking, but also to the representation of lower levels of management. The basis of power at the level where the strategy of a firm is determined in present forms of enterprise is ownership.

But sharing or involvement in decision-taking is not confined to those within a specific enterprise. An important aspect is the way in which firms may agree to subordinate their own freedom of action either in specific arrangements with other firms, e.g. suppliers or customers, or in joint action — often on an industry basis — to deal with external forces such as trade unions, foreign competition or relationships with government.

Yet another set of external influences are those of movements such as consumerism or the protection of minority interests which, while starting as voluntary initiatives, may subsequently be added to the range of governmental agencies. In each case the question arises as to how pressure can be exerted or interests represented. Is it sufficient, for example, that in any future reconstitution of the company membership of the ultimate governing body should be confined to ownership and employees or should there be a wider interest represented? Whatever the extent to which the private employer of the last century was aware of being in a 'negotiated environment' it is clear from the foregoing that the enterprise of today is very aware of it, not only at the individual nation-state level but also through wider regulations of that environment such as the European Economic Community, itself an attempt to produce a common basis for competition, not just through the removal of tariffs but by the 'harmonisation' of trading practices.

Central to this whole trend towards wider involvement is the question of accountability. Whereas it was once sufficient for the owner to make the most profitable use of his resources subject to very minimal social constraints and obligations, the view of the firm today is very different. It is seen as being entrusted with powers and resources for which it is accountable not only to the suppliers of capital but to those of other factors of production, notably labour, and to the community as a source of employment, a provider of goods and services, and a contributor, both positive and negative, to the quality of the environment. While in the past it may have been sufficient to be profitable it is now required to provide not only jobs but satisfying ones and it has to be much more politically and socially sensitive. This is all in the culture in which it is operating as a producer. But it may have to survive by selling in very different cultures; it may even have to operate in several national cultures and their associated political frameworks. Where the result is a multinational company then there can be special problems of accountability to any one nation-state.

While the firm remains the key unit it has to cope with two conflicting pressures. On the one hand if it is of any significant size or complexity then it has to provide for delegation to smaller units for many reasons. Product and process characteristics, specialised or dispersed markets, the need to involve staff and avoid alienation, and local community interests all work for delegation. Joint actions with other firms, whether trading ventures, common services or negotiations with trades unions and governments, all imply a larger unit possibly on an industry basis. The very dispersal of decision-taking and variety of managerial outlooks makes it much more difficult to get a coherent reaction from firms. Indeed it can be claimed that in the face of much criticism they have so far shown little convincing argument that they should be allowed to continue to enjoy their present autonomy in many respects.

Yet except where the state has — through nationalisation — replaced firms by an alternative unit of organisation, usually on an industry basis, they remain the key units. They can, however, be regarded as falling into four main types for the purpose of this study:

(1) *Private firms*
Sole proprietors
Partnerships
Private limited companies
Unquoted public limited companies   Chapter 3

(2) *Corporate Sector*
Quoted public companies   Chapters 4
                                              and 5

(3) *Foreign and multinational companies*   Chapter 6

(4) *State-owned sector*
    Nationalised industries   Chapter 7
    Companies in which the state
    has a major interest   Chapter 8

Two sets of issues are common to all forms of enterprise. The first is governmental influence and regulation. The general case for and features of such intervention are set out in Chapter 2. The second is the representation of interests other than capital and management. This is discussed in Chapter 9. The various implications and questions for future policy are discussed in Chapter 10.

Before proceeding to the particular types of enterprise, however, it is necessary first to examine their relative importance in the context of a mixed economy and then to consider the issues that arise in the growth of any business as it moves from one stage of management to another as a background to the subsequent study of the problems of authority and power sharing in larger enterprises. Section 1.2 is concerned with the former while sections 1.3 and 1.4 explore the issues posed by the latter including the emergence of a separation of ownership and control.

1.2 The Enterprise in the Mixed Economy

Any society has to devise a means of organising economic activities. In very primitive societies the tribe or family may be the group operating self-sufficiently. Modern industrial societies are based on a high degree of specialisation of tasks among both individuals and groups. This requires both a network of communications and widespread dispersion of decision-taking. Even an absolute dictator has to have a system of delegation of command and if there is also to be sufficient incentive for economic performance then there has to be decentralised control over the use of resources. Therefore, although in the present century a number of attempts have been made to establish highly centralised planned economies, the problems of economic scarcity and of incentive have compelled them to experiment with decentralised systems even to the point of restoring — if only to a limited degree — the use of markets. At the same time, those Western countries that have sought to meet the deficiencies of the free enterprise system by greater state intervention and replacement of market forces have found this to present very acute difficulties in the pursuit of either efficiency or stability.

British business has evolved from the self-employed person through the craftsman employing assistants to the small firm owned by one person who had complete control. Early attempts at larger ventures were in the hands of government and the Church. With the need for greater resources for trading ventures, powers were granted by the Crown to groups of venturers but it was only with the industrial revolution that new forms of enterprise became more widely needed. As long as the exploitation of new means of production — first with the switch from the domestic to the factory system, and then with the application of power and machinery — could be financed from the initial capital of one individual, subsequently reinforced by profits ploughed back into the system, then no new forms were needed. The development of the canals and then the railways could only go ahead with new institutions, the company on the one hand, and the development of a banking system on the other.

As the new technology gave great opportunities for cheapening production and expanding output there emerged a highly successful capitalist system side by side with ruthless exploitation of labour and disregard of the environment. The very success of the system led to the shift of much political and economic power to the new owner managers and in turn to an exceptional application of the ideas of laissez-faire. Yet precisely as this movement was reaching its fullest development, countervailing pressures for the regulation of the system were appearing. Governments sought to regulate the powers of private monopolies such as the railways, to regulate conditions of work and to introduce greater safeguards for those who dealt with companies. Opportunities for trade became an increasing concern of government in its dealings abroad but there was no attempt to regulate the conduct of the economy as a whole.

Even at the start of the present century the typical firm was owner-managed and of modest size. Marshall, writing in 1892[11], regarded very large firms such as those running railways as an exception having such problems that they would not be more widely used. It is therefore no accident that the prevailing economic thought was to remain geared to the idea of the small independent firm that was subject to the 'invisible hand' of the market. Yet the next twenty years were to see the start of the movement towards very much larger groupings of firms and the events of the First World War were to throw into sharp relief the deficiencies of British industry. The report of the

Royal Commission on Industry and Trade (Balfour report) 1927-9 with its concern for the size of firm and establishment and the need to rationalise production is all too familiar in the debates of 1976! The rapid concentration of ownership and control within firms, and the preoccupation of governments with the problems of those large firms that have been in industries faced with structural change has perhaps distorted our view both of the roles of firms of different sizes and the future sources of innovation and growth.

If at one end of the spectrum the problem is one of government and its relations with the very largest of firms, including those that are now owned by the State, then at the opposite end is the fate of the small firm. The Committee on Small Firms (Bolton) reporting in 1970[12] not only indicated their importance to the system in terms of both output and innovation but queried their future ability to perform even their present roles given the pressures of inflation, taxation and the whole standing of profitable business in British eyes.

The present 'mixed economy' is therefore to be seen as being 'mixed' in two senses. On the one hand there is the straightforward question of public versus private ownership of business enterprises, and on the other there is the extent to which decisions within the economy are in public and private hands. On the latter there are two aspects. First, there is the extent to which overall economic policy is regulated together with detailed intervention on specific issues such as regional policy or consumer protection. Second is the impact of the greatly expanded non-market sector of public services for which the government is almost solely responsible. The scale of its impact on resources is such that it requires the transfer of resources to meet public investment and current expenditure through taxation and borrowing on such a scale that on this count alone the role of government in the conduct of the economy is dominant. This is in sharp contrast to the position even forty years ago. Furthermore, the response of government to structural changes in the market sector has only served to increase the scale of its control over the disposition of resources so that the continued survival of enterprises does depend on public policy.

The question then arises as to what the policy might be in respect of each of the main types of enterprise. Hitherto the private sector as a whole — private and corporate sectors in the classification used here — has been self-financing through the financial institutions that have been evolved over two centuries.

More especially the corporate sector has been both financed and monitored through the working of the capital markets. Relationships are changing in two ways. First, there is a far higher degree of dependence on such institutions as firms find it impossible to be self-financing to the extent previously regarded as normal; second, there are changes in the role of the capital market when set alongside the scale and forms of governmental intervention even when the latter appear to work through existing institutions. As each form of enterprise is examined it is therefore essential to consider future public policy concerning the basis and even the extent of its evolution.

Even with this scale of governmental influence the criteria by which the working of the overwhelming majority of enterprises is judged remains that of the market economy with profit as a key measure of economic performance. But it is not the only criterion. Power and influence, which are to a degree a function of size, are important as is ability to survive. These are apparent as soon as we try to assess the relative sign:ficance of each of the main types of enterprise.

Any attempt to estimate the relative importance of the various forms of enterprise runs into two main difficulties. The first is the choice of test of importance — should it be numbers employed, gross product or investment committed? The second is the absence of data collected on this basis especially for smaller firms. However, in table 1.1 an attempt has been made using employment data for 1968 to estimate the relative importance as *employers* of the various sectors. This is then compared in table 1.2 with the number of firms in each category based on data for 1974. In both cases it should be noted that there have been significant transfers from the public company to the state-owned sectors subsequent to these returns, but at the time of writing it is estimated that they do not alter the order of importance in either table.

On the one hand, the use of employment data is a guide to scale that can be used over time without concern for the effects of inflation on money values; on the other hand, it has to be pointed out that the state-owned sector includes a number of particularly labour intensive and structurally declining industries. Public companies emerge as having the greatest significance though this is concentrated in the minority of them whose shares are quoted and dealt in. The data, being based on employment in the United Kingdom, underestimate their importance once account is taken of those mainly or exclusively

Table 1.1 *Types of business enterprise ranked by importance as employers with examples of industries/trades in which they operate*

Type of Enterprise	Ownership	Control	Industries/ Trades
Quoted public limited companies	Private shares transferable through stock exchanges	Directors elected by shareholders	All except those debarred by nationalising statutes plus professions; rarely in agriculture
Unquoted public private limited companies	Private restrictions on transfer of shares	Ditto	Ditto
Public corporations	Crown	Board reporting to Minister	Railways, gas, electricity, atomic energy, ports, steel (Not 100%), road passenger and freight transport (not 100%), British Airways
Public companies in which state has a major interest	State through NEB some private as for public companies	Board partly appointed by Government	Rolls Royce British Leyland, Ferranti, British Petroleum (49% stake), etc.
Unincorporated firms — sole proprietors and partnerships	Sole owner Partners		Professions, agriculture, fishing, horticulture, retail and wholesale trades, road haulage, hotels, catering and services

trading overseas. Apart, however, from the enterprises owned by the state they represent the smallest number of firms.

Private companies are estimated as coming second in

Table 1.2 *Types of business enterprise ranked by number of firms 1974*

Type of enterprise	Number of firms (estimates)	
Unincorporated		800,000
Private companies*	580,000	591,500
Unquoted public companies*	11,500	
Quoted public companies*		4,000
Public companies in which state has major interest		110
Public corporations**		31

* Companies effectively registered and trading in UK.
** Based on number covered by Select Committee on Nationalised Industries; Electricity and Gas Area Boards treated as subsidiaries.

importance. They are the prevalent form of business ownership in the private sector outside the public companies and those trades and professions in which they are replaced by unincorporated businesses. Updating the estimates prepared for the Bolton Committee studies of small firms, it is clear that unincorporated firms — that is sole traders and partnerships — are the exception outside agriculture and horticulture, fishing and those professions where the company form, at least with limited liability, is precluded by rules of professional conduct. While the number of independent unincorporated businesses is very large — especially if we treat all the self-employed as coming in this category — their contribution to employment is much less than the comparatively few organisations that constitute the two parts of the state-owned sector, which include the largest single employers in industry and commerce.

Lastly the types of activity in which each type is to be found offer several interesting points. The first is the clear restriction of the unincorporated firms to those industries and services having the least demands for capital and their exclusion elsewhere. The second is the wide spread of activities of private as well as public companies. The third lies in the key industries that have been taken into the state-owned sector, many of which through their policies have a bearing on virtually all the others, e.g. public utilities.

A distinction is made between the nationalised industries as such, and the firms in otherwise private sector trades that have been taken into public ownership. The main organisations in the former group cover most or all of an industry either directly or through wholly-owned subsidiaries. Policy issues have then to be judged on an industry basis rather than as one firm in an industry.

There are some omissions from the list because they are of far less total impact than the groups included. Foremost amongst these is the Cooperative movement. The main element in this is the Cooperative Wholesale Society. Originally set up by the retail societies, it has subsequently come to take over the operations of nearly all local societies through Cooperative Retail Services Ltd in view of their failure in the face of increased competition over the last two decades. Other cooperatives include some concerned with agriculture and at least three that have resulted from worker cooperatives being set up on the closure of plants with the collapse or contraction of activities of their previous owners.

Concerns of many types exist side by side in most trades and there may be a clear division of function between them on the basis of size and specialisation. As the Bolton Committee pointed out, the small firm as defined in its studies contributed at least 25% of the value of output in the trades included. It remains an important source of innovation and of new firms, a few of which may attain far greater scale and with it a change of form, though the view cited earlier from Marshall writing in the last century of 'a broad movement from below' of small firms maturing and replacing earlier larger firms is no longer as clear today. Not only is growth more difficult due to the high cost of entry in many trades but there is a high mortality among smaller firms, not only through failure but through absorption into larger firms that are seeking to diversify by buying their way into new trades.

While this gives an appreciation of the relative importance within the economy of the main forms of ownership there is another dimension which cannot be ignored. This is the influence of a minority of very large enterprises — mostly public companies, some publicly owned concerns but hardly any private companies — which are such large employers, generators of value of output and determinants of policy that they have to be treated in a league on their own. These can be taken to be the top 100 enterprises and they present special questions for the governance of the economy as they are, for example, the organisations with which government can be expected to be in regular contact[13].

1.3 Enterprise Management and Growth

The enterprise is examined first in terms of the internal management problems that emerge with increasing scale and complexity of operations. The immediate purpose is to focus on the problems facing the founder(s) of an enterprise, the stages through which they are likely to pass as they react to these problems, and the economic and power issues posed with the evolution from the one man business to the larger enterprise. The ultimate purpose is to bring out the political and structural questions to which the resolution of these internal problems may lead. In so doing it is possible to cover such topics as managerial economies of scale, the differentiation of operating, administrative and strategic decisions, and key questions of structure in relation to strategy.

At the start, in the smallest enterprises there is only one effective decision-taker. All these issues centre on that individual. He may well provide all the factors of production — labour, capital and management. The first step in growth is, therefore, the point at which he takes on his first employee. This is the first test of his ability to delegate responsibility, however small. The second comes when the number of employees has grown to the point where their immediate supervision has to be delegated, perhaps initially to one of their number, a chargehand in industrial terms, and then to someone who is a full-time supervisor. At this point a distinction is being made — even if it is not recognised as such — between operating decisions and other types of decision. Operating decisions are those needed within agreed policies and procedures. They may vary considerably in magnitude; supervision is only the first level at which they occur. But once the management task has been divided, two further questions appear. One relates to the number of such supervisors whom the proprietor can manage, an application of the concept of span of control; the other concerns selection and development of supervisors and therefore the ultimate question of management succession. The concept of span of control applies at all stages. At the level of supervision the span is bound to reflect the degree of control that the supervisor has to apply to the worker on the one hand, and the manager to the supervisor on the other. Both clearly involve several variables.

First among them is the nature of the task and of the consequent need for consultation and decision involving the coordinator, be he supervisor or manager. This can be expressed in terms of the frequency with which such contact is required, the scale of the decision involved, and the capacity and willingness of the parties. If the situation is one where, as in one-off production, perhaps of a complex and unfamiliar type, consultation has to be frequent then this must reduce the number of persons with whom a given manager/supervisor can maintain contact. An alternative would be the size of the decision in terms of funds to be committed and over what period of time.

Most critical of all is the capacity and willingness of the parties. This second question concerns knowledge and skill, incentive to delegate, training and development. At the core is willingness to delegate. So far, however, the argument has concentrated on growth over time, but even without growth there is the problem of management succession.

This has three aspects. First there is the problem of identification of an individual with a task whether it be running an entire firm or some much lesser responsibility. This is often an immense asset at the early development stage, and continuing personal interest often in matters of detail remains an important aspect of management control. But it can be carried to the point at which it threatens the ultimate survival of the enterprise. This is where the second problem emerges, that of ageing, leading to a slowing down and a conservative approach that is resistant to new ideas and circumstances. From here it is only a short step to the third, that of ultimate succession.

Herein lies one of the dilemmas of the small firm, as Boswell has pointed out particularly clearly[14]. The firm, in his view, passes into a 'transitional' phase, at which dynastic succession may present a real difficulty. The traditional family succession approach presumes the existence of a successor within the family group. When due allowance is made for the operations of both heredity and marriage there remains the earlier problem of how well — or how badly — the successor has been prepared, especially if dominant founders hang on too long, not giving their intended successors a fair chance to develop.

So far, however, our growing firm has remained relatively unspecialised in its management. It has remained essentially a small firm with a versatile top manager. But this is likely to change with only a modest increase in size. Thus specialisation occurs, not only as it engages in diverse activities, but even if it does not, then through specialised management. Advisors and supporting staff are introduced for such functions as accounting, personnel, marketing, etc. The firm now requires a team answerable to a chief executive, whom we are assuming to be the founder proprietor.

If the first major step in management is the recognition of separate supervision then the second is the existence of specialisation within management. The problems of coordination are now greater as delegation is no longer confined to operating decisions. There is at least a form of joint decision taking among managers on main procedures and over what may be called administrative decisions. For the men who set about building a firm from the smallest beginnings, this is a major step in power-sharing even though they are assumed, so far, to have retained ultimate control. Here a further reason for change is likely to lie. To reach this scale it is quite likely that others have had to be brought into the business, if only as investors, and it may be that the stage of joint control has already been reached. Even if succession stays within a family they have to agree on courses of action; there may be rivalries among them.

Clearly, the next stage is that at which there has to be joint decision on key strategic questions that lie at the core of the definition of an independent firm set out in section 1.1. These concern the continued separate existence of the firm, its principal activities and the investment needed to facilitate them, its key appointments and the main features of the style and structure of its management. The assumption that ultimate power to take these decisions lies with one or more persons who are both owners and managers in the enterprise has now to be modified and then dropped.

The modification is that the key owners withdraw from management, leaving this to hired professionals, and retaining for themselves ultimate control through their majority on the Board of Directors of a company. Just as the idea of being able to transmit ownership and management from one generation in a family to another is a characteristic of private firms, so is the notion that they have a responsibility for running it, which means direct personal involvement of at least one of them as a manager.

Clearly if they have no members able and willing to assume such a role, and owning families can be quite ruthless as to their own members in this respect, then the outcome is a new form of joint control in which effective power is increasingly shared with professional managers whose personal stake in the shares of the firm remains lower by comparison. With the passage of time and continuing growth a firm might well be approaching the separation of ownership and control associated with much larger concerns. However, the really successful, fast-growing firm is likely to have reached this stage of evolution as it has moved from being a successful private company to becoming a public company.

The managerial problems can be viewed in two phases. The first is to draw a distinction between levels of management role, notably between what Andrews has termed 'supervisory' and 'central cadre' management.[15] The second is to apply to the latter the concept put forward by Penrose of the 'receding managerial limit'[16].

Andrews has distinguished 'supervisory' management, that which is directly concerned with the supervision of operatives, and the cost of which is therefore related to the span of control, from 'central cadre' management, that which is concerned with overall planning and control. This distinction is important for several reasons, connected with the cost of management and the issue as to whether management is subject to economies or diseconomies of scale.

Supervisory management, in this context, increases in step with the numbers to be supervised, provided that the span of control remains constant. If the span contracts, and more supervisors are needed in relation to a given number of employees then, whatever the cause of this change, the outcome is a higher average cost of supervision. If, on the other hand, the span can be increased, as might follow from greater self-direction of work by employees with more participative systems and/or a change in their payment system, making them more self-regulating, then the opposite effect on costs would follow.

But as Melman has pointed out[17] the overall trend has been for a higher proportion of employees to be doing managerial, technical and clerical tasks, a tendency common to expanding and declining industries. This he puts down to changes in the nature of the management role which we may term 'widening' and 'deepening' of management influence. 'Widening' occurs where management seeks to extend the breadth of its influence by new responsibilities for, say, public relations, employee welfare, research and development. 'Deepening' is more detailed control within a given area of influence, such as is brought about by management services such as work study and operations research or by closer budgetary control. Either way more resources are involved and it is in the nature of their involvement that we may see a bridge to the concept of a 'receding managerial limit'. The bridge lies in an observation of Sir Francis Bacon cited by Plant[18] 'There may be three parts of business, the preparation, the debate or examination, and the perfection. Whereof, if you look for dispatch, let the middle be the work of many, and the first and last the work of a few'.

The founder of a business may well have performed all three stages for himself. His ability to find the time, especially for the search and analysis of alternatives prior to decision may well have been a serious constraint once he has got going. He may well have pondered on these issues before starting but once the business is in hand he comes up against a limit on his managerial time and capacity. As the firm grows, he may succeed in building up a management team. But his rate of growth, other things being equal, will largely depend upon that team and his and its ability to develop further.

This is not an easy task as the team, like the founder at an earlier stage, has finite resources which may be severely stretched at times. To a limited extent it may be reinforced by use of external agencies such as consultants and research agencies. But the process of choice, against the accumulated values and objectives of the firm, cannot be delegated or contracted out. Only the middle phase can be so treated.

What then are the constraints on the management team itself and especially its ability to augment itself by new development and recruitment? There are two: its own time, which is an outcome of the pressure upon its resources, and the time that is needed for any newcomer to learn the methods and ethos of the firm. Of course, the whole team has to be learning as it adapts to its environment where knowledge is increasing continually.

But so far it has been assumed that the enterprise has remained a single unit for management purposes. This does not imply only one physical establishment or activity but a sufficiently compact and homogeneous set of activities capable of being managed as an effective firm. With the growth in both the geographical spread of activities and the range of products and markets in which a firm is engaged there is a challenge to its 'widened and deepened' management, which may by now have acquired all the traits of a bureaucracy even though those in charge may deny this. The question that then arises is not only the separation of strategic from other decision levels but even the emergence of more than one level of strategic decision taking.

Thus the very large firms that have emerged partly by direct growth, partly by merger, may take one of two forms. They may attempt to run as single 'unitary' businesses through bureaucracies supported by complex data processing facilities or they may be loose 'federations' such as holding companies with subsidiaries that enjoy a high degree of autonomy. Studies of the relationship between strategy and structure show that the most prevalent tendency, first in the USA and now in the UK is towards the adoption of a divisionalised structure with the central enterprise investing in and overseeing perhaps many subsidiaries and divisions to which there is substantial delegation of power[19].

However, by the time an enterprise has reached this stage of evolution it has almost certainly passed another, the separation of ownership and control.

1.4 Separation of Ownership and Control

Even in the private firm with a family or group firmly retaining ultimate control, effective everyday management is often shared with, even wholly delegated to, managers whose claim to authority stems from a kind of professionalism in management. The public company has long been regarded as offering very great opportunities for the transfer of power. The immediate task is, therefore, to demonstrate why this should be so.

The starting point is the increase in scale of enterprises and therefore in the financial resources needed to sustain them. The whole point of 'going public' is to be able to appeal to a much wider investing public so as to receive much larger amounts of capital. But the very safeguards offered to this wider investing public — limited liability, the transferability of their shares not only without restriction, but through a highly sophisticated and well-informed market, the stock exchanges — create a very different relationship of investors of funds and managers of enterprises.

Once we leave the enterprise that is effectively owned and controlled by an individual — or even a small group — having a particular preference for continuing to operate independently, we move to the more typical public company which has attracted investment capital, the owners of which are concerned about the return on their capital and/or the appreciation of the value of their shares in the firm.

To the shareholder it is what its earning power, particularly its dividend, produces in the opinion of the stock market as represented by a price at which he could sell his share that matters. To the Directors it is what the firm as a whole has earned on all its capital employed, including consideration of what level of dividend the Board elects to pay having regard to how the stock market will value shares in the company relative to shares in other companies in comparable situations. The extent to which a Board is sensitive on this point reflects their dependence upon or independence of the market and their assessment of any threat of a take-over bid.

In theory the stock exchange performs two functions in a market economy. It redistributes profits and it evaluates company performance. If firms were to distribute to the maximum, then resources would be coming into the market for re-allocation to whosoever appeared to the market to offer the best prospects. Equally, if firms show poor performance, then, at least in theory, the stock market provides not only a sounding board against which performance can be judged, but a mechanism through which take-overs can be initiated which might then lead to a change in control aimed at improving performance.

Where a firm is felt to be less immediately sensitive to stock market pressures, either because it is a private company and therefore not quoted, or because although a quoted public company, it is regarded as secure from attack, then the Directors may feel able to take bolder decisions than where they are more sensitive to stock market opinion. In looking at enterprises, therefore, there are both advantages and disadvantages in each form. But overall, every firm in the private sector is ultimately subject to the market for its product. This is the rationale of the system, whatever the degree of independence that some larger firms appear to have developed.

The combination of scale, the nature of the interest of the shareholder in his investment, the opportunities offered by the stock market, and the opportunities open to a Board of Directors, place the latter in a very powerful position. Effective control may pass into the hands of a largely self-perpetuating group, whose personal stake and interest is discernibly different from the owner-manager of both the smaller firm and the public company that retains owner-manager dominance, whether through share ownership or merely through the mechanics of Boardroom succession.

The question that has then to be asked is what evidence is there of the extent of this tendency, and how is it developing? For this the principal UK studies are those made by Sargant

Florence of data for 1936 and 1951 as followed up by Radice[20] and Holl[21]. In his first study Florence analysed the shareholdings of the 82 largest UK companies in 1936. At that time only four of these companies had a person or family in control of more than 50% of all voting shares, but there was owner family dominance in 23 companies. Such dominance was assumed to exist if the person or group held 20% or more of the shares with no other person or group holding 10% or more. At the same time he found that there were 25 companies where another company or a financial institution had a similar dominance. In contrast he found no dominance, that is no person or group having even 10%, in seven of the companies.

In his second study he used a very much larger sample — 268 companies — and these covered a much wider spectrum of sizes of firms. This time he extended his range of tests to include the collective shareholdings of the Directors and the inclusion of Directors among the top 20 shareholders. These data have been further analysed by Holl using additional data compiled by the Department of Applied Economics, Cambridge. On this basis a sample of 183 companies shows management control in 127 cases compared to owner-control in only 56.

Radice examined all firms in three industries, food, electrical engineering and textiles, that had net assets of £5M in 1963. He found that out of 86 firms, 28 were owner-controlled, 42 management controlled, and 14 were transitional. The remaining two had control through, in one case, non-voting shares and the other 'pyramiding'[22]. Radice also showed that there had been little change in the overall situation from 1957 to 1967. Radice and Holl both reported increased dispersion of share ownership which would facilitate effective control by holders of smaller blocs.

1.5 The Enterprise and Society

It is a far cry from the self-employed person or even the very small employer to the kind of corporate enterprise that has come to dominate so many branches of trade and industry. The proprietor of the one-man business, apparently accountable only to himself, has given way to an enterprise owned by one set of people — or by other enterprises — directed by a second group and looked upon by society as a provider of employment, a source of exports, a place for training future employees, a source of tax revenue and a whole host of other expectations.

The corporate enterprise has come to be regarded as the norm and legislation is framed accordingly so that the small firm becomes an aspirant for exemptions and special treatment rather than the model against which all other enterprises are compared.

In these circumstances it is surely appropriate to contrast the two approaches to enterprise accountability. On the one hand there remains the original concept of ownership as the source of authority with accountability in the first place to the owner(s) of the enterprise. Partnership and Company law reflect this and the formal constitutions of corporate enterprises give it practical expression. Yet the self-employed citizen has always had obligations to others whether under common law or through successive statutes. Perhaps most important is the extent to which individuals enter into contracts which limit their sovereignty and specify obligations to those with whom they trade and those whom they employ.

The alternative approach based on the range of interests that have to be considered in the direction of any enterprise is therefore equally well established[23]. The student of economics has to recognise that what a firm can achieve is limited on the one hand by internal systems, such as the technical system in the form of methods and resources, and the information system represented by the accounting system; on the other hand the firm is a part of a wider economic system and a socio-political system which encompasses both internal and external relationships[24]. The student of business policy or corporate strategy is consequently concerned with decisions about objectives, responsibilities and constraints[25]. Each firm has to identify these in its own situation and given its own choice of ethos and style.

This is represented diagrammatically in figure 1.1. On the left are the suppliers of factors of production, the inputs to the firm which include management itself; these merge with wider interests whether of finance and investment or of community relations. On the right are the users of the output, principally the immediate and ultimate consumers of its products but also the wider community represented ultimately by government. At stake is a more fundamental issue, namely whether there is a convergence or a divergence of interests, and therefore whether the situation is sustainable. If it is not, then 'constitutional' arrangements may be of little avail.

Three approaches are considered here, the shareholder approach advocated by free enterprise theorists, such as Hayek

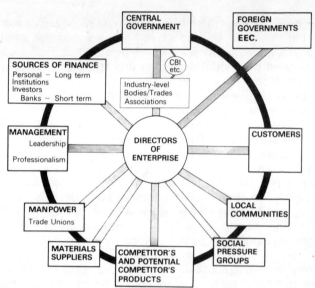

FIGURE 1.1 Forces affecting enterprise management

and Friedman, the stakeholder approach, as portrayed by Dahrendorf, and the Marxist approach[26]. The first two imply the survival of something akin to the present system; the third assumes its almost total replacement.

The first view denies that the situation in respect to corporate enterprises is any different from that of the small firm under capitalism. In the balance of forces within the enterprise it is the shareholders' interest that must prevail, whatever the apparent roles of the directors, and firms can fulfil their social purposes by concentrating on profit maximisation. While it is acknowledged that information systems hardly ever permit profit maximisation as envisaged in parts of economic theory, the continual striving for profits as the basis of survival, let alone growth, is the key to the efficiency and the social justification of enterprises. Firms should not therefore embark on the kind of spending, whether within themselves or in relation to society, that Galbraith depicted in respect of the larger corporations; they should confine themselves to seeking maximum profits in the interests of their shareholders, and distributing these as dividends so that shareholders could decide on where to invest, not the boards of directos[27].

While this may be an acceptable view for smaller enterprises it is clearly in sharp conflict with the evidence on how larger firms are directed in almost any major Western country, let alone the framework of influences of government and society.

On the one hand, the rugged individualist as a type is portrayed as performing a key role in the economy and his values and style are what need to be sustained and extended. Yet all the pressures of society as reflected through government and even the representatives of business point to a very qualified acceptance of such an ideal. Indeed, it can be argued that while abundant lip service is paid to it, the practice is significantly closer to the second approach, that of convergence of interests. Factors as widely different as the values of the private educational system, the basis of public honour and esteem, and the emphasis on 'team spirit' have been blamed for this outcome[28].

This is not to deny the existence of an influential body of people actively subscribing to this approach among the business community, especially in the small firm sector but also in what may be broadly termed the City. On the contrary, one of the dilemmas is the extent to which many whose roles and role performance are very different continue to claim adherence to this approach[29].

The second approach, that based on a convergence of interests, starts with a recognition of the power situation within and around the corporate enterprise. It recognises that the firm is not a single individual but as Cyert and March put it, a coalition of individual and group interests[30]. The starting point of their behavioural theory of the firm is therefore the way in which a firm arrives at decisions on objectives and then on specific policies. This is seen as a process of debate and negotiation from which agreed objectives emerge. Policies are then developed by comparing expected and attained performance to current reality as perceived by the organisation. These policies may challenge and even change the previously agreed objectives. Throughout, the assumption is that for the enterprise to survive a form of consensus has to emerge, whatever its period of survival.

The stakeholder approach to the modern enterprise starts from the premise that managers will seek to maintain such a consensus. To do so they have to develop harmonious relationships with all the interests involved, and to accomplish this they are presumed to take a non-sectional view of their own role. By this is meant that they will not impose their own personal interests to the exclusion of consensus. The point here is that they are not 'neutral' balancing agents setting off the claims of finance, labour, suppliers or customers against one another; they have a self-interest which is identified with remaining in office to enable them to pursue certain goals that they perceive as being in the long-term interest of all parties to the enterprise.

This view of their interest is linked to the idea that power can be derived from office held, as in a bureaucracy, as opposed to that based on ownership. Whereas in smaller firms ownership is clearly the basis of power, in larger concerns office held, including the professional skills and expertise needed to perform it, emerge as an alternative source of power. This has led to the development by Marris of a theory of the performance of firms based on the need to remain independent and therefore in office[31]. The enterprise is seen at least as an uneasy coalition of economic interests if not a potentially harmonious system.

In sharp contrast is the Marxist view that the firm is no more than a potentially unstable vehicle for economic exploitation. It relates power to ownership and sees the so-called managerial revolution as no more than a change in specific exploiters. The founder capitalists are seen as having been replaced by financiers who in turn have given way to a technocratic management class that exercises power for the protection of its own kind through the exploitation of workers and consumers. Furthermore this class is common to both capitalist and non-capitalist societies as Burnham argued[32]. To those who take this view, the sooner the system is replaced the better and the outcome is some form of socialism, having at least a facade of workers' control, but associated with a strong state direction with which all personal interests are assumed to be capable of alignment.

In practice the common pressures of markets, public opinion, sectional interests and their representative bodies, government and the attitudes and ideas among 'professional managers' reduce the significance of this difference between a sectional and a consensus view of enterprise management. This is not to deny the extent of conflict and of thinking in conflict terms among both employers and managers on the one hand and trade union activities on the other, but it is an assertion that, for better or for worse, UK enterprises are influenced towards maintaining some form of consensus, at least at enterprise level, and this can be seen in such pronouncements as have been made on the social role of business and business management by representative bodies.

What is clear is that, as in other aspects of company affairs, some firms are in effect setting new standards in the acknowledgement of a wider basis of accountability, at least to the extent of recognising issues upon which they have to take a more socially responsible view as opposed to a narrow sectional interest. This is, however, in answer to both governmental and sectional or privately stimulated pressures. Thus lobbies on environmental questions or consumer protection or on aspects of human relationships at work (discrimination) have been successful in their own right. They have spearheaded a considerable intervention by government leading to a marked extension of statutory requirements and controls. By far the most pressing is the question of accountability to employees, the issue of worker participation, more fully discussed in Chapter 9.

Central is the issue of to whom is an enterprise to be accountable in future? Is it to remain apparently only accountable to owners but having a range of statutory and contractual obligations to others? Is it to be as the TUC has proposed, a bi-partite body representing owner/shareholders on the one hand and the employees through their trade unions on the other? Or is it to be a tri-partite body as in the Netherlands where the state nominates 'independent' members to create a balance of interests represented?

The evolution of the enterprise like that of its 'negotiated environment' poses questions about the further evolution of the forms of enterprise appropriate to the needs of society.

This study is therefore set in the following framework. Activities occur in groups and places that can be broadly defined as 'plants' or 'establishments' which are owned and administered by 'enterprises' or 'firms'. Decisions in such enterprises are of three kinds: operating, administrative and strategic. The key decisions that distinguish the 'independent' enterprise are those of a strategic nature — whether to continue in existence, in what direction and style, and through whom? Such independent enterprises may be run as single 'unitary' or more loosely 'federal' or as 'divisionalised' enterprises. What is then of interest is the interaction of power to determine or influence policy at the level of the enterprise including the extent to which this is partly — or entirely — transferred to industry level and the ways in which decisions at both enterprise and industry levels interact with the endeavours of governments to guide the overall conduct of the economy. As a first step the principal features and justification of the present 'negotiated environment' within which the enterprise works are considered in Chapter 2.

Throughout there are two further influences at work, one of

immense political significance — the trade unions. While the main arguments concerning employee participation are deferred to Chapter 9, the trades union presence at every stage now involves a much wider range of interests. At the level of the plant or establishment there has to be negotiation and consultation, now with the added backing of legislation to facilitate the extension of trade union membership even as a condition of employment. At company level there is the same pattern but on a wider scope than at plant level and now with the added possibility of some form of worker-directors or alternative arrangements. At industry level there is an established practice of negotiation between employers' associations and groups of trades unions. Lastly, at national level governments not only consult but virtually negotiate with the Trades Union Congress through its General Council and permanent officials.

The other area is that of professional standards and conduct where self-regulating institutions exert very great influence on the evolution of acceptable practice. With the increasing 'professionalism' of management this raises the question of possible codes of conduct for the very people whose roles are the subject matter of this text, those with ultimate responsibility for the long-term direction of enterprises.

Notes and references

1   Van Der Haas, *The Enterprise in Transition,* Tavistock Publications 1967, Ch. 2.

2   E. Emery, *Systems Thinking,* Penguin Management Readings 1969, Part 3.

3   P. Sargant Florence, *Logic of British and American Industry,* Routledge & Kegan Paul 1953, Part I.

4   E. Penrose, *Theory of the Growth of the Firm,* Basil Blackwell 1959.

5   R. Marris, *Economics of Managerial Capitalism,* Macmillan 1964.

6   R. S. Edwards and H. Townshend, *Business Enterprise,* Macmillan 1958.

7   D. Channon, *The Strategy and Structure of British Enterprise,* Macmillan 1973.

8   P. Sargant Florence, *op. cit.,* Ch. 1.1

9   H. Liebenstein, *Economic Theory and Organisational Analysis,* Harper International Reprints 1965, p. 153 ff.

10 P. Sargant Florence, *op. cit.,* Ch. 1.1

11 A. Marshall, *Economics of Industry,* Macmillan 1892.

12 *Committee of Inquiry on Small Firms,* Cmd 4811, HMSO 1971.

13 D. Channon, *op. cit.*, Ch. 9.
14 J. Boswell, *The Rise and Decline of Small Firms,* Allen & Unwin 1973.
15 P. W. S. Andrews, *Manufacturing Business,* Macmillan 1949, Ch. 4.
16 E. Penrose, *op. cit.*, Ch. 4.
17 S. Melman, *Dynamic Factors in Industrial Productivity,* Oxford University Press 1958.
18 A. Plant, *Modern Business Problems,* Longmans Green 1937.
19 C. Channon, *op. cit.*, Ch. 7 & 8.
20 M. Radice, Control type profitability and growth in large companies, *Economic Journal* 1971, p. 547 ff.
21 P. Holl, Effect of control type on the performance of the firm in the UK, *Journal of Industrial Economics* 1975, p. 257 ff.
22 Pyramiding: the device whereby a holding company controls through subsidiaries with a combined capital which may be a multiple of its own.
23 J. Child, *The Business Enterprise in Modern Industrial Society,* Collier Macmillan 1969.
24 D. C. Hague, *Managerial Economics,* Longmans 1968, Ch. 1.
25 A. Ansoff, *Corporate Strategy,* Penguin Books 1968.
26 J. Child, *op. cit.*, Ch. VI.
27 A. Rubner, *The Ensnared Shareholder,* Penguin Books 1966.
28 J. P. Nettl, Consensus or elite domination, *Political Studies,* Vol. 13, 1965.
29 T. Nicholls, *Ownership, Control and Ideology,* Allen & Unwin 1969.
30 R. Cyert & J. Marsh, *Behavioural Theory of the Firm,* Prentice Hall 1963.
31 R. Marris, *op. cit.*
32 J. Burnham, *The Managerial Revolution,* Penguin Books 1942.

STUDY QUESTIONS

1 Taking any industry not under public ownership identify the principal organisations that appear to regulate or speak for it, and their scope.

2 How would you decide whether a firm was 'independent'?

3 Why is the separation of ownership and control of interest to society?

4 Account for the continued survival of the small firm.

2
GOVERNMENT AND THE NEGOTIATED ENVIRONMENT IN BRITAIN

2.1 Evolution of the Roles of Government and Business

The concept of the 'negotiated environment' is based, first, on the role of government in creating and regulating a framework within which individuals, enterprises and groups can interact, second, on the extent to which they then seek to regulate their immediate environments by collective action and, third, on the interaction of government with them in pursuing their goals and in seeking to further political and social aims. At first the role of government, once the 'mercantilist' system was being abandoned, was confined to creating conditions under which a largely self-governing business community dominated the direction of the economy and was free to develop such institutions and arrangements as appeared to further its interests. Yet even at the height of laissez-faire, it was evident that merely establishing a general body of law within which individuals were apparently free to act left major abuses and excesses which were to arouse consciences to the point of forcing statutory minimum standards of provision and conduct. As long as there continued to be confidence in the ability of the capitalist system to sustain economic progress, and as long as the prevailing body of political and economic opinion remained so strongly supportive of the free enterprise system, with a minimal role for the state in economic affairs, the main pressure for intervention or regulation was that generated by the business community itself with, as a second element, the emergence of trades unions to protect the interests of wage-earners.

If the repeal of the Corn Laws in 1846 and the last of the Navigation Acts in 1849 represent the final landmarks in this movement for a laissez-faire society, it is equally true that the first landmarks of the new collectivism and paternalism had already been passed with the Factory Act in 1833 and the legislation on railways and on companies in 1840 and 1844 respectively. If the passing of the Reform Act 1832 had swept away one political power based on hereditary privilege in favour of the industrial business classes, the establishment of friendly societies and the new craft unions around 1850 marked the first step in a new collective movement for the wage-earning classes.

Initially, the business community was concerned with maintaining and extending the opportunities open to the new order. Businessmen got together on matters of local and wider interest such as the needs of their localities, as local government appeared as the instrument to provide much of the infrastructure, or questions of access to foreign markets at government level. The emergence of trades unions evoked a strong reaction among employers and led to much closer joint action which was later to spread to other sources of challenge to their established positions, notably that which resulted from new sources and forms of competition.

However, the most immediate effect of changes both before and after the First World War was on the extent to which there was a move to regulate competition. In the years leading up to 1914 there had been a series of important mergers and agreements to restrict competition such as those which attended the foundation of the Imperial Tobacco Company and the arrangements between it and British and American Tobacco (BAT's) which were to last for close on seventy years. The earlier reliance on the law in restraint of trade gave way to widespread collective action, collusion and even the involvement of government in protective arrangements now that free trade had been abandoned with the McKenna duties in 1915, and there was a move towards the concept of Imperial Preference finally attained in 1932.

Faced with surplus capacity in traditional industries, the loss of markets with technical change as well as widespread economic nationalism, there was a need for structural change, though this was only slowly recognised. Throughout the rest of the nineteenth century there was a gradual return to regulation of the conduct of various aspects of business and the appearance of interventionist measures designed to correct what were already seen as fundamental weaknesses in our industrial system. The Great Exhibition of 1851 was itself a major event in this process of influencing the outlook and actions of business men, engineers and designers. The new technical facilities of railways, town gas and, later, electricity, the telegraph and telephone were all to lead to regulation of monopolies in public utilities, to the compulsory amalgamation and nationalisation of telegraph and telephone services, and to increasing control over prices and even profits. But the laissez-faire philosophy still dominated trade policy and was to continue to do so until 1914. Yet in addition to the better known intervention in wages and the labour market, the last Liberal Government provided for a Development Fund to stimulate industrial and scientific innovation. It also acquired the government's stake in what is now British Petroleum in 1913 when it purchased a controlling interest in the then Anglo-Iranian Oil Company.

The First World War transformed the situation. The deficiencies of British industry compared to that of Germany were thrown into sharp relief as early as 1915. Emergency measures had to be taken, many of which had lasting effects. A system of controls in the allocation of resources and eventually on prices had to be introduced. To achieve this there had to be a major extension of the government machine and this was greatly helped by the development of self-governing arrangements by industry through trade and employers' associations. There were important innovations in research and in the whole structure of communication between government and business. Although much of this was dismantled very rapidly in 1919, the experience had been gained.

These were soon to be put to new uses as governments were compelled to intervene more and more in the face of rising and persistent unemployment, especially after 1930. The report of the Balfour committee had pointed the way to a structural change in industry through what came to be known as rationalisation. This involved mergers, sometimes under strong banking and even government pressure to bring about larger units and enable surplus capacity to be scrapped. The outcome was a range of interventions including subsidies, guarantees, grants and direct intervention in the rationalisation process in steel, shipbuilding, coal, cotton and wool. Protection was linked to plans for rationalisation as in the steel industry from 1932 onwards, with the result that normal processes of competition were partly replaced. Only in the field of overall budgetary policy did the old beliefs prevail; Keynes was not to get his new conception of such policy accepted until the exigencies of the Second World War put him in a position to convince government of their relevance.

Yet the 1930's are strewn with new interventions ranging from the Special Areas Acts to the Agricultural Marketing Boards. The laissez-faire view of industrial location was still official Board of Trade policy when evidence was laid before the Barlow Commission in 1937,[1] but an interventionist policy had been launched two years earlier. A range of special 'Commissions' were set up to handle issues in a whole range of industries, some of which became the objects of direct intervention as in sugar beet, dyestuffs and shipping and ship-building.

The Second World War carried the process even further than the first, initially in much the same way, the machinery of government being extended and supplemented in conjunction with the trade associations of the various industries. There was also tripartite cooperation at national and local levels including government, employers and trade unions. In government the sheer mechanics of controls led to the system of 'sponsoring' departments. The system involves each of a number of departments assuming responsibility for the welfare and progress of a defined group of industries, not only in terms of controls imposed by government, but as a first step in government-industry cooperation and even a form of indicative planning. As a part of this policy isolated enterprises were brought into public ownership e.g. Short Bros.

In contrast to 1919, the post-1945 period saw on the one hand an extension of governmental control and an attempt at national economic planning. At industry level, apart from the extension of the public sector to include the Bank of England, railways and associated road, harbour and shipping interests, coal, electricity, gas and steel, there was a complex web of controls over resources, building, the raising of capital, and the location of activities. There was even an attempt at reorganisation through joint action in a number of industries dominated by smaller, but highly individualistic firms through the Industrial Development Councils authorised by the Industrial Development Act 1947.

On the other hand, through both existing and new institutions there was an attempt to revive the market economy in a more vigorous form than pre-1939. This had two main features. First, the Monopolies Act 1948 inaugurated a process of change in attitudes and policies that reflected the pragmatism of the British approach. Although modelled on American practice in so far as its investigatory role was concerned, the new commission could only investigate situations referred to it by government, and all monopolies established by government were outside its purview, as were labour practices. Its main impact in the first eight years was on the climate of opinion through exposing the nature and extent of restrictive practices, while concluding that it would be wrong to stop one set of businesses using them while others were free to do so. In 1956 the next stage took the form of outlawing a range of practices collectively enforced unless those engaged could show that the practices were in the public interest on any one of a range of grounds. Individual enforcement, notably of resale price maintenance was not brought to an end on a similar basis until 1963. But the effect of these measures combined with new groupings in trade and industry, especially in the distributive trades, was to restore the vigour of competition in many sectors but at the same time to force those who sought to continue to act together to merge with one another, especially after 1964.

Second, the new institutions of the state sector were not removed wholly from the market economy. On the contrary, the new 'state capitalism' placed emphasis on 'breaking even', on competition between one state concern and another, and between state and private enterprises. In particular, in key sectors such as transport and energy the customer was left free to choose between modes or sources according to his own interests.

By 1952 economic recovery and a change of government had brought a slowing down in the extension of interventionism, some direct reversals with denationalisation and the demolition of much of the physical controls of the previous decade. Nevertheless, government now had immense influence on the industrial scene through public ownership not only in the power and transport industries, but also in about one hundred other companies, set up or acquired from time to time. Through the three industrial estate corporations it owned an expanding acreage of industrial space in all the development areas, and through the Atomic Energy Authority and the National Research Development Corporation it had a stake in the sources of new ideas in the key expanding industries. Overall, its buying and sponsoring power dominated industries for which it was the main home market, enabling it to dictate their organisation and policies as it was to do in the regrouping of the aircraft and nuclear power equipment industries in later years.

The range of exhortations, inducements and subsidies showed no sign of contraction; on the contrary both in their own right and as side effects of tax policies they were to become more important even if more discontinuous as time passed. The philosophy until the early 1960's emphasised the reliance on market forces and competition, notably with the progressive strengthening of Monopolies and Restrictive Practices legislation in 1956 and 1963. Only towards the end of the Conservative government was there a major development in relationships with industry, the establishment of the National Economic Development Council and its supporting bodies in specific industries in 1961-2.

While governments reorganised here and there, the aircraft industry, the post office, computers and the private sector in civil aviation, the private sector itself was in the first phase of a merger boom which was to reach its peak in the late 1960's to the accompaniment of a new wave of interventionist policies from the Labour government. The most important features over this period were the operations of the National Board for Prices and Incomes and the Industrial Reorganisation Corporation, together with the provisions of the Industrial Expansion Act 1968.

The Prices and Incomes Board, although immediately concerned with price increases and wage/salary awards, did undertake a review of underlying policies and productivity which stimulated ideas and moves on questions of structure and control. The Industrial Reorganisation Corporation was concerned with facilitating the restructuring of key parts of the private sector and therefore was a notable new departure in interventionism. Established against the background that a more interventionist policy was required than the institutions appeared willing to exercise, the IRC chaired by Lord Kearton with Charles Villiers as Managing Director, figured in a series of important mergers, notably those which brought about the GEC/AEI merger and the British Leyland take-over of the British Motor Corporation[2]. Some of these mergers were in direct opposition to what might have been the outcome if left to the market, as for example in the case of George Kent Ltd, which was denied to the Rank Organisation. Backed by borrowing powers from the Treasury the IRC sought to restructure a number of key industries. Of necessity, those in difficulty and seeking government financial assistance found themselves objects of its attention. One consequence was a further extension of government holdings in companies and these are just some of the many to be transferred to the National Enterprise Board. The short life of the IRC ended with the change of government in 1970 as did the National Board for

Prices and Incomes, but the retreat from interventionism was short-lived.

Although proclaiming a change of policy away from what were termed "lame ducks", the new Conservative government found itself faced with the collapse of Rolls Royce and of Upper Clyde Shipbuilders, itself a product of a merger of Clydeside shipbuilders including Fairfield's, itself in turn the centre of an earlier reconstruction involving government, private finance and trade union support. While steadfastly refusing to prevent the liquidation of both companies, the government undertook to take over that part of the Rolls Royce undertaking that was considered vital in the aircraft industry for defence and provided support to enable a truncated Upper Clyde Shipbuilders to continue operations. This they were able to do partly under the Industrial Expansion Act 1968, partly by special legislation and partly by the Industry Act 1972, under which power was taken to advance up to £570 millions in the first instance to assist ailing firms in development areas.

2.2 Intervention in the Market Economy

Governmental intervention in the conduct of enterprises in the market sector can be examined in four stages: 1 there is the regulation of the internal government of enterprises; the reasons for, and the forms of such intervention have to be reviewed; 2 the extent to which, for whatever reason, government seeks to have decisions made on an industry rather than an individual firm basis, and the implications that this can have for the individual firm; 3 the types of decision that government seeks to influence at the level of the firm and the ways in which this influence may be given effect; 4 the ways in which governments influence the choices of firms in general through their interventions in the conduct of the market economy as a whole.

1 Some of the earliest forms of control and intervention have concerned the internal government of enterprises. From the first joint ventures involving royal charters to the legislation on partnerships and companies the grant of privilege has carried obligations. Over time, the latter have become more specific and onerous. The original aim was to protect those who had dealings with bodies corporate by making sure that they knew that such firms were acting within their powers and by offering

safeguards against default on obligations. It remains the right of the creditors of a company to instigate proceedings for its compulsory winding up if there is no other way of ensuring that their debts are recovered. But whereas the earlier aim was to protect those trading with companies, the more recent legislation has concentrated on enabling the shareholders themselves to have the opportunity including the information which would permit them to exercise control over the conduct of the firms in which they have invested. This reliance on disclosure of information has latterly assumed a much wider significance with the recognition that a much wider public has an interest in the conduct of a given enterprise — employees, suppliers, customers and those who are indirect stakeholders, such as those whose pensions or insurance provision are related to the investments of financial institutions in equities. In particular, information is the basis for financial comment and even possible external challenge to the present balance of power within a company.

These are the important aspects of external vigilance on the conduct of firms. There are, in addition, specific powers in respect of companies under which inspectors may intervene to investigate aspects of company affairs though the evidence to date is that such action is taken reluctantly and on a very limited scale. What is now more pertinent is whether in any future reform of company legislation there ought to be a radical redefinition of the interests to be considered, to take account not only of employees as sought by the TUC but consumer and other interests. Indeed, the whole basis of sanctions to managerial authority and the accountability of those directing enterprises is a matter of debate.

Given their importance and the opportunities for independent action by directors it is inevitable that the main body of legislation is concerned with companies. Furthermore, in view of their significance to the economy, the quoted public companies occupy a special place and this is associated with the market mechanism through which their affairs are monitored — the stock market. Government has sought to influence the conduct of the market partly through pressure to stiffen the rules and conventions that govern take-over and similar transactions, partly by requiring that mergers that pose questions of public interest may be referred to the Monopolies and Restrictive Practices Commission, and partly by encouraging a more positive collective action by the main investing institutions. To this must then be added the direct action in the market of government agencies such as the Bank of England, the National Enterprise Board and the former Industrial Reorganisation Corporation. One outcome is the continuing debate as to the future form of regulating machinery for the stock exchange; does the market need an equivalent to the Securities Exchange Commission in the USA? Intervention to date has been associated with rescue operations for specific firms such as Burmah Oil or Rolls Royce, and with attempts at reconstruction in key industries where government has a major interest as a customer or sponsor, e.g. aircraft and atomic power station plant. The more general aim has been to ensure that the market works fairly for investors as a whole and not to the exclusive advantage of those with 'inside' knowledge or power derived from the virtual disenfranchisement of the majority of shareholders as in the case of the Rank Organisation. This has been largely associated with the exceptional wave of merger activity over the past twenty years.

2   The second main impact on firms as such is where government seeks to act on a much wider basis such as an industry or sector, either in economic planning at national level or in determining codes of practice or standards of provision of support on an industry or product basis. Thus in planning future policy for the economy as a whole, including the nature and scales of investment in public services, government may seek information on intentions. This has hitherto been done partly by consultation with representative bodies, partly through the 'Little Neddies' — the Economic Development Councils for particular industries under the auspices of the National Economic Development Council — and partly by direct consultation with a limited number of the largest firms each being representative of an industry.

In future the provisions for disclosure of information under the Industry Act 1975 together with the planning agreements with a number of firms now being sought represent an extension of this approach. At the same time there is a further extension of the machinery for consultation on a range of standard practices such as material and product standards, safety and health hazards, training standards and consumer protection safeguards. These are largely handled by semi-autonomous agencies set up by government but acting subject to advice and consultation with the trades and industries concerned. Services provided from public funds are also handled through such agencies, notably the Employment

Services and Training Services Agencies of the Manpower Commission. Here the consultation takes in both employers and trades unions with provision for other relevant interests such as education, minority groups and the disabled.

The issue that all these pose for the individual firm — except possibly the very largest companies — is that of representation and consultation. The firm is dependent on a trade or employers' association or Chamber of Commerce. The whole question of the effectiveness of such bodies and their interaction with government is considered in the last section of this chapter.

But the range of legislation and of regulatory bodies has two further aspects. First, they are an important aspect of the process of 'harmonisation' within the EEC. It is clear that removal of tariff barriers is only the first stage in establishing a larger market open to competition from firms in the member-states. Specifications and trade practices not only differ materially between countries but are often a much more effective form of national protectionism. Their codification and standardisation is likely to be a long process but an essential one if the aims of the Community are to be achieved. The second aspect is the resulting apparent avalanche of papers, whether demands for information, new regulations or mere advice. The smaller firm in particular finds this difficult enough at the national level let alone on a wider basis.

3   The third type of intervention is where the government or one of its agencies seeks to influence specific choices of firms in order to attain some wider political policy objective such as that involved in regional policy. Faced with the greater propensity of new firms to emerge and existing firms to expand in certain regions than in others, and linking this to the persistence of higher rates of unemployment in those regions with the poorer showing in new developments, the policy for over forty years has been to divert at least some of the growth to the areas defined as being in need of assistance. To achieve this there has first been a system of licensing of extensions and new premises for industrial purposes whereby substantial developments could not be carried through in the more prosperous areas in which they originated unless it could be shown that they could not be carried on anywhere else. This has been backed up by a monitoring of the progress of medium or large companies in order to anticipate their likely opportunities for job creation and the pressure that might be exercised upon their decisions. This, coupled with the normal process of planning approval and the operation of a succession of financial inducements linked to selected areas in which government has sought to encourage new development, constitutes an impressive set of pressures. But the decision whether to go ahead, and if so where, together with the risks that attach to such a decision, remain the task of the firm. At most it can be prevented from starting in particular places.

While there are specific choices of this type there are also wider aspects that are caught through such measures as price control. This is really part of the fourth category since its aim is related to overall prices and incomes policy in the context of inflation. But price control, being related to levels of profit in particular 'reference periods', may have a marked effect on the short-term policies of firms both within the home market to which it applies, and in terms of the profitability of exports or overseas activities as against home operations.

4 National policies can be seen to fall into two main groups: those that concern the relationships between enterprises such as competition and monopoly, and those that relate to the level and pattern of economic activity. Taking the former, it has already been observed that there is an element of contradiction in that government on certain issues encourages firms to cooperate and in other matters is anxious to sustain competition. This then presents a problem, for example, in attitudes to effective export performance. It may well be that for certain types of export activity firms may have to cooperate either in consortia for specific contracts or in the penetration of particular markets. Yet within the home market they may be in competition. Alternatively, in order to secure sufficient economies of scale to withstand foreign competition fewer but larger firms may be thought appropriate, perhaps only one main UK firm, and this then leads to two problems. On the one hand this could be one of the 'gateways' of the Monopolies and Restrictive Practices legislation where practices would be tolerated if they were a condition of support for the one UK firm or consortium. On the other hand, competition in the home market is now only possible from foreign firms. The type and vigour of competition may be sustained but this is dependent on the closer integration of the UK in an international market with all its attendant implications for the balance of payments and for harmonisation, as discussed above. The next step is then the impact of policies on competition of the wider negotiated environment, the Community itself.

The outcome is governmental involvement in what were previously private negotiations to regulate the environment in any one country. This is further strengthened by the operations of multinationals. These very powerful concerns may be so large as to be virtually independent of any one government, especially if their base is not confined to one country as with Anglo-Dutch Shell and Unilever. Equally they may act in close cooperation with their own national governments. This may result in their policies being closely related to the political pressures to which they are subject in their country of origin, as with American multinationals, or close political and economic links as with several European groups. Collectively, however, these giants may have such independent resources and ability to switch resources from one country to another to be beyond the effective control of any one nation-state.

Before leaving the question of competition there is, of course, the transfer of certain industries and companies to the publicly owned sector. This may mean a switch from the full force of the market economy as other criteria are applied, but in most cases government has so far kept the majority of such enterprises within the framework of the market economy. Indeed, even the Industry Act 1975 is now intended to work through the institutions of that market and using most of its criteria.

There remains the effect on firms of the principal means by which government seeks to regulate the overall performance and use of resources in the economy. Although in wartime and for short emergency periods in peacetime governments have resorted to rationing and other 'physical controls', the main weapons are monetary policy, taxation and attempts to regulate the general levels of prices and incomes. While this is not the place to discuss their relative merits in terms of economic policy two features do call for comment.

The first is the extent to which they affect the balance of power in decisions within and about firms. To rely on monetary policy while placing the main responsibility firmly on the management of each firm does also place an added emphasis on the attitudes and decisions of banks and other financial institutions. If the main emphasis is on the use of fiscal policy then the tax-gatherer may be put in the position of arbiter on the fate of firms, as tended to happen during the period of the tightest application of the taxation of 'close companies' in the late 1960's. If physical controls are used then those administering the system acquire this influence. Whenever decisions that could vitally affect the future survival and policy of a firm are transferred from those whose livelihood depends upon that firm to others, then the first question that has to be asked is on what criteria do they then act. To this has to be added a nagging doubt, namely, is this a type of decision for which they are equipped by background and training?

Here one is faced with some of the key dilemmas of the mixed economy where government is strongly interventionist and under continual political pressure to intervene even from members of the business community who now see it as their main or last hope of assistance. The pursuit of 'instant tuning' of the economy has characterised successive regimes of each main party and has created not only the familiar 'stop-go' situation but increasingly violent changes of direction and methods of intervention not only with each change of regime but within the life of any one government. The search for an 'industrial strategy' in the Winter of 1975—6 is typical of the problem. If this is then repeated for governments throughout the trading world then political instability and the prediction of changes in regimes and their policies becomes an increasing concern of business leaders.

The second feature is, therefore, the need for closer understanding of the business world and its decision problems by politicians and civil servants, and of political forces and their implications by managers.

2.3 Roles of Collective and Governmental Agencies

Clearly, a modern 'mixed' economy in which government and private interests interact presents a need for continuing contact between them. Our next task is to see how the private sector communicates with government and to examine the ways in which government seeks the advice and cooperation of the private sector.

Grove[3] has distinguished three main types of organisation — sectional, vocational and geographical. Sectional bodies are those that seek to protect or advance the special interests of a group of firms in a trade or a cause which cuts across trades. In the first category are trade and employers' associations; in the second we find 'pressure groups' which may be for a cause at a particular moment, as with the organisations for and against British membership of the European Economic Community, or concerned with some continuing interest, e.g. Aims of Industry. Vocational bodies are concerned with professional and technical standards, having memberships which may be common across all industries, e.g. accountants, or confined to one industry, e.g. locomotive engineers. Their interests may extend well beyond considerations of qualifications to codes of conduct or to cover important aspects of technical, professional or managerial practice.

Some such bodies are national; others are confined to particular localities and there may continue to be several trade or vocational associations on a locality basis. However, the most obvious examples of geographical associations are chambers of commerce and of trade, and regional industrial development associations. The first two are 'umbrella' organisations in the sense that while the former may be, and the latter are, based on individual membership, they cut across trades and perform a variety of functions on behalf of those in a locality. Industrial development associations are promotional bodies to attract new firms and new business to a region. All such 'geographical' bodies which straddle many trades have a representative role to local government, to regional bodies and either collectively or separately to central government.

In practice some bodies are in more than one category. Some associations perform as trade and as employers' associations while also participating on regional and national policy issues, either directly or through some form of federation. Representation can be clarified up to a point by distinguishing between technical or specialised matters, broader local issues, and wider national questions. On the first, trade and vocational bodies in various combinations may have established communications with central government. On the second, chambers of commerce and of trade may have local contacts with public bodies both local and national. As for the third, the main channels are those of the national 'umbrella' organisations, notably the Confederation of British Industry.

To appreciate the different foundations upon which these organisations operate it is necessary to examine what resources, services and members' support they can command. Thus, some trade associations may have a minimal secretariat, hardly any specialised support staff, and operate on a tight budget which means that few, if any, services can be offered to members; the whole influence of such an association depends upon its active membership which, in turn, means a few key individuals. Much depends on the scale of membership among the firms in an industry or area. At the other extreme are associations that can offer extensive trade services to their members, and advise on current legislation and regulations, statistics and possibly inter-firm comparison data. While legislation on monopolies and restrictive practices may have curbed much of the earlier activities of some trade associations, the general increase in legislation has enhanced the need for information and advice over a wide field. This is especially true of employment and here the employers' associations, which are equally varied in scale and support, have an important function.

At the local level, the 'umbrella' organisations are equally varied. On the one hand are major chambers of commerce in centres such as Bristol, Glasgow, Birmingham and Manchester having substantial advisory services, especially in relation to foreign trade. On the other there are the many local chambers of commerce and trade which are usually without any full-time staff and primarily concerned with the distributive trades. There is an Association of British Chambers of Commerce, which seeks to represent the chambers at national level and to act on their behalf on national matters. However, there are serious disagreements between the principal chambers of commerce in major regional centres and the national body which reflect the contrast between the UK situation and that elsewhere in Western Europe. In most West European countries chambers of commerce are powerful bodies having compulsory member-ship, control over training and therefore over the quality of entrants into the various trades, and wide powers and services that are financed by levies on all member firms. They are tantamount to a 'closed shop' among firms similar to that aimed at by trade unions among employees. Clearly, to match their services British bodies need to be more broadly based, possibly on a wider area than the local boundaries to which they have been confined hitherto.

The situation is only partly met by the activities of the national 'umbrella' bodies. The Confederation of British Industry (CBI) endeavours to act on behalf of employers, more particularly larger employers, and provides centrally and through its overseas representation a range of services to both business and government. Its membership embraces most nationalised industries and it is uniquely placed to represent the larger employer's point of view and that of trade associations. The Association of British Chambers of Commerce is one of a number of would-be spokesmen for small firms outside manufacturing.

These then are the representative bodies. The question is now, how do they operate?

The process of government involves a continuing dialogue between those in government — politicians and civil servants — and those outside. This starts with the anticipation or preparation for a change in government policy, and here there is a tradition rather than a statutory obligation to consult. But this then poses three questions. Whom does the civil service consult? On what basis are the consultations carried on? Is there time for effective consultation?

In effect, the government consults those who have made themselves known to it and demonstrated both their influence and ability to assist government with information, advice and possibly the subsequent execution of policy whether by involvement in its machinery or by securing a measure of cooperation among their members. To achieve this position an outside body may have to work on at least three parts of the government machine. The first is the civil service itself. By approaching the relevant departments, by submitting papers and demonstrating a body of knowledge and influence, the association concerned may at least get 'sounded' on developments if not represented on formal advisory bodies which a department sets up for particular purposes. The second is to go straight to the Minister which, if backed by approaches to others in his party in parliament, must at least cause him or her to ask the civil service to evaluate this new source of pressure or opinion. The third is to approach the party in opposition with a view to getting an issue raised.

The relationship develops not only by persistent questioning and campaigning but by active involvement in debate and subsequently in the working out of policy. The independence of the participants remains but each has a better understanding of the points of view of those each represent. On the one hand, the representative body has to be confident it can carry its members with it in any understanding that emerges; on the other, the civil servants can only speculate as to what the Minister might accept or need, and on key issues he is subject to decisions of the cabinet.

The question who is consulted is, therefore, answered with the assertion that it is any body that demonstrates that it has a good basis for being heard, and this basis has nothing whatsoever to do with size. The second question, the basis of consultation, opens up the ways in which opinion can be sought. It may be a direct request for comment or points of view; it is more likely to be a tentative proposition which enables the department to test opinion; this may even take the form of a consultative document or a 'green paper'. If a more controversial wide-ranging search is envisaged then there are several ways in which 'kites' may be flown. A Minister, or still better a party member, may advance some proposition in order to test the reaction, if any. Once an association or representative body is accepted it may find itself invited to comment on any document put out by way of a feeler of this kind. On more specific technical matters there is likely to be a formal system through which such consultations can occur. The outcome may be memoranda, interviews with civil servants, even a deputation to a Minister, at which points of view can be put across. In this way it is conceivable that legislation can be influenced before or when it is drafted. Subsequently, it may be thought necessary to get amendments considered in either House and that involves negotiation with MP's who are, for whatever reason, interested in the industry or the issue.

Subsequently, as we have seen, there is likely to be consultation and even involvement in the application of the policy especially where regulatory or advisory machinery has to be set up. Once again, influence may lie in being one of the bodies that are invited to put forward names for consideration for such advisory groups or for future investigation committees. However, it is clear that this is a time-consuming process and one of the key questions is, therefore, how effective this can be if there is, on the one hand, pressure for quick legislation and/or a heavy legislative programme and, on the other, a problem of time and resources for quick and effective consultation with members. Otherwise the most that can be hoped for is, on the government side, quick consultation with officials or spokesmen for an industry and, on the industry side, adequate anticipation of the sort of issues that they are likely to have to react upon and alert understanding of the views and interests of their members.

All too often these conditions are not met. On the side of government the speed with which legislation is introduced and pressed through Parliament may not only fail to give time for consultation but even for adequate deliberation except in the House of Lords. The spate of legislation in 1974-5 is an example of this.

On the side of all but the largest representative bodies there is the question of how they can react over so wide a field in so short a time on such puny resources, whether full-time officers or the part-time leaders who are, by definition, usually extremely busy people in their own organisations. The time allowed for response is usually such that it is not possible to consult the membership and the issue may well be one on which the body has yet to pronounce an opinion. A study of communications at regional level showed that the time taken to consult was generally well beyond that required for a response[4].

Of course, many representative bodies have been encouraged by government so that it had a channel through which to consult if not to administer. But like so many functions performed for government it is at industry's expense and one of the problems facing representative bodies is not only the limitations of their resources but their vulnerability in periods of economic stress.

While these remarks apply to collective bodies set up by industry and commerce, the central 'umbrella' bodies are in a special position. On the one hand, they have greater resources and are in a better position to anticipate governmental moves. They are closer to government and to circles in which ideas are exchanged which might be translated into future policies. On the other hand, they have a dual problem in relation to their memberships.

The first issue concerns for whom they really speak. A problem exists with the CBI, for example, in terms of the size of firm and the nature of the interest for whom it speaks. Is it the board-room of the large company in manufacturing industry? If so what about (a) not-so-large firms, (b) management other than the board-room, (c) firms that do not fall into its 'supporters club'?

The second concerns their ability to represent the views of the membership, when the leaders and key officers are so closely linked to government, but the majority of members are not even in London anyway, may have a much less sophisticated view of government relations, and indeed show all the suspicion that those at the grass-roots level in any large body have of those at the centre.

Already in commenting on the representative bodies we have seen something of the mechanisms through which they consult. Now we look at these from the standpoint of government. This involves a distinction between, first the continuing process of consultation described above, then formal consultation at departmental and national levels, and lastly regulation by quasi-autonomous agencies.

Formal consultation at departmental level is partly through a network of advisory committees at local and/or national levels, either directly to a department on a type of issue or to an agency responsible to a department, e.g. Employment Services Agency.

These committees may be expressly advisory or have other functions concerned with the interpretation and application of policy which nevertheless enable them to act or to be invited to do so in an advisory capacity on new developments. In addition, there are ad hoc consultations on specific topics to secure cooperation and ideas on matters where the department or an agency is the body which takes the action or handles the advice once secured. At national level consultation is undertaken on both a departmental and an interdepartmental level, the pinnacle of the system being the activities of the National Economic Development Office. This organisation services two types of body, the National Economic Development Council, and the 'little Neddies', Councils and Committees on specific industries or common topics. Instituted as a major feature in national economic planning in 1962, the Council is made up of the principal ministers concerned with economic affairs, with the Prime Minister or the Chancellor of the Exchequer in the chair, representatives of the CBI, the TUC, the Nationalised Industries and 'independent' members. It considers papers on broad economic and industrial policy, mainly derived from the staff of NEDC itself. These have been recruited partly from the civil service, in particular the Treasury, and partly from industry, trade union research departments, universities and consultants. They in turn have a network of advisory committees set up ad hoc to deal with specific topics such as transport for exports to Europe, and management education, and they in turn may sponsor specific studies to provide a firm basis for forward planning. Such advisory committees are appointed in consultation with representative bodies and may be virtually a direct representation of them though the members are appointed by and report to NEDC.

Side by side is a group of Councils for specific industries where there is thought to be some issue of public policy or of government-industry interaction in forward planning. Thus the first report of NEDC in 1963[5] pointed to a number of sectors where bottlenecks or deficiencies were expected to be obstacles to more rapid economic growth. From this developed the ideas of councils for specific industries where action by government, nationalised industries, private firms and service functions such as transport, education, or research was thought necessary. A notable gap in the whole of this structure, as of the central representative bodies, is the City itself which relies on its direct communication through the Bank of England as discussed in Chapter 5, section 5.4.

This machinery has been used to varying degrees by governments over the past thirteen years. While direct discussions between the Prime Minister, key economic ministers, CBI and TUC has been a feature of economic policies of recent administrations, the NEDC structure remains a potentially powerful forum for the exchange of opinion and the formulation of overall economic policy.

Both industry as represented by CBI and the trades union movement through the TUC see the NEDC as a means of sharing in the evolution of policy and of influencing government. From the government's standpoint it is a means of securing wider support for measures and an important opportunity for discussing new approaches that may first be floated in papers put forward by the Director-General. Clearly one critical feature is the relationship of the NEDC to the Treasury as the centre of government economic policy, but that is a field that lies outside the scope of the present text.

There remain the regulating bodies set up under a range of statutes which affect the policies of firms and industries. Perhaps the most important of these are the Monopolies Commission and the Prices Board. The first is an investigatory and advisory body, recommending to government, which is then free to decide what action, if any, to take. It may, for example, be asked to decide whether or not a merger referred to it is in the public interest. The Prices Board has to operate price controls, and therefore considers, within the criteria laid down by government, whether or not to allow price increases for which applications have been made on behalf of firms or industries.

Where controls are in force they are usually administered by a department rather than an agency, and there is usually provision for some form of appeal to an administrative tribunal but not to the courts. In some fields where there is regulation of business practices, e.g. restrictive practices, the interpretation and operation of the policy is divided between a public office or body such as the Registrar of Restrictive Practices and a specially constituted court, in this case, the Restrictive Practices Court. Here the procedure is essentially reversed in that a practice is assumed to be against the public interest unless the Court is convinced that it is not for one or more of a number of permitted reasons.

The full range of regulation is now very much wider and more detailed than ever before in peacetime. Its administration and the reaction of business enterprises present a significant problem and cost to firms and their representative bodies. The combined effect is to curtail freedom of action and impose a range of new responsibilities on directors and managers as individuals as well as their companies or corporations.

To sum up the evolving 'negotiated environment', it appears as a set of overlapping networks of consultation, negotiation and decision. Even the part that is formalised within the machinery of government relies on advice, both formally sought and informally maintained with those representing the interests of business managements. Granted the quality and resources of such representative bodies are often surprisingly poor, even in comparison with those of the trades unions, their position at least offers an opportunity for influence and there is growing evidence of the concern not only of directors but of managers at many levels at the extent to which their viewpoint is not being represented in current discussions on industrial and commercial policy. The earlier defensive frameworks of the period of restrictions on competition have been under strong attack and even the collective action of employers' associations has perforce become largely defensive in periods of national policies on prices and incomes. As will be argued later in Chapter 5, part of the response to the new turbulence has been the merger and the takeover bid. It has also found expression in new joint ventures especially in export markets. Even here, however, it is a response to pressure from the client governments with which contracts have to be arranged.

The sense of independence at the level of the firm rather than the industry remains strong and is reinforced by the persistence of very individualist approaches by chief executives even in very large enterprises. The values and aspirations of the founders of private firms continue to extend into fields where far more complex relationships are prevalent. Our study can therefore begin with the traditional nursery of business management, the small private firm.

Notes and references

1   Royal Commission on the Distribution of the Industrial Population, (Barlow) Report, HMSO 1940.
2   R. Jones and A. Mariott, *Anatomy of a Merger,* Pan Books 1970.
    A. Knight, *Private Enterprise and Public Intervention,* Ailen & Unwin 1974.
3   J. Grove, *Collective Organisation of Industry,* Longmans 1962.
4   V. E. Line, *Communications between Government and Industry,* Foundation for Business Responsibilities 1969.

5   NEDC, *Conditions Favourable to Faster Growth,* HMSO 1963.

Study questions

1   Trace the evolution of governmental intervention in industrial policy since 1960 indicating the main factors affecting it.

2   Examine the reasons for government support for any one of the major mergers that has involved government support or pressure since 1960.

3   In what circumstances may government seek to apply criteria different from those of the market to the policies of an industry?

4   Examine the ways in which government and business may consult on future policy.

3
THE PRIVATE FIRM

3.1 Private Ownership and Small Businesses

Private firms have been defined as those raising their capital by private investment by the founders or those whom they persuade to join them. They therefore include unincorporated businesses such as sole proprietors and partnerships, private limited companies and, in practice, the unquoted public company and the company not limited by shares. At the root of all such enterprises is the idea of independent private ownership, the traditional entrepreneur of the capitalist system. Immediately we find ourselves in an area of economic, political and social mythology which is sustained by the absence of reliable data and compounded by a reluctance to cooperate in relieving the general ignorance.

There is a fundamental ambivalence. On the one hand, the private firm is the epitome of free enterprise, rugged individualism, efficiency measured by consumer satisfaction and good labour relations, and the victim of hostile state bureaucracy, the manipulations of larger companies, not to mention the exactions of tax collectors. On the other hand, small firms are seen as complacent, parochial obstacles to efficiency which is assumed to lie only with larger scale production, mass marketing, mergers and professional direction.

At the outset there is a sharp difference in the legal position of the sole proprietor, the partnership and private limited company. The *sole trader or proprietor* is numerically by far the largest of all the forms of enterprise and ranges from virtually self-employed individuals to modest organisations employing a small number of persons. The proprietor is the sole owner of the enterprise and is personally liable for all its debts to the limit of his (or her) personal estate. As a form of enterprise it gives him full control over the disposition of assets, profits and the very existence of the business. Its disadvantages are clear. He cannot limit his personal liability nor can he provide a means whereby others can put additional capital into the business and have any direct involvement in its operation. Its scale is therefore narrowly limited to what he can invest in the first place, plus what he can plough back. While there are many thousands of such businesses they tend to remain small and to have a continual turnover of proprietors through bankruptcy.

The sole proprietor who joins forces with one or more others to form a firm having larger capital resources can, of course, do so in the first instance by a form of *partnership*. The Partnership Act 1890 provides that in an 'ordinary' partnership, in the absence of agreement to the contrary, all partners share profits and losses equally; in any case they all have equal rights in the running of the firm which is not a separate person in law in England (though it is in Scotland). Partnerships are most common in professions where the code of conduct assumes that the professional man stands by his advice and service without a limit to his personal liability.

As a form of ownership, partnerships are not separately taxable as companies are, but they have a snag deriving from this lack of separate identity at law. They are based on contracts between partners that have to be reviewed with each change of partner. The only circumstance where partners can be introduced with limited liability is where there is a 'limited' partnership under the Limited Partnership Act 1907. This is a rarely used form in which the limited partners have no part in the decisions, a far less satisfactory position than that permitted in a private company which first became available only a year later in 1908.

Sole traders and partnerships when viewed from the second frame of reference, that of power, are clearly very different from one another. In the former the owner is in sole control; in the latter there is joint control. Only in the limited partnership might the unlimited partner — if there is only one — enjoy the same personal power as a sole proprietor.

The independent proprietor who seeks a suitable form of ownership for expansion is much more likely to choose the *Private Limited Company*. This offers him all the advantages of a registered limited company while still retaining the essentially close-knit relationships of the smaller enterprise.

Already, however, terms are being used with which some readers may not be familiar, such as 'registered limited company'. 'Registered' means that they derive their legal status from incorporation under the Companies Acts as opposed to those originally operating under Royal Charter, or those set up under special legislation, the so-called 'statutory' companies, such as insurance companies, building societies, cooperative societies and even trade unions. 'Limited' means that the shareholders liability is limited. The point is that 'unlimited' companies are both permitted and exist. They are uncommon and they are the only companies that do not have to publish and file copies of their annual accounts with the Registrar of Companies. The store group C&A is one of the few firms of any size that are in this position.

The method of limitation is normally by shares, though it can be by guarantee. The latter form whereby members agree to be responsible for debts up to a certain sum is often used by non-profit making organisations. The term 'limited by shares' describes the normal situation whereby the capital is divided into shares of a declared nominal value. Once that has been paid up in full to the company the shareholder has no further liability.

The first principal feature of a private limited company is that its membership is restricted to from two to fifty members. The upper limit may only be exceeded where employees become shareholders. Secondly, it is not permitted to advertise through a prospectus for public subscription for either shares or debentures (loan capital). In the past it enjoyed the privilege of not having to file and publish copies of its annual accounts, but this has now ceased to be the case. Lastly, some limit is placed on the transferability of shares, if only to prevent the company from passing into outside hands against the wishes of the directors.

It is a relatively easy matter to establish a private limited company. A minimum share capital, whether limited by shares or by guarantee, of £100 is sufficient, provided also that there is at least one director and a secretary. This has led to its widespread use, not only by businesses but even by individuals when confronted, for example, with heavy taxation demands, e.g. TV performers, pop-groups. The use of the private company in this context eventually led the government in 1965 to check this practice by introducing the concept of a 'close company'

The 'close' company is one in which five or fewer shareholders have effective control. They have been required to distribute as dividends — and thereby become personally liable for income tax upon — all investment income and a stated proportion of their trading profits, unless it can be shown that retention of such profits is necessary for the development of the business.

As for the scale of the private company sector, there were 641,201 registered in the UK in 1974, though many were inactive. This compares with only 16,658 public companies of which 10,270 had share capital, and of these barely 50% had quotations[1]. Of these approximately 3000 can be regarded as actively trading.

The Bolton Committee defined small firms as in table 3.1[2].

Table 3.1 *Small firms as defined in the Bolton Committee studies*

Industry	Small firms			
	Definition: maximum of	As % of all firms	Employ- ment as % of all firms	Average numbers employed per small firm
Manufacturing	200*	94	20	25
Retailing	£50,000+	96	49	3
Wholesaling	£200,000+	77	25	7
Construction	25*	89	33	6
Mining & quarrying	25*	77	20	11
Motor trades	£50,000+	90	32	3
Miscellaneous services	£50,000+	90	82	4
Road transport	5"	85	36	4
Catering	All'	96	75	3

*employees   + turnover   "vehicles
'excluding multiple chains

The Bolton Committee estimated that nearly a quarter of GNP was attributed to the small firm sector, while in manufacturing and other activities covered by its studies, small firms accounted for 29% of all employment, by either measure a significant element in the economy[3].

If one then takes into account the whole range of activities not covered by the censuses of manufacturing and distribution then the small firm sector is even more significant. The self-employed in a strict sense are all separate firms and their members in the professions, agriculture, horticulture and a whole variety of personal services, let alone the value of their output, make this even more so. They not only constitute an important sector in their own right, but also as they interact with larger enterprises for whom they provide essential services. Indeed, it can be argued that the small firm sector is vital to the flexibility of an economy otherwise dominated by larger organisations.

Despite the continued process of merger and absorption in large concerns, the continued influx of new firms in the years following the report has assured no drastic change in the situation, though as the Bolton studies indicated, there had been a sharp reduction in the number and significance of small firms in manufacturing industries over previous decades. Indeed, one noteworthy outcome has been the lower importance of small firms as a whole in the UK compared to other members of the EEC[4].

The advocates of the small firm do not stop at these aggregate measures of its significance. They argue that in innovation, adaptability, and as a source of future large firms, the small firm has a special significance. The problem, it is asserted, is that small firms have to face special difficulties in respect of finance, access to external services, and the impact of governmental requirements that are in some way 'unfair'. While the Bolton report pointed to a range of reforms that would assist small firms, there is neither a blanket endorsement of the claims, nor any proposal for subsidy on the scale, for example, of the Small Business Administration in the United States.

The traditional view, so vividly expressed by Marshall[5], was of a continual renewal by new firms being launched, existing ones maturing and being consolidated, and a broad movement from small beginnings to larger scale being a possibility for firms with average access to knowledge and skill. The alternative view is that this, even if it were ever possible, is no longer a valid expectation for two reasons. The first is that growth encounters obstacles of such severity that they amount to a virtual blockage; this is seen where the costs of entry into a trade become so high as to preclude new entrants from below. The second lies in the extent to which new ventures, especially those requiring substantial investment, come increasingly from existing large firms, especially now that diversification has become so widespread a policy. If this negative view is upheld then why is it that new firms continue to proliferate? Indeed are they coming forward on a scale sufficient to sustain even the present small firm sector?[6]

Three very different studies may help to illustrate this. The first is that of East Midlands manufacturing firms mady by Boswell[7]. He examined the origins of 64 firms and concluded that the most powerful factor was the desire to be independent, supported by an initial innovation that the founder(s) set out to achieve. The majority of those studied had previously worked in medium or large firms. They had seen opportunities for improvements in performance, innovations in products, methods or processes that they sought to develop. In the study, 27 out of the 64 involved some form of joint venture, only 7 of which were family based[8]. The majority of such ventures involved professional colleagues, but the majority of the firms were clearly one-man foundations in the first instance.

This interest in developing an idea, often first developed in a very different context is borne out by studies of firms in the West of England that the writer has supervised. In these there was not only the improvement of something being done by or for an existing larger firm, but an important spin-off element. This arises where a product or process is developed in one industry, in this case aero-space, and the firm responsible for it has no interest in exploiting further. It therefore allows it to be developed for a wider market by sub-contractors or even former employees.

A further sample of some 47 aspirants to running their own business in the West Country showed that the great majority were not, as yet, running their own concerns, but sought to do so, partly to become independent, partly to continue living in the region, and partly to develop a product or idea that stemmed from their present work.

This combination of a desire for independence coupled to an idea, sometimes arising even from a hobby interest, runs through many of the cases assembled by Clarke[9]. In presenting what are admittedly a set of success stories he demonstrates the importance of grasping opportunities. This characteristic of entrepreneurs is, of course, associated with a major question as to the nature and origin of opportunities. Are they foreseen, even created by the entrepreneur, or is he carried along by opportunities that are offered to him but whose rationale he neither understands nor attempts to analyse?[10]

This could be one of the key differences between those who succeed and those who merely survive, if indeed they even get that far. Studies of technical and commercial innovation such as those of Carter and Williams[11] and Political and Economic Planning (PEP)[12] contrast sharply the innovators, those who adopt other people's innovations, and the parochial sleepers who appear to just survive if not stagnate. In both studies there is a concern for a more innovative or 'progressive' approach, with the implication that 'sleepers' may be particularly common among those firms that are reluctant to admit that they can learn from outside their own concerns.

The question to which this line of argument leads is therefore the extent to which the owner-manager situation is favourable or unfavourable to adaptation as a condition of survival, let alone growth. Those cases cited by Clarke of a decline among small firms illustrate this lack of adaptation in parts of the retail trade and are in sharp contrast to the success stories in the same field[13].

Therefore we need to look first at the operating context of the owner-manager, the extent to which he has to share decisions in his business. One way of doing this is to consider the ownership form used in those trades covered by the Bolton studies.

Tables 3.2 and 3.3 show the legal status of small firms in manufacturing and non-manufacturing trades. Table 3.4 analyses the extent of owner-management still further. In manufacturing, the private limited company is clearly the dominant form; partnerships are confined to the lower size-ranges as are sole proprietorships. The significance of the latter is far less than in four of the non-manufacturing trades, as set out in table 3.4.

Table 3.2 *Legal status of small firms — manufacturing*

Size of firm (no. of employees)	Quoted Cos %	Non-quoted Cos %	Un-limited Cos %	Partner-ships %	Sole pro-prietors %	Total
1—24	0.0	77.2	2.6	7.4	12.6	100
25—99	1.0	94.6	1.1	2.3	1.0	100
100—199	5.4	91.7	1.6	0.7	0.7	100
1—199	0.4	81.0	2.3	6.2	10.0	100

Bolton Committee: *Research Report No. 17*

Table 3.3 *Legal status of small firms — non-manufacturing*

Industry	Quoted cos %	Non-quoted cos %	Un-limited cos %	Partner-ships %	Sole Pro-prietors %	Total
Catering	0.0	6.5	0.0	24.7	68.8	100
Construction	0.0	72.4	0.2	9.1	18.3	100
Motor trades	0.0	46.7	0.3	21.4	31.5	100
Retail distribution	0.4	34.5	0.6	22.6	41.8	100
Road transport	0.8	35.2	0.0	19.5	44.5	100
Wholesale distribution	0.7	82.7	1.8	4.6	10.2	100
Total	0.3	33.3	0.4	20.3	45.8	100

Bolton Committee: *Research Report No. 17*

The greatly reduced use of the private company, especially in catering, stands out along with the much more frequent use of partnerships and the leading position of sole proprietorships in catering, retail distribution and road transport. Only in construction and wholesale distribution does the private company predominate. These reflect differences in the amount of capital that is required both by the nature of the activities and the scale of operations. Important in the former are the period and amount of credit given, the working capital for all purposes, including credit facilities, and the scale of investment in fixed capital. The variations also reflect the opportunities for credit offered by suppliers as well as the number of employees.

Table 3.4 *Owner managership and controlling interests in small firms*

(a) Number of partners or shareholders having controlling interest					
	1	2	3-5	6-10	11+ Total
Manufacturing	39.4	46.3	13.0	0.8	0.5 100
Non-manufacturing	42.0	46.6	10.0	0.5	1.0 100
(b) *Working partners or shareholders*					
Manufacturing	20.8	45.9	29.9	2.2	1.2 100
Non-manufacturing	25.2	44.8	27.4	1.3	1.3 100

Bolton Committee: *Research Report No. 17*

On the basis of table 3.4 ownership and control by one or two persons dominates in both manufacturing and distribution so far as small firms are concerned. Using the approaches set out in Chapter 1 the key decisions of an independent firm and the strategic decisions lie with one or two key people, whatever the ownership form that is followed in at least 85% of small firms.

The next step is therefore to consider the age and state of development of such firms. Taking the Bolton studies first, their conclusion was that most small firms had been established for many years with at least half of those wholly owned by one family already into the second or third generation. They had at least survived one of the key changes, that of management succession. It is argued that one problem facing men and women who launch businesses on their own account is their close identification with all aspects of its operation and therefore the question arises as to their ability to develop a successor and to enable him to take over at a time when he can make his own mark on the development of the firm. Drucker has instanced outstanding examples of failure to do so[14] in much larger concerns where the founder's domination has been near-catastrophic in its consequences. Boswell explores this, including in his survey an interesting analysis of the extent to which founders have indeed had any offspring to whom to hand over[15].

Clearly one problem is that of the development of the founder, the interests that he retains or acquires, and the extent to which he is able to grow with the business as it develops. This therefore poses two questions. One is the nature of the relationships that can build up in a one or two man business; the other is the 'management capacity' of the firm and the ways in which it can be augmented.

The conventional image of the small business is that of a relatively informal organisation in which the whole allocation of managerial and other tasks is built around people as opposed to people being fitted into some hierarchy of roles. Individuals have roles that are both wide in scope and continually adjusting to changes in the situation confronting the firm. There is relatively little managerial specialisation and virtually no management support staff. The enterprise is too small to carry such costs. Managers are therefore involved in a mixture of operating, administrative and strategic choices without always being aware of their significance. Relationships both within management and between managers and managed are likely to be much less formal and the proximity of one to the other facilitates good communications and an immediate awareness on the part of the owner-manager of the pressures upon his work force. If, as is likely, he lives in close proximity, sharing some of the values and experiences of the community in which his firm operates, then he has every opportunity to be much more sensitive to questions of social responsibility in that community, and this may be reflected in his active membership of local clubs and societies.

But at the same time he and his colleagues, if any, are likely to be severely stretched if only to meet the full demands on his time in running the concern, even if he is one of those who has sought to opt for a quiet life by not pursuing growth beyond a very limited scale. This has several consequences. One is that if more demands are made upon him by government it is not just rugged individualism, but the practical aspect of the time available that may make him so antagonistic to what those used to the padding of larger organisations see only as desirable statistical returns or convenient means of tax collection. Another is that while he has a breadth of commercial awareness that more specialised managers in larger firms find difficult to equal he also lacks the time, and perhaps the training and knowledge, to investigate many facets of his operations. He has little or no 'organisational slack'.

The real problems for anyone seeking to grow to a much larger scale appear to be those of finance and management. Finance is critical if only because so many firms start with marginal capital resources. Studies point to the extent to which small firms are continually stretched financially to the point of not being able to invest on any planned basis. But ability to search out sources of finance, at least to the extent of identifying possible lenders or investors, appears to be a key attribute of successful entrepreneurs.

In periods of financial stringency small enterprises are especially vulnerable on one score, that of trade credit, as they make more use of this source than larger concerns. The Bolton report explains this in terms of the trades in which they predominate, but concedes the pressure on small firms to give credit, including that from larger concerns[16]. Davis and Yeomans investigated this in their study of the effects of firm size[17]. They concluded that in a period of financial constraint the pressure would bear more heavily on smaller firms. Indeed the extent to this has subsequently led the CBI to exhort larger firms and nationalised industries not to exploit their bargaining power in this way[18].

As for the managerial limit, this is not confined to the terms depicted in Penrose's analysis; it is very real in respect of the form of external management support open to small firms, the relationships that develop with it, and in particular, the extent to which external agencies, such as management consultants, bank managers, accountants, university and college staffs, or trading associates are either able or willing to give the kind of support that is required.

The question left outstanding must concern the extent to which the business community is able to regenerate itself through the influx of new entrepreneurs. The Bolton Committee, while concerned at the possible threat to the supply of entrepreneurs, was unable to quantify it. Boswell, on the other hand, expressed serious reservations based on his study of stagnant and declining firms.

3.2 The Private Limited Company

The private limited company offers most of the advantages of incorporation while retaining the opportunity for effective private control. While some of the privileges as regards privacy have been withdrawn, the fact remains that here is one of the easiest, cheapest and most readily available forms of incorporation to be found in any country in Europe.

Some idea of the comparative popularity of the private limited company is afforded by table 3.5 which indicates both the total number registered and the number of registrations that were effective. An exceptionally large number of new registrations occurred in 1972 and 1973, itself the record year, but the number in liquidation or in course of removal was high again in 1974, the previous peaks being 1968 and 1972 (peak year).

Table 3.5 *Changes in number of private companies registered UK 1965, 1970, 1973 and 1974*

	1965	1970	1973	1974
All registered 31 Dec.	522,963	542,858	620,953	641,201
New companies	36,076	30,090	67,178	42,362
In liquidation or course of removal	19,196	39,626	37,024	58,375
Effective registered 31 Dec.	503,767	503,232	583,929	582,826
Department of Trade, *Companies in 1974*, HMSO 1975				

The published data do not distinguish between public and private companies in respect of nominal capital but an idea of the high proportion of very small companies, the great majority of whom can be regarded as private is given in an analysis of new registrations in 1974. By far the largest number have a nominal capital not exceeding £100!

Whereas the earliest approaches to company law were highly restrictive in the granting of the right to incorporation, the provisions for private companies since 1908 have made them a most attractive proposition. It is only their separate liability for taxation since 1965 that has led a few firms to revert to alternative legal forms.

This becomes apparent as soon as the proprietor(s) of a business seek incorporation. They need not even go to the trouble of forming a new company as it is possible to acquire an existing company currently held by a firm specialising in such work. Such firms offer 'shell' companies from £25 which is slightly cheaper than the formation expenses of a new private company, currently around £100.

The choice of a private limited company as a first step is normal unless there is a desire for secrecy, as the Companies Act 1967 introduced the principle that publication of accounts in the sense that they have to be filed with the Registrar of Companies was a price of limited liability; to escape this obligation the company must be an unlimited one. It is also unusual to start as a public company; this is subsequently achieved by re-registration and flotation as described in section 3.3.

To register a new private company only two persons are needed and in any case the number at this stage may not exceed fifty. In view of the evidence already presented in table 3.4, the likelihood is that two or a few more persons will be involved. They seek registration of a company for which they must select a suitable name under which it will trade. At this stage an approach to the Registrar for Companies is made to check whether the name is available. This control has two purposes. The principal one is to prevent any confusion in the public mind through the use of the name of any existing company or of one so close as to imply a connection that does not exist. The second is to ensure that the firm is not described, for example, as an 'Insurance Company', when it is not, with the use of words which imply a connection with the Crown or a public authority, or which 'in the opinion of the Board of Trade is undesirable'[19]. Provided the proposed name is not rejected outright it is probably safe to proceed to the preparation and submission of the principal documents:

    (i)   Memorandum of Association
   (ii)   Articles of Association
  (iii)   Statement of Nominal Capital
  (iv)   Declaration of Compliance
   (v)   Notice of Situation of Registered Office
  (vi)   Particulars of Directors and Secretary

The Memorandum of Association need only state the company's name, its objects, domicile (whether England or Scotland), share capital (if any) and that the liability of members is limited. In our projected private company all of these have to be included. Perhaps the most important operationally is the objects clause since the company can only trade within the purposes prescribed therein. In practice this is made very wide in its scope, first by initial drafting, and second by subsequent amendment. The only thing in the Memorandum that the company cannot subsequently amend, is its country of domicile.

The Articles of Association are the working constitution of the company and a private limited company cannot rely solely on the model set presented in table A of the Companies Act for two reasons. First, a private limited company must expressly provide in its Articles for restrictions on the transfers of shares, on invitations for public subscription to shares or debentures, and on the number of members. Second, the Articles may be so drafted as to give the company many more distinctive 'private' features fundamental to private control that a public company would not be allowed to adopt.

The restriction on the transfer of shares is fundamental to the idea of a private company. The precise form varies, but a typical one would specify that all transfers required the approval of the Board of Directors or be first offered to existing members. One effect is to rule out the possibility of an unsolicited take-over succeeding. Linked to it is the restriction that no invitation may be made to the public to subscribe for shares or debentures. This effectively limits its raising of share capital and debentures to those whom it contacts privately, a very powerful limitation on its ability to raise funds. The last of the restrictions concerns the number of members, which may not exceed fifty, except where employees are admitted to membership.

What are perhaps less well known are the other restrictions in Articles that private companies can make. One important topic is the balance of power both in the Board and among the shareholders. Thus the first directors may be relieved of any obligation to rotate and may even be made life directors. The requirement that directors retire automatically at 70, unless re-elected by special resolution, does not apply to private companies. All the directors can be re-elected on a single resolution at the annual general meeting. There may be a provision that in the event of any further issue of shares being made it must be offered in the first instance to existing members, even in the proportions of their existing holdings. Lastly it is still the case that a private company need only have one director and a secretary, giving a 'Board' of only two!

There is no requirement that the share capital is to be of any particular sum — or indeed that it should be 'paid up'. The company is acceptable as a separate legal entity conferring upon its members the privileges of limited liability, of its own perpetual existence as long as there are shareholders alive, and able to trade. There are indeed very few limitations on who may set up a company. In practice the founders of most private companies are persons who intend to conduct a business for a particular purpose, not professional company promotors. There is no law against anyone holding a share in a company; the only limitation is on an undischarged bankrupt and those committed of certain type of fraud from acting as directors or taking part in the management of companies.

The company is now free to operate. In practice this means that the management of its affairs lies with the Board of Directors subject to such control as the shareholders are able to exercise through general meetings. Powers vested in a Board of Directors by the Articles of Association cannot be interfered with by the members through general meetings and, in law at least, they have little other means of direct action. Furthermore their remedies even in general meetings are limited to the approval of the Annual or other reports and accounts, the election and continued tenure of directors, and the approval of changes in the Memorandum and Articles and in the capital, whether nominal or issued, where these are sought by the directors.

In private companies, except where the owners have withdrawn from everyday management, this is not a difference of substance as the directors are both managers and key, if not dominant, shareholders. As long as there is agreement within the controlling group or family then the issue of shareholder control over directors has little significance in a private company. If, however, this should cease to be the case then the way may be open for a radical change either by one party buying out the other, or by the introduction of a third party as in an agreed merger.

The main problems facing a private company are thus those of maintaining its own growth from the resources of its existing members. To admit newcomers would be to alter the balance of power. However, this means that a private company has to plough back profits as a major means of financing its growth, and to do so may present problems due to the nature of company and personal taxation. If control is to remain in the same hands in successive generations then inheritance and wealth taxation present special problems.

To sustain their company the directors have not only to aim at a reasonable rate of profit, but possibly to limit dividends in order to retain sufficient funds. At the same time the threat of death duties or capital transfer tax on shareholdings means that precautions have to be taken by way of insurance policies to cover the expected assessment on transfer at death or by gift. Otherwise there may be no way of maintaining the particular private ownership of a firm. Without such precautions private ownership could ultimately become impossible. Furthermore many private companies fall in the 'close company' category, that is they are effectively in the control of not more than five persons.

Since 1965, company taxation is primarily on the profits of the company as such but also on the sums distributed to shareholders. Both the company and the shareholders are subject to capital gains tax and now to a capital transfer tax, which covers both legacies and gifts.

There are two important consequences of this basis of taxation. The first is that it offers governments the opportunity to transfer resources from all companies operated at a profit to public expenditure and therefore it implies a transfer of funds from private to public investment. This may be carried to the point at which the inadequacies of the funds remaining, coupled with the rate of return seen to be earned on private investment, discourage private investors to such a degree that government may feel obliged to offer funds back in a variety of ways. But criteria used by government for such advances may be quite different from those of the private sector as a whole. What is more frustrating, however, is the instability of government policies in such matters. Not only do governments of opposing persuasions reverse each others' measure on gaining office, but the belief in 'instant tuning' of the economy leads to repeated changes in detailed policies with investment a particularly vulnerable victim.

The second consequence is indeed the rate of return. This is affected directly by the tax on distributions. The company has to pay the income tax to the Inland Revenue and this, so far as the company is concerned, is tantamount to a distributed profits tax. The outcome is encouragement to retain profits for re-investment in the company. This is further reinforced where restrictions are placed on dividend increases when prices and incomes policies are in force. While the result may then be that retained profits are reflected in the value of the shares, that increase in value becomes, for the shareholder, a capital gain and therefore taxable.

The position of the private company calls for two special comments, one on share valuation and one on the problems of the close company. On share valuation the point is that, if as argued already, the private company has to aim at a high level of retention in order to finance new activity, then this is ultimately reflected in the valuation of the shares of any member on transfer whether on death or otherwise. If the aim is to retain control by a family then this implies a particular cost in terms of insurance cover on the persons concerned. The extent of the difficulties facing private companies where key shareholder(s) die leaving a need to realise part or all of the shares at a valuation has been such that special facilities have been created to assist in such situations. The Estate Duties Investment Trust Ltd (EDITH) was established in 1953 to advance the funds required by becoming a minority shareholder on a temporary basis. If private funds are not subsequently forthcoming then the next step would be re-registration with a view to the ensuing public company making a flotation.

The essentially private nature of most private companies, therefore, faces a substantial challenge to its very survival. No wonder that the cynics concluded that the only beneficiaries — apart from the Inland Revenue — from Capital Transfer Tax would be the insurance companies!

Before the Finance Act 1965 companies controlled by five or fewer persons were required to make a 'reasonable' distribution of their income within a 'reasonable' time. Otherwise surtax might be levied on the controllers on the entire income of the company as if it had been distributed in dividend. Then in 1965 such companies were defined as 'close companies' and a series of stringent rules applied to determine what tax liability was due.

In practice this put most private companies in the position of having to justify their investment plans to the Inland Revenue. It placed a premium on distribution as opposed to the retention emphasis in other company taxation and it led not only to a sharp fall in new company registrations but to some firms exercising their right — when obtained by the Companies Act 1967 — to become either unlimited companies or partnerships. Alternatively 'close' company status could be avoided by 'going public' and putting not less than 35% of the equity on the market.

Subsequently, the rules were relaxed so that by 1973 some 80% of private companies previously covered by the 'close' company rules had reverted to a position nearer to that which had obtained until 1965. The outcome is that those that remain in this category still have a requirement to distribute an adequate level of income based on 'an excess of relevant income over distributions' together with tight restrictions on loans and other forms of distribution to participators or their associates.

The term 'participator' used in this context means anyone owning or having an option of share capital, a loan creditor, anyone who might receive distributions from the company or who is entitled to have that income or assets applied for his benefit.

More fundamentally, the taxation possibilities raise the question of how valuable are the advantages of limited liability. Any judgement on the outcome in recent years is difficult if only because of the much wider economic and financial difficulties with which all businesses have had to contend. But it is already clear from the first reports of the Diamond Commission[20] that one consequence of the general level of taxation of all companies has been a marked change in their methods of financing with a switch to borrowing, the interest on which is an expense allowable for tax purposes, with a consequent rise in the gearing ratio, i.e. the ratio of equity or ordinary shares to preference shares and debentures.

So far as the private company is concerned what is at stake is the future scale and form of the private firm sector, for it is not only taxation that is involved; there is the whole question of the future of smaller businesses and of future sources of new developments.

3.3 'Going Public'

So far our study of the private firm has stopped short of any attempt to gain access to the capital market as this would presage a radical change in its context of operation. This is not to assert that as long as it is a private firm it is answerable only to its owners. Small firms are heavy borrowers, making much more use of commercial banks than larger concerns. The banks, like other lenders and creditors, keep a close scrutiny on the affairs of those to whom they have advanced credit and may well bring pressure for an expansion of the capital base of a private company. Equally they may have sought additional security for advances made to such a company from the key shareholders involved. For a variety of reasons a private company may be obliged to seek additional resources, and these may ultimately bring it to the point where it has to 'go public'.

The first reason is growth and the need for additional capital beyond that the existing shareholders are prepared to put up, or that the company can plough back from earnings. Normally this would appear to be a hurdle for a fast-growing company but conditions of inflation, coupled with the level of taxation, have compelled companies with much more modest growth to seek additional funds. Up to a point these can be met by additional borrowing, but even here the bank, if it is a commercial bank, let alone a merchant or industrial bank, will be impressed not only by trading prospects but the scale and marketability of the share capital. An increase in the latter would make them more ready to continue and to increase the funds they are prepared to advance.

While growth is mentioned first there can be little doubt that for many years the most frequent reason for 'going public' has been the demands of death duties on shareholders' estates[21]. As these have to be valued not as in a quoted share but on some estimate of the going worth of the business there are even problems of assessing the amount due. Mention has already been made of EDITH and there are parallel arrangements under the auspices of individual merchant and industrial banks.

Further pressures favouring a public issue may be the desire to escape from close company status or the spreading of risks by proprietors themselves. Indeed key shareholders in private companies have long sought to limit their commitment to their own firm by preferring to direct the business into borrowing to the fullest extent so that they might spread their investments in wider and more marketable outlets.

For any or all of these reasons a company may wish to go public, but it can only do so if, as already indicated, it is seeking at least £250,000 and putting on the market at least 35% of its future equity, and is in a position to meet the requirements of the stock exchanges as to its past record. Normally this requires at least five years trading for even a quotation, let alone permission to deal. Furthermore its finances must be such that it can face costs of making the issue. At this stage this phrase is taken to mean the conventional costs of the actual process. The true total cost is of quite a different order, as is shown below.

How then does a private limited company set about changing itself into a public one, seeking a quotation, and finally making an issue? The first step is to so amend its Articles of Association as to remove those provisions which give it private status, that is the restrictions on the transferability of shares, and on the number of members. If, however, more extensive changes are needed — in objects, capital or where the company has been limited by guarantee — then a new public company has to be registered and the whole business is then transferred to it. The second step is to file a prospectus or a statement in lieu of prospectus. These two steps are relatively simple. Changing into an unquoted public company is easy; what is much more complex is the process of seeking a quotation and later of floating the company through a public issue, whatever form that takes.

It is inevitable that these steps will only be taken for fundamental financial reasons and with professional advice and support from the company's bankers. Attention has already been drawn to the apparent cost of making an issue. The true cost and the difficulty of reaching a point at which it is feasible to contemplate such a move must now be considered.

At the centre of these questions is the so-called 'Macmillan gap' first publicised in 1931[22]. The Macmillan report argued that there were deficiencies in the financial facilities available for firms engaged in domestic operations which did not exist where international trade was concerned. In particular there was a need for closer cooperation between banking institutions and industry in what might be termed medium-term finance, and there was a specific difficulty where new quotations of growing companies were involved. The commercial banks did not sponsor them in the way that issuing banks and merchant banks did for overseas investments. Accordingly they recommended new jointly-backed institutions, of which the more recently merged Finance Corporation for Industry (FCI) and Industrial and Commercial Finance Corporation (ICFC) were the most important successors. When the Bolton Committee studied the problems they came to a very similar conclusion to the Macmillan report forty years earlier 'that sound borrowers for purposes of a kind which it is suitable to finance by means of bank loans have seldom or never been refused adequate accommodation by their bankers'[23]. The Bolton Committee added that the institutions developed subsequently had filled the gap. But there is still a problem for the firm which is seeking finance beyond the normal duration of bank loans but below the scale at which merchant banks and similar institutions are interested, let alone a flotation being successfully launched.

This is a point brought out in the study of Davis and Yeomans[24] who analyse the cost of issues in relation to both method of flotation and size of issue. They challenge the Bolton report's conclusion that the Macmillan gap has largely been filled by pointing to the costs to an aspiring private company both of handling a flotation and of the cost to it of the terms upon which that flotation is made.

These terms depend upon which of the three methods in general use is chosen. They are Offer for Sale, Placing, and Offer by Tender. The company could make a Direct Offer to the public, sometimes called an Offer by Prospectus, in which the company bears the risk of the issue being unsuccessful. In practice this means that the Issuing House assisting the company would itself underwrite or share in underwriting — sub-underwriting — for a commission not exceeding 10% of the nominal value. This method is rarely employed for shares nowadays.

An Offer for Sale, the most frequently used method, is in two stages. In the first the company sells all the securities that are subsequently to be offered for sale to an Issuing House at a fixed price. The Issuing House may well have been concerned in its industrial banking role with the 'nursing' of the company over a period of years, or it may have been brought in at this stage following a period of support under other auspices, such as ICFC or one of the special investment companies that have become more numerous since the Bolton report was published.

These are companies backed by an insurance company or a merchant bank, having both a financial and a management input in the firms that they act for or even own. Thus Venture Capital, chaired by John Bolton himself, limits its interest to that number of firms that it can effectively help in a management capacity. Assistance, as opposed to direct management, is

offered by many financial institutions, though most bankers still
heed the warning given by Dr Goldschmidt to the Macmillan
Committee that 'a banker must never forget that he cannot and
must not be an industrialist'[25]. However, the merchant banker is
now about to perform one of his accepted banking roles, that of
the second stage in the offer for sale at which a prospectus is
issued offering the shares at a price at which the offer can be
expected to succeed.

The wording here is important. The Issuing House is
concerned that the issue is taken up, mainly for the criticism and
reflection on it and its client that must follow if it is not, but also
because it will have to take up the balance except to the extent
that it has sub-underwritten the issue. Basically the Issuing
House is dependent on a successful sale for its profit; it is not
being paid to make the issue in any other way. The price at
which it offers for sale is therefore critical, and the study of
Davis and Yeomans concentrates on the discount implicit in
such a price. In order to ensure success the price is usually 10—
15% below that which subsequently materialises with normal
trading in the stock under stable market conditions.

Four arguments can be put forward for such a discount. The
first is the greater risk associated with small firms by the capital
market, particularly in terms of credit-worthiness; there is no
clear evidence against smaller firms on grounds of profitability.
The second is the need to protect underwriters and other
institutions involved, all of whom are investing clients' money,
not their own. The third is the risk that institutions may find
themselves left with too high a holding in any one company to
meet their preference for spreading risks. Spiegelberg quotes
the example of Robert Fleming where a holding approaching
10% of a firm's equity was regarded as excessive[26]. Lastly there
is the uncertainty as to the effect of the interest aroused in a
company when an issue has been made.

The effect of this discount on the cost to the company of the
additional funds raised has to be set against the advantage of
now holding a marketable investment. But there is another
element in the package, namely that the firm must now be able
to maintain its dividend record under an entirely new degree of
continuous expert scrutiny and this must affect its freedom to
act compared to that which existed when it was an owner-
managed private company. An Offer for Sale, however
successful, therefore puts the firm into a different league, with
new opportunities but also new constraints. While it is the most
widely used method, and one that can perhaps produce the most

disposed allocation of shares, thereby reducing if not averting any threat to the balance of power, it does involve the highest cost in terms of the amount of discount in the offer price compared to subsequent performance.

In complete contrast is the second method, that of placing. Once again the entire issue is sold to an Issuing House at a fixed price, either for resale to institutions at a higher agreed price, or for partial resale, the balance being held by the Issuing House. Only a few institutions are likely to be involved and while this method is cheaper, in a direct sense, there are two snags. One is that it cannot normally be used for equity shares if they are to be quoted, unless the amount handled in this way is comparatively small. The other is that a quotation must have been secured by the company. To do so those arranging the placing will have to make sufficient shares available for dealings to begin. The main advantage of placing is clearly the reduction in uncertainty and this is reflected in the lower rate of discount.

The third and last method open on a first flotation is that of Offer by Tender. All the shares are allotted at the highest tendered price offered over a stated minimum price. All the shares will then be allotted at that price at which they are all taken up. This is deliberately aimed at eliminating speculators on new issues and results in a far smaller rate of discount than in the previous two methods. As a method it clearly depends on high demand for the issue and therefore the judgement as to timing is even more critical.

Whichever of these methods has been employed, the outcome is a public company with shares that are dealt in on the stock exchanges. The firm has now passed the hurdles of quotation and permission to deal. But as we have seen earlier, it may still have a strong private interest in effective control so we cannot take it out of the owner-managed catergory, though it is no longer limited to private contact financing. Indeed it is subsequently able to seek to raise further funds by rights issues to existing members. This method involves a direct invitation to offer for shares to existing members in proportion to holdings and with priority to acquire those not so taken up. Such an approach may dispense with outside financial institutions, be cheaper to undertake, and retain the existing balance of power. Such issues should not be compared with bonus or capitalisation issues where no new capital is raised but undistributed profits are converted into issued capital thereby retaining the funds in the concern.

However, due note must be taken of the recent history of the capital market. The collapse in share values in 1974 and the general lack of confidence has made it extremely difficult to float any companies in the ways described above, therefore forcing us to reconsider the ways in which the private sector is to survive, and the innovations in company finance that these may entail.

Notes and references

1 Department of Trade, *Companies in 1974*, HMSO 1975.

2. Committee of Inquiry on Small Firms, Bolton Report, Cmd 4811, HMSO 1971.

3 They excluded those in agriculture, fishing, horticulture, and the professions.

4 K. D. George and T. S. Ward, *Structure of Industry in EEC*, Occasional paper 43, Department of Applied Economics, Cambridge.

5 A. Marshall, *Economics of Industry*, Macmillan 1892, p. 175.

6 Bolton Report *op. cit.,* ch 2.

7 J. Boswell, *The Rise and Decline of Small Firms*, Allen & Unwin 1972.

8 Boswell *op. cit.,* p. 53.

9 P. Clarke, *Small Businesses: How they Succeed and Survive*, David & Charles 1972.

10 A. Alchian, 'Uncertainty, evolution and economic theory', *Journal of Political Economy* 1950, p. 212.

11 C. F. Carter and B. R. Williams, *Industry and Technical Progress*, Oxford University Press 1957.

12 PEP, *Attitudes in British Industry*, Penguin 1965.

13 Clarke *op. cit.*

14 P. Drucker, *The Practice of Management*, Heinemann 1955, ch 10.

15 Boswell *op. cit*, p. 89.

16 Bolton Report *op. cit*, ch 12.

17 E. W. Davis and K. A. Yeomans, *Company Finance and the Capital Market*, Occasional Paper 39, Department of Applied Economics, Cambridge 1974.

18 CBI, *The Responsibilities of the British Public Company*, 1973, p. 15.

19 L. C. B. Gower, *Principles of Modern Company Law*, Stevens 1969, p. 254.

20 Royal Commission on the Distribution of Income and Wealth, Reports 1 and 2, HMSO 1975.

21   J. K. Ghandi, 'Some aspects of the provincial new issue market', *Bulletin of the Oxford Institute of Statistics,* 1964, p. 244.

22   Committee on Finance and Industry, (Macmillan) Report, Cmd 3897, HMSO 1931, para 392.

23   *Ibid.,* para 225. *See also* Committee on the Working of the Monetary System, (Radcliffe) Report, Cmd 827, HMSO 19 pp 324-5.

24   Davis and Yeomans *op. cit.*

25   Macmillan Report, para 390.

26   R. Spiegelberg, *The City,* Quartet Press 1973, p. 30.

Study Questions

1   Account for the continued survival and popularity of the private limited company.

2   'Clogs to clogs in three generations'. How valid is this adage and what are its implications for policies towards the survival of small firms?

3   Why is finance thought to be a problem for the fast growing private firm and what can such a firm do to get over the problem?

4   Discuss the advantages and disadvantages of 'going public'.

4

THE PUBLIC COMPANY

4.1 The Quoted Company Sector

Here we are dealing with far fewer firms, some of which command immense resources, and a few of which are of major importance, not just to one national economy but to many, exercising economic power on a greater scale than smaller developed nation-states. Behind them all we are looking at an intricate and concentrated financial network, which effectively concentrates even greater economic influence. Questions have to be asked at each stage about the future relationships that these are to have at the level of the single nation-state and in wider federations such as the EEC.

Let us begin by looking at the quoted company sector based in the UK. This phrase 'based in the UK' is intended to cover two of three situations that arise in the subsequent analysis. The two are companies based and operating within the UK, and companies based here but mainly or entirely operating overseas. The third is the unquoted subsidiary of a company based abroad.

Table 4.1 shows the number changing from and to private company status and is comparable to table 3.5 for private companies. As there was no comparable peak in 1973 it has been omitted.

There is a striking fall in the number of conversions of private to public companies which is linked to the paucity of flotations of previously private companies.

Thus the *Annual Abstract of Statistics* gives data relating to only 1,168 quoted companies trading in the UK in 1972. Yet these had a combined gross trading income of £707 millions and an average weekly employment of 5,832,000! Clearly, they made up in scale of operations for any smallness of numbers compared to other forms of business ownership.

Table 4.1 *Changes in number of public companies registered UK 1965, 1970, 1974*

	1965	1970	1974
All registered 31 Dec.	16,411	16,639	16,658
New registrations	239	172	134
Conversions:			
private to public	197	112	60
public to private	149	111	120
In liquidation or course			
of removal	1,100	1,214	1,105
Effective registered 31 Dec.	15,311	15,425	15,553

Department of Trade, *Companies in 1974*, HMSO 1975.

This is, however, only a first impression. Within this group a minority exercise great influence. Before the merger wave of the past two decades, Sargant Florence[1] showed that the hundred largest quoted companies earned 20% of the aggregate profits of industry and commerce, and that some 1700 companies earned 40%. If this concentration were not striking enough he pointed to the fact that in manufacturing industries the 93 largest companies controlled 65% of the net assets.

More recent studies by Utton[2] and George[3] show that this process of concentration in the larger public companies has now gone further here than in the USA even when disregarding the transfer of large companies in steel to the public sector. Add in that sector and one has a high degree of concentration of ownership, let alone market power. While the data used in these studies do not always refer to public companies, very few private companies are anywhere near the top 100 companies by assets controlled. Indeed, a recent study by Whittington[4] shows that private companies becoming public quoted ones through flotations account for 9 of the newcomers among the 100 largest companies in 1968 as compared to 1948.

Equally, when we examine those institutions that are in a position to judge and influence the performance of this sector we are coming to grips with a major centre of power, second only to government itself. Indeed, one of the issues is the concurrent but often divergent influences of these two centres of power.

Already the reader will have noticed a change of emphasis with the introduction of other sources and forms of control than those derived from ownership. These began with the discussion of the separation of ownership and control in Chapter 1 and have now been extended to other forms of power exercised by one firm over another. The discussion which follows on share ownership and control must be viewed in this context; we are not asserting that share ownership is the sole source of power to be considered — far from it. Nevertheless, the issues here are striking enough to command our immediate attention.

The move from the relatively close relationships of the participants in a private limited company with owner-management and minimal outside interests through the transitional phase of 'going public' to the situation of the large quoted public company involves a radical change in ideas on ownership and control. While the founders or their successors may remain in command, the basis of their power and the environment in which they now have to operate are new. This is illustrated by several features, foremost amongst which is the pattern of share ownership. Here there has been a marked change in the role of the private investor in comparison with financial institutions in recent years.

Two studies carried out by the Department of Applied Economics at Cambridge bring this out in respect of quoted ordinary shares in 1963 and 1969. They are summarised in

Table 4.2 *Beneficial ownership of quoted ordinary shares in UK companies in 1963 and 1969 and in 30 large UK companies in 1975*

Category	Quoted cos 1963	Quoted cos 1969	30 large quoted cos 1975
Persons, executors and trustees resident in UK	54.0	47.4	42.1
Charities and non-profit making bodies	2.1	2.1	4.2
Insurance companies	10.0	12.2	14.9
Pension funds	6.4	9.0	15.2
Investment trust companies	7.4	7.6	4.7
Unit trusts	1.3	2.9	2.0
Banks	1.3	1.7	2.1
Stock exchange	1.4	1.4	0.1
Other financial institutions	2.6	1.1	0.5
Non-financial companies	5.1	5.4	2.2
Public sector	1.5	2.6	0.8
Overseas	7.0	6.6	3.5
Unallocated nominees			7.7

Source: Royal Commission on Distribution of Income and Wealth Report No. 2, Cmd, 6172, HMSO 1975, tables 1 and 6.

table 4.2 which is derived from the second report of the Royal Commission on the Distribution of Income and Wealth. This shows, in addition, the results of an analysis of holdings in 30 large companies in 1975. Yet the Diamond Report makes the point that by percentage of ordinary shares issued, the change in the period 1963-73 for quoted companies was even more striking.

In 1973 financial institutions already held 41.6% of the equities in UK registered and managed quoted companies, with the insurance companies leading the field with 16.2% followed in descending order of importance by Investment Trust Companies, Private Pension Funds, Unit Trusts, and Public and Local Authority Pension Funds.

The effect of this and of the second change, the greater dispersion of private shareholdings themselves with some two million private shareholders having mostly very small stakes in companies, is to create an even more dispersed share ownership in which it becomes even less likely that any one shareholder will have a dominant influence. Against this, three factors must be set.

The first is a direct consequence of this dispersion. It is that effective control can be exercised on the basis of a much smaller proportion of shares, certainly well below the conventional 51%, if the rest either do not vote or do so at random or by granting proxies to the group in control. The second is the

Table 4.3 *Portfolio turnover in equities 1971*

Investory type A	Equity purchases as % average market value	Equity sales as % average market value	Portfolio turnover (purchases × sales)
Insurance companies	12.9	7.3	20.2
Pension Funds:			
Public	19.6	14.0	33.6
Private	19.2	6.0	31.2
Local Government	25.8	12.4	38.2
Investment trust			
companies	15.4	12.1	27.5
Unit trusts	39.7	33.8	73.6
Private investors	14.0	17.6	31.6

R. Dobbins, 'Institutional shareholders in UK equity market', *Accounting and Business Research* 1972.

difference in the individual behaviour of any institutional investor from that of private shareholders as a whole. There is a presumption that the institutions, and in practice this means their investment managers, will exercise a much keener, professional view over company affairs and act accordingly. One way in which they will act is to keep down their involvement in any one firm, thereby reinforcing the disposal argument. Another is to move quickly in and out of stocks.

Dobbins analysed portfolio turnover in 1971 by setting sales and purchases of equities in quoted companies against their average market values for the year as set out in table 4.3.

In only one group, private shareholders, did sales exceed purchases, itself an indication of the change already referred to. Clearly, the most volatile were the unit trusts, with a relatively high turn-round of their portfolios. The pension funds came next and then the investment trust companies. The insurance companies were by far the most stable.

Clearly, these reflect the different aims and interests of the various categories. The question that emerges is, therefore, to what extent the third factor, joint pressure by institutions, is a possibility. This is potentially a very important influence having a substantial effect on the power balance, but posing real dilemmas of knowledge and expertise for the institutions.

It would therefore be wrong to assume that because there is widespread dispersion of shareholdings in equities in general that the outcome is a relatively independent position for companies on this evidence. Quite apart from the very great inequality in the size of holdings that persists, leading to owner-management of a minority of even large public companies, there is the question of pressure from individual or collective action by institutions. To put this into perspective, however, we have to consider first the comparative insignificance of the new issue market as a source of funds, and second the effect of the sharp increase in the gearing ratio that has occurred over recent decades.

Over the period 1962-72 equity capital raised for cash accounted for only 4.5% of the investment funds of quoted companies compared to 76% from retained profits with loans and other forms of borrowing accounting for the balance. Taking 1972, for example, all share issues by 1,168 quoted companies involved £1,621 M of which only £440 M was for cash. This compared to increased bank loans of £315 M and in creditors of £1,198 M. Gross income for the same period was £5,707[6].

This high degree of self-financing on the part of the UK

companies, while in sharp distinction to the practice in other West European companies, has meant that as long as companies could sustain this situation they could enjoy a high degree of independence, not only of the stock market but of the financial institutions as a whole — not just those that act as institutional investors. Three comments are necessary here.

The first is that the position has been under attack because of the combined pressure of taxation and inflation. The effect of these on the whole process of depreciation and of funding re-investment, let alone new investment, has been such as to force firms to seek external finance, particularly by borrowing.

The second is that the financial institutions were originally developed to finance trade, becoming highly proficient at financing international transactions, and thereby acquiring great knowledge of dealing in money but far less of managing businesses that were themselves changing with the longer lead time associated with much modern production.

The third is that both companies and financial institutions have acquired 'knowledge gaps'. On the company side, the poor understanding of finance has made both for tragic mistakes and to a great dependence on financial advisers, whether internal or external. The writer recalls hearing a participant in one of the first executive courses he ever taught emerging from the first session on finance and accounting with the words ' its like religion, you have to believe in it'. While he later, whether through belief or not, rose to be head of a very large industrial group, his reaction was the reciprocal of the merchant banker who, twenty-five years later, when talking to the writer about a company to be studied, observed that 'it is in manufacturing industry which we in the City are currently frightened to touch, it is in high technology which puts it right out of court, and if that is not enough, it is connected to the aero-space industry'.

These attitudes, and the deficiencies in knowledge and skill that they honestly reflect, cannot be separated from this analysis of power and its use. The point that emerges is that inflation and corporate taxation are putting serious strains on the liquidity of much of UK business at least in the short period, and that this has brought a growing number of companies to the point where external financial support from traditional sources has not been forthcoming on a sufficient scale, leading to the question of governmental support, whether by guarantee of borrowing or direct investment. This, in turn, has raised even more profound questions of future power and accountability.

At the same time dispersion of interest in companies has

never been greater. The Diamond Commission reports that, in addition to 2 million shareholders, there are 13¼ million members of occupational pension schemes and 14 million savers through life assurance alone. These are very significant interests to be set against the arguments of those who would further reduce, if not eliminate, the interest and influence of investors in the running of companies. Where this balance of power between different immediate investors becomes apparent is when a public company is involved in a major step that calls for shareholder consent. The most obvious is where a take-over is concerned.

Let us look at three celebrated take-over battles, one in the early days (British Aluminium) and two more recently (GEC/AEI) and (PO/Bovis). In the first case one group, Tube Investments acting jointly with an American group, Reynolds, had quietly acquired 10% of the British Aluminium equity by market purchases before they put their proposals for a take-over to the British Aluminium board, who then revealed that they had already arranged a deal with the Alcoa group on terms which they judged to be in the interests of their company. As a result a fierce battle developed between the bidders and their backers on the one hand, and the company and the rest of the merchant banking community on the other. The bid succeeded when key institutions — including in this case the Church Commissioners — favoured acceptance. In the second, an important part of the battle for AEI was the series of meetings between Sir Arnold Weinstock and his associates with groups of institutions in each major city. The majority favoured Sir Arnold and GEC took over.

In the third case there was a division on the P & O Board, followed by widespread debate backed by conflicting views of the financial advisers to the Board and the dissentients. In this case both the private shareholders and the institutions rejected the merger at the time, a decision well justified in view of the terms agreed less than two years later.

But the institutions are not always sufficiently strong or united to overcome the general body of shareholders, as seen in their attempt to oust 'Tiny' Rowlandson from the post of Managing Director of the Lonrho group, in which the exceptionally large number of small shareholders was sufficient to rally to Rowlandson's support and survival.

Potentially, therefore, what matters given the particular distribution of shareholdings in a quoted company is the degree of interest that its affairs arouse among the professionals who manage the institutional holdings. As the study by Midgley[7] points out, during most of the time shareholders are conspicuous by their absence from annual general meetings, and the latter distinguished by their brevity. The reasons for this lack of interest have been very fully explored by Sargant Florence; he suggests the reasons are lack of knowledge, inertia and the existence of the easier remedy of selling out if dissatisfied. To these might then be added the dynamics of conducting a meeting in the absence of any organised opposition or restrictions on voting rights[8].

This is not to imply that all such meetings are havens of peace and quiet. Interested groups such as trades unions have begun to attend and make themselves heard. The pressure of shareholder opinion, both private and institutional, on the Distillers Company over the thalidomide compensation issue is a case in point. But organised steps to liven up such meetings like that taken by Mr William Gammell who organised a bus load of shareholders to attend the 1964 annual general meeting of Crown Cork are rare and there is no equivalent to some of the investor pressure groups that have sprung up in Sweden for example.

However, there is one feature of share ownership which does call for further comment, and that is the practice of nominee-shareholdings. These are shares held on behalf of an undisclosed party by an agent, such as a bank or trust. The issue here is whether a firm ought not to know who its shareholders really are, especially where shares are acquired through nominees in the early stages of a take-over bid. At present there is no requirement at law to disclose the identity of the holder and this is justified on grounds of the delicacy of disclosure for such parties as the Royal Family, foreign potentates and individuals. The code of conduct for take-overs developed by the City Panel goes some way to meet this by requiring disclosure of the identity of the bidder once acquisitions have passed the 10% mark, and then requiring that no further bids proceed *sub rosa* using nominees as had occurred in the Philips/Pye transactions.

Lastly, in what circumstances can the shareholders make themselves felt? Essentially this is only through a general meeting, though large and influential shareholders may bring informal pressure to bear on directors. The principal opportunity is the Annual General Meeting at which the accounts and reports are received and approved, retiring directors re-elected or new directors elected, and the auditors reappointed. Otherwise an extraordinary general meeting is required for other matters or when called by the directors, either on their own account or at the requisition of shareholders having not less than 10% of the paid up capital carrying voting rights. Voting is initially by show of hands, but a poll can be demanded if the Articles permit and then proxies can be exercised on behalf of shareholders not present. The proxy system, however, favours the board who can invite members to authorise them to act for them.

4.2 The Role of the Board of Directors

Whereas in the case of private firms a close relationship of shareholders and directors was implicit, the very nature of the public company brings out forcibly the distinction between the general body of shareholders and the Board. If the separation of ownership and control already described then follows it becomes all the more necessary for us to understand the division of powers between them. In particular, it is essential to examine on what basis 'professional manager' directors are able to conduct the affairs of companies towards different priorities to those conventionally associated with 'owner-managers'.

Accordingly, this section explores the basis of the power exercised by directors, the issues posed in their transactions on behalf of the companies they direct, and the evidence as to the objectives they seek to pursue. It is also timely to comment on the nature and membership of UK company boards in view of the preference in some other countries, notably within EEC, for a two-tier structure of a board of directors and a board of management. These studies then provide a suitable back-cloth to subsequent discussions on the future composition and accountability of boards of directors before we turn to the question of how that accountability is assessed by present approaches to company auditing.

How do they get appointed in the first place? When a company is newly formed they may be among the original subscribers and be named in the Articles, but in a public company they are subsequently elected by the annual general meeting for periods of office, retirement being by rotation except where the Articles specifically provide for a longer period of appointment. In practice, this process gives a board almost full control over whom it may invite to join its membership, the qualification being necessary to cover those situations where a director has to be appointed to represent a particular interest, for example the firm's financial advisers or bankers, or a particular group of shareholders. Furthermore, the board can co-opt, confirmation following at the next annual general meeting. The only check on this otherwise apparently impregnable position lies in the requirement that directors have to be elected individually, and not as a group, except where this is agreed in advance, and subject always to the requirement that once a director reaches 70 he must retire at the next annual general meeting. He can, however, then be re-elected for the normal term!

The directors may also have service contracts with the company as managing or working directors, and they may also be employees of the company in that they may have been appointed to management posts, possibly carrying a title such as 'special director'. In effect the service contracts are negotiated between themselves, that is between the managing or working directors and the board, subject only to the contracts being available for inspection by the shareholders.

The possibilities of abuse, particularly where a take-over threat is believed to be imminent, have led to a further check being exercised under the City Code. Once a bid has started, any change in existing service contracts being drawn up would require approval by the shareholders. This all adds up to an impressive position. What then are the directors powers and to what checks are they subject?

As to their powers, it is clear that they alone can decide and act for the company except where the Articles require that the shareholders approve a particular change. The shareholders in a general meeting cannot cancel or otherwise interfere with decisions taken that are within the directors' authority. They can only take over from the directors in the event of default of action on the part of the board. The only ways in which the shareholders can act is by so amending the Articles as to compel the directors to pursue a particular course, or by the removal of the directors. The latter is indeed their main sanction. To remove a director, a simple majority at a general meeting is sufficient, but special notice (21 days) must have been given and the director concerned has the right to be heard before a decision is taken. In practice, there is a further constraint where he has a service agreement, represented by the cost of ending it.

Subject to these two limitations the board, provided it acts as a board and not as isolated individuals, has almost complete power to act on behalf of the company, even to the point of negotiations to bring about an end to its independent existence whether in a merger or take-over situation. It is clear that while some aspects of the duties owed by directors to their companies are akin to those of trustees, their role is at least that of agents having few restrictions upon their power to act. This includes the right to delegate first to a managing director or directors and second to managers, but they cannot abdicate their responsibilities as directors in so doing. In practice there is a role as director which is distinct from that of being a manager. The director, whatever his special title and management duties, remains one of a group collectively responsible for the whole business of the company.

What duties does a director, as such, owe to his company? Broadly he has two types of duty[9]. He has a fiduciary duty to act in the bona fide interests of the company as he and his colleagues see them, but subject to the restriction that in this, employees, customers, and all others except the shareholders are irrelevant as determined in the News Chronicle case[10]. When that newspaper was closed down the Cadbury family, the controlling group, sought to compensate the employees, but this was successfully contested by one shareholder. Clearly, the judgement of what is in the bona fide interests of shareholders, whether it is maximum distribution of dividends as Friedman[11] or Rubner[12] argue or a more 'responsible' attitude towards all stockholders as argued by K. R. Andrews[13] or Dahrendorf[14], is of fundamental importance to the whole conduct of companies. Where mergers are involved or take-over threatened there can be some very debatable situations.

Taking one case already referred to, the battle for control of British Aluminium, when the Reynolds Tube Investments syndicate approached the board of BA, they were told that a deal had already been agreed with Alcoa. The terms included the acquisition of BA stock at 59s per share and the retention on the new board of the existing BA board members, including the Chairman, Lord Portal. When the battle ended the shares changed hands at 86s, a very different price for the shareholders, and the board was replaced in its entirety.

Or to take an even more controversial step, when the Savoy Hotel group was threatened by a bid from Sir Charles Clore and his group, the directors transferred a key asset from the company to its pension fund, of which they were life trustees, thereby preventing Clore from gaining control of it even if he gained control of the company. Accordingly he withdrew. The Savoy Hotel was able to retain its independence, but was this in the best interests of the shareholders?

The directors, provided they are acting within the proper purpose of the objects clause of the memorandum, the flexibility of which we noted earlier, may exercise unfettered discretion. The problems remaining are then those of conflicts of interest and abuse of confidence. Conflicts of interest may arise on a business transaction where a director has a personal interest, e.g. a contract with another company of which he is also a director. In practice, the Articles provide a measure of protection to directors provided that they disclose to the board that there is an interest and its nature, though not necessarily its scale. A conflict of interest would arise where there is an opening for a secret profit and take-over situations present a number of opportunities for this that the City Take-Over Code has sought to check. As in the British Aluminium case already quoted, there may be an agreement as to future tenure of offices such as membership of a reconstituted board. While the Code attempts to regulate such transactions, the most difficult to check is the profit secured by 'inside' dealing, that is where a party has prior knowledge. This is, of course ,not limited to directors by any means. On the contrary, it poses very considerable dilemmas for a number of parties to such transactions.

The second duty of directors is to exercise care and skill. In this they cannot be expected to do any more than would reasonably be expected of anyone else in this role and there is no clear code of practice as there might be in a profession. How then do they appear to operate? This can be examined from two different standpoints, their method of working as a board, and their general aim and conduct.

As for method of working there are two issues, the type of board and the role of chief executive. The first concerns membership. Typically, UK companies rely on a single-tier board with at least one chief executive, probably some executive directors who also have full-time managerial posts and a number of ordinary or part-time directors. The roles of Chairman and chief executive may even be combined. This is in sharp contrast to the practice elsewhere of two boards, a board of directors representative of shareholders, and in some European countries of employers and the state, and a board of management appointed by the directors but being wholly full-time executives. The first body is then essentially supervisory taking key financial and policy decisions on the basis of proposals from the management board.

Two issues arise immediately. The first concerns the projected Fifth Directive of the EEC Commission on the

European Company with its provision for a two-tier structure with employees being represented on the higher body, a proposal initially opposed by such bodies as CBI on the ground that a single executive body should be retained to take all major policy decisions. The second concerns the domination of UK boards by the full-time members.

On the one hand, the working directors who may well have been promoted from senior management with nominal shareholdings have the knowledge of the firm and are directly concerned with its future. The ordinary directors may have been sought because of their special interests such as trading and financial contacts and knowledge, political experience or even their public standing which can be of help to a firm. Their dilemma is how far they accept the leadership and the information supplied by the existing working directors, especially the chief executive, as illustrated in the events at Lonrho, the Rank Organisation and the collapse of the London and Counties Securities.

While they are primarily sought by the board for their contacts and advice they remain responsible as directors to the shareholders at large. Indeed, they may have a special duty to safeguard their interests against those of a powerful management group. In one sense they are a key component in the information network of the financial institutions. But the need for part-time directors with professional management experience to strengthen the independent members of boards is one of the recommendations of the Catherwood report to the British Institute of Management[15].

The second issue concerning the conduct of boards concerns the role of chairman and chief executive or managing director. Once again UK practice has been to combine these more frequently then elsewhere, but there are strong arguments for their separation, certainly in companies of any substantial size.

Every board has to elect a chairman who, if available, takes the chair at all general meetings of shareholders as well as meetings of the board. The formal duties of a chairman are clearly vital to the effective handling of business. To perform this task he has to be very fully informed, whatever the quality of the advisers at hand at the meetings of the company.

The Catherwood report makes a strong recommendation for the separation of the two roles, arguing that the chairman ought to be in a position to take a broad view of the company and its responsibilities. In practice, he and the managing director as chief executive have to be able to work together, a factor to be borne in mind by whoever is involved in appointing either of them. The chairman may of course be appointed by reasons of his holding in the company, but increasingly he, like the managing director, is a professional! The precise powers and duties delegated to a managing director will vary from one company to another. There is no general definition any more than there is for the role of chairman, except in so far as the Articles stipulate various matters concerning the conduct of meetings.

The picture that emerges is of a potentially very powerful group whose members are admitted by invitation and whose chairman and managing director are selected by, though not necessarily from within, the group. Should this be qualified in any way?

The answer is that in particular companies the real power situation may have to reflect forces that are not contained by the ownership/control model that we have been discussing up to this point. One obvious factor is finance. If a company finds it necessary to seek significant and extended external finance by borrowing, then it is probable that the lender will seek or even insist upon some form of representation at board level, at least for the duration of the advance. This is the basis for the representation of banking and other financial institutions. But a similar pressure may be extended by a dominant supplier or customer leading to the suggestion or even stipulation that it be so represented.

The outcome is, inter alia, a complex information network through which ideas for new links and associations can be fostered, including close associations to the point of amalgamation. A feature of this network is that it is increasingly concerned with questions of securing greater control over what has been described earlier as the turbulence in the environment. Managements are concerned to regulate the sectors in which their firms operate and this poses questions as to the objectives of the groups in effective control.

4.3 Accountability and Audit

Any evaluation of the performance of an enterprise has to start from some definition of an agreed purpose, some acknowledgement of its ethos and style and an appreciation of the means at its disposal. De jure, the public company is in the position that shareholders alone matter whereas, de facto, suppliers of finance and organised labour appear to exercise the main power. The particular company may still be aiming at what it calls profit maximisation or some equally conventional economic measure of performance; it may, however, be already in transition to a different set of aims in which the long-run survival of the enterprise as an employer is as important as maintaining a minimum acceptable rate of return on the assets it uses, or where a wider range of non-pecuniary and social aims has at least been partially introduced. Equally, the firm may not be clear where it stands and what rules it is seeking to apply. Even if we accept a more conventional criterion, by what can the shareholder, whoever he is, judge performance?

Surely, as Bird[16] suggests, the shareholder is only able to judge by the clues he can obtain as to future performance and the only indicators available are the firm's dividend, its share price, the annual reports and accounts, and such comment as these arouse. This is largely historical, not predictive. What the shareholder wants is some measure of managerial and technical competence in the forward planning of the firm's operations. This, he suggests, involves the selection of the optimal period for planning revenues, the choice of the best available alternative course of action based on detailed analysis, correct selection of those actions which will yield the maximum increase in cash income, having the optimal use of the various forms of credit available, and early perception and reaction where circumstances change, whether externally or internally. This exacting specification calls for a very alert learning system in the firm as well as for well-developed competence at strategic search. The overall criterion is still net return on assets employed rather than some less precise formulation in terms of strategic viability as argued for by Ansoff, but the two views are pretty close.

The question emerging is how can anyone external to the firm's management be in a position to assess this? To some extent, past performance in so far as it gives any indication of the balance between successes and failures is at least a starting point. What would be more instructive is some indication of what forecasts had been made, and upon what assumptions the targets had been set and what results were achieved.

The adequacy of the systems used might be judged in some form of management audit but the comparisons that shareholders or their advisers might make would have to take other factors into account, notably the attitudes of the parties — shareholders and directors — to risk.

This whole field of analysis of company performance has been deepened and extended in recent years but it still comes up against a number of key problems. The first of these is the question of what information are firms prepared to reveal as to their plans, even projects contemplated in the past. The traditional secrecy of a competitive system, coupled with suspicion and fear about the use to which information might be put, has been accentuated by the reaction of business men to the growing demands for information by government, with all the latter's secrecy, both as to its own expectation and the data that it has acquired, even when the data are aggregated to preclude identification of individual enterprises. This has been evident throughout the debate on the Industry Act 1975 with its requirements for disclosures, particularly in respect of planning agreements.

The second problem is the state of the art so far as corporate or strategic planning is concerned. This also poses a further dilemma: in many industries relatively long lead-times are inevitable; the capital market, and in practice governments, have a preoccupation with shorter term performance and results. There is a real difficulty in adjusting to widely different lead times, but it is not insuperable.

The main difficulty, however, has lain in the nature of the audit and the annual accounts, which record stewardship over a period of time that has long since elapsed, with the emphasis on integrity, accuracy, and the correctness of judgements in accounting practice terms, as opposed to the assessment of the business decisions taken. Furthermore, the interpretation of published accounts calls for professional knowledge of their contents, particularly where changes occur in their basis, whether of the items themselves — a change of accounting practice — or of their scope — as where a company has been expanded by acquisitions, making the comparison over time difficult.

Nevertheless, the requirements for publicity are a powerful check on the otherwise secret world of business. The trouble is that the business community has become increasingly adept at handling many aspects of publicity, not least that involving the financial press[17].

The auditor's report continues to play an important part. It is essentially a check on the state of accounting practice in the company including, therefore, a comment on the extent to which a 'true and fair view' is given in the figures, and therefore their basis, as presented in the annual accounts. Where the auditor is unable to give a favourable opinion on some aspect of the accounts then he can do one of three things, any of which is a signal to all concerned and may trigger off further enquiries.

The first, a qualified approval, will refer to those items upon which he has reservations, as for example where he feels unable to come to a conclusion as to the fairness of the view given by the accounts as presented to him. The second is an adverse opinion, as where he takes exception to the treatment of an item that is so significant as to affect the view given by the accounts as a whole. The third and last is to refuse any opinion at all.

The auditor's report is to the shareholders, not the directors, and it is the shareholders who appoint and fix the remuneration of the auditors — otherwise the Department of Industry does so. The auditors are heard at the annual general meeting and cannot be removed except after special notice and after they have had an opportunity to be heard by the shareholders. This forms an important part of the process whereby accountability is currently seen to be exercised.

At the Annual General Meeting, in addition to the accounts and the auditor's report upon them, there will also be a report from the directors, probably supplemented by an address from the chairman, all of which are circulated in advance. These at least offer an opportunity, albeit a limited one that is rarely exercised, for the shareholders to question and to accept or reject the views of the board. But as seen earlier, their powers remain very slight, quite apart from the dynamics of the meeting which normally work heavily in favour of the board, as they are limited to not approving or receiving papers, and to their voting in the election of directors. Nevertheless, the fact that the meeting is held in public with the press present, the report and accounts having been released in advance, is a significant check provided the directors are being sensitive to shareholder and outside opinion. Where this does not appear to be the case, as in such situations as the transactions of Newman Industries in 1975-6, or where there are complex overlaps in their interests, or simply dominant leadership by a powerful chairman as in Lonrho, the Rank Organisation or the London and Counties Securities cases, even powerful institutions may find it difficult to get full information, let alone influence the outcome. Indeed, the deplorable state into which some companies have been seen to degenerate all too quickly does raise the question of the adequacy of present monitoring.

Three parties are involved here. The first are the directors themselves and more especially the outside or part-time directors. The extent to which both their detachment from executive involvement and their independence from the chairman or chief executive permit them to act as stewards of the interests of shareholders as a whole is partly a matter of their perception of their role, partly a function of the information offered to them and partly a personal matter as to how far they are prepared to intervene. Reaction to disagreements on policy may be such as to provoke demands for their resignation without any immediate opportunity for the issues to be considered by the shareholders.

One of the disquieting features of recent cases is the quality of the information available, both in terms of the willingness to reveal it and as to the care and skill of the second of the parties, the auditors. The criticisms of auditors' reports have raised questions about the state of professional skill as well as the importance of judgement in the assessment of accounts or transactions. This has even led to substantial settlements in compensation.

The third party is the firm, often accountants, who act as financial advisers, whether in addition to being auditors or acting independently. Once again this is a matter of professional judgements, but where the advisers are financial institutions there may be a problem of the nature of their interests and the use they may be able to make of 'inside information'. The dilemma was well illustrated in the case of Flemings as advisers to Pergamon Press in their negotiations with Leasco.

These parties can be studied most closely when there is a challenge to the essentially 'one-party' state in which most companies operate most of the time. If there is no split among the existing board then the challenge has to come from an outside source and this usually means another company which has begun to acquire shares and which may seek a change of policy if not a take-over of effective control. This is discussed in Chapter 5. Alternatively, there may be a split among the present board which is brought into the open through resignations, and this may then trigger off new comment and interest in the firm concerned which may stimulate interest among possible suitors for merger or take-over.

Otherwise we are back to the question of how far shareholders are able and willing to be actively involved and, in particular, the role of the professionally managed investors, the institutions. Even here, however, there is a limit set by the provisions of the Companies Act with admittedly ultimate safeguards through the powers of the Department of Trade and Council of the Stock Exchange.

4.4 Company Law and the Regulation of Quoted Companies

While Chapter 3 examines the influence exerted by the stock market and Chapter 8 the interventions on issues of policy by government, this is a convenient point at which to take note of the two main means of overall regulation of the conduct of quoted companies, company law and the rules and moral sanctions of the stock exchanges. At the moment even the legal framework is in a state of flux, innovations having been made through a range of legislation and further revision of the Companies Act deferred pending the outcome of the Bullock Committee on Industrial Democracy in the private sector[18].

The aim in both legislation and the sanctions of the stock exchange is basically identical, namely to extend, initially by example, then by exhortation and lastly by legally enforceable sanction what is currently accepted as good practice to all companies. An important feature of the whole approach is therefore publicity.

The Companies Acts having initially conceded the privileges of incorporation and limited liability, their main emphasis lay in protecting the rights of those who traded with companies, in particular their creditors. Only later did the emphasis switch to ensuring that shareholders had the opportunity to influence the fate of their investments. While on the one hand there has been even greater tolerance of the freedom of action allowed to directors, for example in the interpretation of objects clauses and their revision, there has also been a rising demand for greater disclosure of information at two levels. The first is the immediate financial or other personal interest of the directors in any transaction including their own terms of remuneration and compensation where they are working directors. The second concerns the conduct of the enterprise as a whole and the interest therein of a much wider public not confined to those working in the concern. This wider interest revolves around the performance of the firm and the need for information as a basis of comment and possible action. The press has an important role here in publication and comment on results and other information.

The extent to which the data and the procedural opportunities under company law are used by shareholders is a matter for them. Such aspects of this as the role of the institutions acting in concert are dealt with in Chapter 5. The only provisions for intervention under the Companies Acts are of two types. The first is where there is a failure to carry out a statutory obligation such as holding an annual general meeting within the required period, and the second is where circumstances arise in which an inspection is initiated by the Department of Trade.

The difficulties here are the scale of the resources at the disposal of the Department and the reluctance to resort to a full investigation because of the publicity involved. Even a preliminary study could tip off offenders and give time for covering action. In 1974 the Department started with 123 inspections outstanding; it received 438 applications of which 158 were approved[19]. The first step is a request for books and documents for inspection before proceeding to the appointment of inspectors, a step which arouses widespread publicity and almost certainly a suspension in dealings in the shares of the firm concerned. The outcome is a published report which may make very severe criticisms of the conduct of named individuals in a manner which might not be admissible in a court of law. The main long-term consequence is the highlighting of issues that call for new codes of conduct if not for strengthening of the law itself. Such evolution of codes of conduct is central to the self regulation of the City as a whole. This again is an issue which is discussed in Chapter 5.

There remains the extent to which the shareholder can act through the Courts as opposed to general meetings of shareholders. In general, the tendency has been to expect shareholders to seek redress through the machinery of the company and not through the courts but there are four circumstances in which he can seek the help of the courts:

(i)   the company has acted or is proposing to act, ultra vires;

(ii)   The action taken or proposed, though not ultra vires, has not been approved in the proper manner, for example, by a special or extraordinary resolution at a general meeting, where such a step is required;

(iii)   the personal rights of the shareholder have been or are about to be infringed;

(iv)   those in control are perpetuating what is termed a 'fraud on the minority', that is they are directly or indirectly adversely affecting the business and its assets to their own advantage.

In these cases the shareholder may apply to the Courts for an order stopping the offending action and compelling redress. As an ultimate sanction an application may be made for a compulsory winding up of the company.

A quoted company is subject to the additional requirements of the Council of the Stock Exchanges. This key body plays an important role in the evolution of accepted practice and eventually the law itself. As situations arise where the interests of shareholders are at risk through some practice that is regarded as 'unfair' or prejudicial, the Council may first indicate its disfavour without applying any sanctions to secure observance; at a later stage, this opinion may be consolidated in what is accepted as a convention and lastly as a rule. One major field in which this evolution has been of particular significance is in respect of mergers and take-overs. In this case there has been much pressure from outside opinion to which the City has responded through the establishment of the Take-over Panel and then the development of a code of behaviour which remains dependent on voluntary observance backed, it is true, by 'responsible opinion'. What remains debatable is the adequacy and acceptability of such voluntary regulation. There is a growing minority opinion that the powers of the existing bodies are not enough and the case is put forward in Chapter 5 for an equivalent to the Securities Exchange Commission in the USA.

For the present the combined watchdogs are the Bank of England, which acts as a link between the City and government, the professional bodies such as the accountancy institutes and the Council of the Stock Exchange.

Notes and references

1   P. Sargant Florence, *Ownership, Control and Success of Large Companies,* Sweet & Maxwell 1961.

2   M. A. Utton, *Industrial Concentration,* Penguin 1970.

3   K. D. George, 'Concentration and specialisation in industry', *Journal of Industrial Economics,* April 1972.

4   G. Whittington, 'Changes in the top 100 quoted manufacturing companies in the United Kingdom 1948-68, *Journal of Industrial Economics,* November 1972.

5   R. Dobbins, 'Institutional shareholders in UK Equity Market' *Accounting and Business Research,* 1973.

6   *Annual Abstract of Statistics,* HMSO 1974. A more recent study shows that new equity issues account for only 12% of gross

capital spending with only 4% representing new cash receipts. See G. Meeks and G. Whittington, *The Finance of Quoted Companies in the UK,* Study for Diamond Commission, HMSO 1976.

7 K. Midgley, 'How much control do shareholders exercise?', *Lloyds Bank Review,* October 1974.

8 Preference shares may only carry voting rights if the dividend is not fully paid. Other non-voting shares are now exceptional. There is pressure to enfranchise all shareholders, e.g. Rank Organisation 1976.

9 L. C. B. Gower, *Principles of Modern Company Law,* Stevens 1969, Ch. 23.

10 Parke v London Daily News Ltd, 1962.

11 M. Friedman, *Capitalism and Freedom,* Chicago University Press 1963.

12 A. Rubner, *The Ensnared Shareholder,* Penguin 1965.

13 K. R. Andrews, 'Public responsibility in the private corporation', *Journal of Industrial Economics,* April 1972.

14 R. Dahrendorf, *Class and Conflict in Modern Society,* Routledge and Kegan Paul 1959.

15 British Institute of Management, *The Responsible Company* 1974.

16 P. Bird, *Accountability: Standards in Financial Reporting,* Haymarket 1973.

17 R. Spiegelberg, *The City,* Quartet Press 1973.

18 A committee on Industrial Democracy in the Private Sector was set up in 1975 to report within twelve months; a parallel study is bvein

19 Department of Trade, *Companies in 1974,* HMSO 1975.

Study Questions

1 Examine the role and responsibilities of the ordinary or non-executive director.

2 Consider the case for separating the roles of chairman and chief executive.

3 How can the shareholder be enabled to exercise any active role in the working of a public company?

4 Discuss the possible future scope of company accountability.

5
THE CORPORATE SECTOR IN THEORY AND PRACTICE

5.1 Theory in Transition

Given the importance of the quoted public company sector to the economy and the opportunities for independent action open to boards of directors, the monitoring of their performance becomes a matter of general concern. In practice this has two aspects. There is, first, the self-regulation of the 'corporate sector', that is the quoted companies and all the bodies that participate in the assessment of their performance through the stock market. This is the immediate check, as the market is ultimately one in corporate control. There is, second, the regulation both of companies as such and of the economy as a whole, that is the role of the government and is the subject of Chapter 8; our present concern is with the market in corporate control.

What is of interest is the way in which this market has been evolving especially after a period of intense merger and take-over activity which has been accompanied by significant changes in the structure and strategy of many larger companies. The first step, therefore, is a comparison of models of the behaviour of firms in relation to this market given the changes within companies such as the separation of ownership and control and the emergence of professional management. Earlier models assumed that the stock market had a major role in the direction in which investment might occur through its control, not only over the investment of new funds first appearing, but also through the reinvestment of distributed profits at a time when not only was there more apparent support for profit maximisation as a goal but less emphasis on the retention of funds within companies for investment by their directors. This earlier view of the working of the capitalist system sees the shareholders as the owners of companies;

profits should be maximised and distributed so that they can decide on their use, not the present directors.

Clearly, this view is not accepted as representative of the modern corporation by writers such as Galbraith[1] who depicts the large company as being almost independent of stock market pressures. It has attained such a scale of operations and of redeployment of resources within itself for a variety of purposes as to need to be called to account on quite different social reasons. That the large company may enjoy such independence cannot be denied; it may be able by sheer reputation to attract funds on terms and by means that are not open to lesser firms, but it has at least to pay sufficient attention to the stock market that its standing there is maintained at a level acceptable to its board even though it may appear beyond the reach of a take-over bid. But as both G. C. Allen[2] and Meade[2] have pointed out, the Galbraithian view not only ignores the very substantial sector of quoted, let alone unquoted, companies that exists but it also takes no account of the many ways in which governments and other agencies can bring pressure to bear on even the largest firms.

The extent to which firms can escape the discipline of the market is as easily exaggerated at one end of the spectrum as the power of the market over firms can be inflated at the other. The market retains three basic functions. It acts as a means for allocating new funds among the prospective users on criteria of profit expectation against risk assessment; it may have only a limited role in reinvestment where funds are heavily retained both as a free choice by boards and under the impact of taxation policies which may or may not be concerned with encouragement of investment; but it acts as a monitor of performance in the use of funds already committed and as a mechanism for bringing about a challenge to existing direction where this is thought to be poor.

Whatever the state of the argument about the role of profit as a measure of performance and of profit maximisation as a goal of company directors, the fact remains that profit is a key indicator.

Profit maximisation in its strict theoretical sense is unattainable if only because no firm has the information system or the means of allocating costs to permit it; the most that can be hoped for is an approximation and even this is fraught with persistent problems of judgements about the treatment of items. Nevertheless, it is one of the tests of performance and one of the goals of enterprise. It is, however, only realistic to qualify it as a goal. Firms are concerned with the turbulence of their environment and while profit is an incentive to face that turbulence, measures to control parts of the environment and to protect positions of power have been acknowledged as key business aims. Thus Schumpeter recognised the importance of power and of technical or product satisfaction as well as profit as goals of business men. The problem at this point is how far does the present system reflect this with its apparent preoccupation with short-term profit.

It is this recognition of the importance of power in the sense of both retention and extension of control by a board of directors that has attracted the attentions of writers such as Marris[3]. Starting from the position that, in an increasing number of firms, share ownership is dispersed and the directors are in the position of being regarded through their performance as working directors and not as major shareholders, he set out to explore what policies they might be expected to pursue. In particular, he was concerned to compare their likely impact on the growth and performance of their companies with those of owner directors, that is those with a substantial capital stake. The argument has many points in common with those later put forward by Galbraith, but is set in a non-Galbraithian setting in which holding on to the position of power is subject to the external threat of overthrow through a take-over bid. Marris argues that the directors have a direct interest in extending their influence as they are likely to be rewarded more on a basis of the extent of their responsibilities than on the profits they earn. But to stay there they have to so run the firm that they do not lose control; therefore they have to put it in a situation where it is not attractive to others, primarily in terms of what he calls the valuation ratio, the estimate of what it could yield to an outside bidder compared to what it is currently yielding to the present shareholders.

The one major constraint is the cost of the bid itself. A potential bidder has to be able to convince sufficient share-holders that he can generate a better performance than the existing directors, and he has therefore to be able to show three things. He has to put a higher valuation on the potential earning power of the assets employed than the present controllers. He has to be in a position to carry through the actual bid including raising cash for those who cannot be persuaded to take his shares. He has to be able to put up a convincing management proposition so as to realise the expectation he is arousing at the price he is prepared to pay, which may be substantially higher than that which he offers in the first instance.

One of the questions that is examined more closely in the third section of this chapter is the scale of this 'cost of acquisition' and its implications for the ability of a bidder to carry out his forecasts. The actual cost of acquisition is only the first step; thereafter the enlarged group has to be managed, possibly with extensive integration of the component companies and this may well prove a difficult and expensive task.

Nevertheless, this idea that the take-over threat is a major check on performance is an important one, especially if we then relate it to the second assumption about profits and their use. Whereas the free enterprise idealists all argue for maximum distribution of profits so that investment decisions pass to investors, the whole tendency, reinforced by taxation, is to encourage retention of earnings to the point that the interest of the investor is seen as being in the rising value of his share based on investment by the company with a steady dividend rather than higher dividends which would give him more say in where investment should occur. The problem of monitoring company performance then becomes one of the criteria upon which the company reinvests retained profits, and how the outcome is judged by the market. There are those like Galbraith who argue that large companies can even ignore this check on their activities[1].

Put in this extreme form the argument is that the large company only distributes that rate of dividend that is conventional for its type of business. It does so in the context of an increasingly high technology industrial system in which long-lead times in production, the scale and highly specific nature of investment in both plant and personnel put a premium on central planning to which the corporation makes a major contribution through its ability to regulate markets and influence consumers. What matters to those in charge of the enterprise is its continued independence and this is assured partly by its dividend policy and partly by its use of economic and political power to maintain stability in its markets. Galbraith goes on to argue that the corporation not only cooperates in prices and incomes policies — which include dividend restraint — but switches more of its effort into sophisticated products with a high technology component which facilitates maintenance of protected monopoly positions through entry barriers based on scientific and technical knowledge.

G. C. Allen[2] and Meade[2] have both criticised this portrayal as inaccurate and misleading, not only for its write-off of the whole private firm sector, especially outside manufacturing, but also for its failure to come to terms with the evidence of continued change, notably among the very large firms themselves. Whittington[4] has pointed out the extent of the changes among the top 100 companies in the UK and studies of merger and take-over activities show that the system is much more turbulent. The large company may well have the leverage that Galbraith asserts, but it is rarely immune from competition, if not nationally then internationally and, as Meade points out, there are a whole variety of forms of governmental intervention that both over-ride the actions of individual companies and create forms of Galbraith's own earlier observation — 'counter-vailing power'.

But perhaps the most important checks are those posed by the remaining assumptions when tested in practice, those of information and the role of investors. These can be taken together.

The large company may well be able to sustain its independence of challenges through shareholdings if it is able to finance its growth not only by reinvestment but by borrowing, whether by loan capital (debentures) or in other ways. On the one hand these appear to give it new opportunities. Certainly if it can finance its growth solely by reinvestment then in the short run the controlling group can select their investments on their own criteria, aiming to reinforce their position by warding off any threat of a bid. This they can do by not holding on to unused funds, by diversification and by generally making their business 'more indigestible' to a raider. But they are still constrained by the need to maintain at least average performance in the earnings per share and their growth. Even where borrowing has been used more extensively to finance expansion, the influence of the institutions both directly and indirectly has been increasing. The outcome is a potentially much more professional and better informed monitoring of investment performance with the added threat of joint action among the leading investors.

The market, therefore, while it has changed in the sources through which funds enter it, has emerged even more powerful than in the past because of the scale and concentration of its participants. With so much coming forward through pensions and insurance funds there is potentially a significant switch in power though this has yet to be fully translated into action as the financial institutions have so far shown a much greater tendency to stick to their known trades and not to diversify as manufacturing and distributing firms have done. Indeed they have often remained so cautious as to excite criticism of their reluctance to use their existing power to good effect even on their traditional criteria.

The market retains a major function in two of the roles assigned to it in earlier models, as a means of financing fast growing firms including those that are changing from private to public company form, and as a monitor of performance in quoted companies. But the power lies primarily with the institutions and more specifically with their investment managers, and not with private investors as such, though they have not lost all their influence.

How then should we expect the system to operate? Clearly, it is the role of the market in assessing use of funds already invested that is going to act as a guide to both new investment and challenges to existing boards on the basis of prospective performance.

But before examining the way in which it does operate, the entire edifice has to be set against the evidence concerning the whole future supply of long-term risk capital. The whole argument to this point rests on the assumption that the system can and will provide that capital. This is challenged on two counts. First, the changes in the ownership of capital, including those arising from extensions of taxation, are bringing about a situation where the institutions and the state are the principal sources of funds. Second, the evidence of recent years has been of a reluctance to invest in industry in particular, on the part of both institutions and private investors, if only because of the very poor prospective rate of return, at least in the minds of investors and investment managers. Admittedly this view has been challenged by King[5] who shows that while conventional gross profit before tax did show an underlying downward trend from 1950 to 1973 there was no secular decline in the share of profits after tax, except where stock appreciation is deducted. But what is clear is a marked reluctance to come forward with long-term risk capital, to such an extent that the whole basis of the system has been questioned.

For our purposes, therefore, we have to proceed in two stages. In this chapter we explore further the way in which the stock market acts as a market in corporate control, relying on a development of the ideas of Marris as our model. In Chapter 8 we consider the role of government.

Quoted companies are therefore viewed on a spectrum from

the owner-managed company with a dominant shareholder at one extreme to separation of dispersed ownership from autonomous management at the other. There is a presumption that firms will move from the owner-managed to the professionally managed, and that the majority of large quoted companies have already so moved. Mergers and take-overs are then the main instruments of change.

Clearly, owner-managed firms may seek to change and their reasons for doing so may be quite different from those of the professionally managed firms. There may be succession problems, whether of a personal or a fiscal nature; there may be a straight retirement from involvement in the whole process of direction or a partial retirement where a managerial role is retained though the financing and risk-bearing roles are transferred; or there may be a direct investment choice, namely that the prospects after sale are so much more attractive that all other considerations are eliminated and the business is sold.

Such aims and considerations are much more easily separated from those that are common to all firms contemplating mergers for reasons such as economies of scale and rationalisation. It is argued later that although these are often cited in justification of mergers and raids, their attainment if the change comes off can be a very different matter. We are then left with the valuation ratio argument which we can now consider as part of the wider question of the evaluation of company performance.

5.2 Evaluation of Company Performance

'When you are capitalizing a *perhaps* which you believe to be infinite, the number of noughts that you add on to the market value of the company's capital is not a matter which concerns you as long as you are wrought up to the right pitch of excitement. There is nothing by which the valuation can be tested, for it is all based on profits that are alleged to be going to be earned one day. The market simply riots at its own sweet will, as long as there is a sufficient supply of enthusiasts who will back fancy estimates with hard money, and of speculators who see that the enthusiasm is likely to endure for a time, and buy shares to unload them on the next set of enthusiasts'.[6]

This is not a commentary on any recent affair, such as Poseidon; it was written of the London stock market in 1910. Is it a caricature or does it give us at least a starting point in any study of how company performance is evaluated?

The most important thing Hartley Withers is stressing is the emphasis on expectations of future performance and on what others may think of that future. As shares are the basis of control, share prices are a key element in the assessment of a company and its performance. But the whole emphasis is on what 'the market' expects is going to happen, not just to that one company, but to security prices as a whole.

Indeed this must be the first major observation. A distinction has to be drawn between the general level of share prices and the relative position of the shares in a particular company, both in the market as a whole and the section in which it is found.

The general level of share prices is influenced by four main factors: the volume of business reflecting willingness to buy and sell, the level of interest rates, the current expectation as to future levels of activity, and the present condition of the economy. The volume of business in part reflects expectations as firms are not likely to be as keen to raise funds when prospects are poor. The level of interest rates, while immediately reflecting government policy both as to activity in the economy and methods of regulating it, is also affected by interest rates in other countries, notably when a country such as the UK operates a reserve currency and seeks to attract short-term funds as with the current oil earnings of the oil exporting countries.

The expectations of the level of activity in the economy can reveal the market at its most jittery as well as its most buoyantly self-confident. One of the difficulties here is how others in the market are expected to behave. Thus during the great slump in share values in 1974 the expectation was that they would have to go still further down before investors would enter the market in the hope of a turn. As a result funds were diverted elsewhere, notably into government securities, which were being offered in large volumes to cover the rapidly exploding deficit of public income as against expenditure. When a concerted move to purchase equities was made at the end of the year those concerned found themselves in a situation where no investment manager could risk not buying now that there was an upturn; immediately previously no one dared buy. In part this is not a criticism of their judgement as to likely movements so much as a salutory reminder of the very great difficulty in timing correctly that the market is changing.

In their estimates of future prices those operating on the market behave very much as any other crowd except in so far as they are preoccupied not only with today's price but how they are likely to react tomorrow. A short-term, almost daily or even hourly change in either the general level as reflected in an index or a particular share, leads others to act upon it which can thereby compound it, especially when speculators are also taken into account. The move from the type of knowledgeable direct investment to the divorce of ownership from management and knowledge reflected in the exchanges, far from producing greater professionalism and stability, may be said to have produced greater instability. Keynes pointed this out[7]. He argued that the combination of the ignorance of the investor of the company in which he acquired shares, the day-to-day fluctuations in prices, the vulnerability of any such price to what he called 'the mass psychology' of a lot of individuals to changes which might have no relevance, and the presence of the professionals and speculators brought about an inherently unstable situation. The preoccupation with anticipating the next change was hardly consistent with sober evaluation of a single company, the affairs of which would rarely change with such speed and frequency.

Indeed, this is the touchstone for those studies that have been carried out which suggest that day-to-day fluctuations can be accommodated within the 'random-walk' theory. This has been tested in the US and asserted as a feature in the UK[8]. It states that there is a 50-50 chance of a movement of any kind at any time and that one therefore might as well concede that very short-term movements are virtually at random.

When we then add to this the evidence of persistent differences in the prices of shares in companies where the results do not apparently provide any basis for such a gap, then we have to concede that the market, rightly or not, applies a 'risk margin'[9] as between securities. As we have seen when looking at the flotation of previously private companies, this is partly a reflection of lack of knowledge of new firms, partly a reflection of rules of thumb such as the one cited earlier where manufacturing was regarded as taboo, high technology as doubly so, and anything to do with aircraft quite outside consideration! These rules of thumb reflect the current opinion among those most involved in investment decisions, namely the larger lenders whose operations are regarded as of particular significance.

What emerges is that the first bench-mark, if so firm a term can be used, is an index or moving average, particularly when viewed over a period of time such as the Financial Times Index.

This gives a measure of the movement in prices as a whole. What matters in looking at any one company is the behaviour of its share price.

While subject to all the forces that affect the general level of prices this will be further affected by the risk margin applied to this class of investment and to the specific company, its current performance and expectations, including any indications of forthcoming events, good or bad, and the evidence deduced from, not just given in, its most recent report and accounts. First among these in significance, according to Fisher[10] is the dividend declared, the basis of the earnings per share measure. Second is the last declared statement of undistributed profits, but in view of the arguments advanced earlier in this chapter the evidence both here and in the US is that retentions are of much lower significance compared to dividends. But while dividends remain an important indicator, even during periods of dividend restraint under incomes policies, the past record of the rate of growth of dividends does not have anything like the same significance as an indicator of share price.

If we return to the Marris theory, he asserts that what is crucial is the valuation ratio, that is the market value of the shares as a proportion of the book value of net assets. If for any reason a potential raider concludes that this ratio undervalues a company after allowing for the costs of making a bid then, if he has the resources available, he may bid. From this it is argued that to ward off such a threat a management must do all it can to ensure that the firm is not undervalued. This means using its assets so that they are not idle, and having a combination of dividends, capital profit opportunities and a record of growth of business as to yield a realistic valuation. Since one part of the valuation ratio is the book value of net assets, one step is to ensure that they are not undervalued.

In viewing the performance of a company, the first set of checks is, therefore, its share price relative to others in its field of operations, and if it is a very important company, in many trades, then its standing is assessed against others of its kind. This approach is based on its published accounts and reports plus the intelligence available to the market both from the firm and from independent sources. It is true that the firm is in a position to influence market opinion to the extent that both the precise content of what it communicates and the level of optimism or pessimism that the chairman or chief executive conveys are an important element in that intelligence. But the market has its own sources of analysis and comment —

specialists in company analyses, the monitoring done by the institutions and the larger brokers, and press, TV and academic comment. Published data are supplemented where possible by informal contact and there is a continual search for data on the one hand, and a concern in companies on the other, to influence opinion through control over what is said and published. The pressure for information starts with the requirements of the Companies Act from which no limited company is now exempt as to the form and content of published accounts. All the signs point to an extension of the requirements on disclosure in future, notably in view of the provisions of the Industry Act on disclosure to government and of the Report of the Accounting Standards Steering Committee on the scope and context of accountability, known as the Corporate Report[11].

The presumption so far has been that this external assessment may trigger off action to change the situation. There may be direct pressure by one or more key shareholders to secure improved performance. This poses the question of the responsibilities of the institutional shareholders and with it the possibility of joint action on their part. As to the first, like any other shareholder they are free to move their funds elsewhere if they think this in the best interests of their clients and themselves. However, a situation may develop where they are in a position to take a more direct line possibly through any director who represents their interests or by direct approach to the managing director or chairman. This can often be a very effective, if discreet, means of securing change to better performance over a period. Alternatively there may be a situation where many institutions are involved and there is the chance of joint pressure as through the joint committees established by the main pension funds and some of the other institutions.

The problems here are (a) the attitude to joint action with one's competitors and (b) a reluctance to become involved in the management problems of a firm in a very different type of activity. The institutions may feel that knowledge of management is confined to their admittedly specialist activities and no basis for becoming involved in the affairs of industries that are remote from their experience.

There is therefore bound to be a dependence on those pressures upon the managers in a given industry where comparison with their compatriots is possible. Thus the directors of a firm in a given industry may have access to inter-firm comparison data for the trade(s) in which they are engaged.

They are also aware of the market performance in competition with their rivals both at home and abroad and, through trade sources, have a far better idea of what each other are doing than is generally conceded. Furthermore their own concern to retain their present roles provides a powerful incentive to avoid being put in a position where such external pressure, whether of a bid or more direct action, would arise.

Lenders, notably the banks, have had to keep a close eye on their client's affairs and have often been instrumental in bringing very strong pressure for change. What is increasingly evident is pressure for information, if not for much more powerful action, from trades unions and employees generally. The concern of employees for their job prospects is understandable.

The provision in the Industry Act 1975, whereby the National Enterprise Board may acquire part of the equity in a company, represents a new extension of a form of performance monitoring through the mechanism of the market, and it remains to be seen to what extent the criteria used will be different from those used by the system so far.

In a sense this already occurs in so far as departments of state seek to anticipate where calls are to be made on their services or where opportunities may arise for pressure to be exercised on firms as part of specific policies such as that on the distribution of industry. With the opportunities for financial assistance offered by the Industry Acts 1972 and 1975, observation of this kind is almost certainly going to be maintained.

Throughout, the key is the quality of the information available, whatever the evaluating body. This therefore involves the questions already raised in Chapter 4 on the basis for auditing performance and those of disclosure of plans and intentions. In this there are at least two considerations to be borne in mind.

The first relates to the earlier quotation from Hartley Withers. There is an element of window-dressing in published statements and in the whole process of seeking a 'good press'. The company is trying to give as good an impression of itself and its prospects as possible. But this particular arena has shown itself to be gullible. Take the remarkable saga of Mr Howarth and the El Sobrante gold mine in California that was held before the shareholders of E. J. Austin in 1969 where the share price trebled in as many days![12] One does not, however, need to go to such bizarre examples to find the relevance of this point. The second is consideration is the consequent need for professional analysis of accounts and forecasts, especially in view of

the complexity and very definition of items within modern
company accounts.

5.3 Mergers and Take-Overs

If take-overs are the main means by which the capital market
seeks to enforce better use of existing resources, then they have
to be seen in the context of very widespread mergers, the great
majority of which are agreed amalgamations even among public
companies. In this section we must begin by examining the
motives for mergers, bearing in mind that both parties may be
seeking some new alliance, and then consider the agreed take-
over before tackling the unsolicited take-over bid. By so doing
we may be able to unravel the real aims of the parties as
opposed to the arguments to which they give voice during the
process. We must also endeavour to compare subsequent
events with the arguments and claims made to see what light
can be shed both on the motives for, and the general effects of,
mergers and take-overs.

The scale of the merger/take-over movement in the past two
decades has been exceptional in the UK whether compared to
earlier periods or in contrast even to the USA let alone other
countries. Except in relation to the USA the legal framework has
been particularly conducive to such developments and it has
been reinforced by government policies which have been
directly aimed at achieving mergers, though often on criteria
that might conflict with those of the market.

The scale of this process has been such that merger and
acquisition has become the dominant reason for the deaths of
both public and private companies, with the situation among
quoted public companies that deaths have exceeded births over
many years, bringing about a net decline in the number of
quoted companies effectively in operation 1962-70.[13] The
implications for the future of the corporate sector and for public
policy are very great indeed, as the outcome could be that the
share of private sector output of the top 100 firms could have
moved from 25% in 1953 to 67% by 1980.

The term merger strictly means an amalgamation of two or
more firms to form a new legal entity which then replaces them
entirely. It is often difficult to distinguish in practice from an
agreed or voluntary take-over. A take-over occurs where one
company acquires a controlling interest in another. It is said to
be an agreed take-over where the parties, however they have

been brought together, decide to combine their interests in this way. Such an arrangement does not imply that in all circumstances effective power now moves to the acquiring company, as that power lies with the board on which the original directors may be at least as influential as the new. The contrast is with the unsolicited take-over bid where one firm makes a bid for the shares of another with a view to acquiring control. Where this happens the terms and circumstances may still be such that the directors of the 'victim' recommend acceptance, and in most cases this is what happens.

However, the directors may resist the bid and this they may recommend for a range of reasons. It may be only that the price offered is not regarded as good enough, or it may be a much more realistic bid to retain control, possibly with an eye to alternative alignment with other companies, or to a counter-bid from one such company. Where a contest develops, whether through resistance or a counter-offer the outcome is far less certain. Indeed, less than 50% are successful as against over 90% among agreed mergers and uncontested bids. But of far greater significance is the effect of a contest on the terms upon which a bid is likely to succeed. In his study Newbould[14] found that the effect of a bid on the price of the shares of 'victims' was an average increase on the pre-bid situation of 33% where it was *not* contested compared to 74% where a third party entered the fray and 77% in cases where the directors contested the bid. The outcome of this on the whole logic of bids and mergers calls for our consideration when we study the strategies that lead firms to such situations. The bidder has to justify the step in terms of subsequent performance on a revalued business where the market will also have raised its valuation of the bidder's shares, in Newbould's analysis, by almost 10%.

Where then do the parties see the opportunities for a more profitable operation once the deal has been carried through? To answer this we have to explore the possible motives of the parties, that is the companies concerned as opposed to third parties to the take-over process itself, such as financial institutions.

At the outset we have to recognise some of the circumstances in which a firm may seek to be taken over, and eliminate these from our argument before analysing the potential acquiring firms. The process is not merely one of raiders seeking unwilling victims. At any time there are firms that are seeking alliances and absorption and they are just as likely to be the initiators. Indeed one of the important checks that those whom they sound out must make is the true nature of their situation. Does it in fact reflect the picture as presented or is there a problem ahead, if not already there, which prompts this desire to be taken over?

The most straightforward reason is where the firm has been built up by an individual who has no clear successor. It may be simply that the owner(s) would have preferred to retain management and control but are unable to do so, having no one available, or that they are reluctant to rely in these circumstances on a hired management, feeling perhaps that their own interests and those of the management do not automatically coincide. Equally, it may be simply a question of the value of the enterprise to them being better realised on sale of the concern than retained under their control.

But equally there may be problems of financing the continued operation of the firm even where there have been no errors of judgement. These problems may, of course, be present both in failure to achieve and in over-achievement. While it may still be possible to raise the finance required the cost of doing so may be prohibitive.

While these factors may all be reflected in the terms upon which the acquisition can be carried through, the aspect to be considered by a potential purchaser or partner is the opportunity for new economic advantages which could follow.

Such advantages are conventionally presented as being those of economies of scale, particularly where the combination is what economists describe as horizontal or vertical, in contrast to those designated as lateral or conglomerate. A horizontal combination is one at the same stage in a particular industry. A vertical combination is one that takes in either the previous stage (backward integration) or the succeeding stage (forward integration).

The effect of each of these can be considered in terms of costs and of prices and competition. Horizontal combination offers opportunities for economies of scale in the purchase and handling of materials, and if followed up by horizontal integration, that is the physical concentration of production in fewer and larger plants, these can offer opportunities for economies of scale in manufacture. Vertical combination eliminates the profit margins at the stage(s) acquired and may reduce purchasing costs in backward combination and market development costs in forward combination. Where physical processes can be brought together, production and transport economies may follow.

But of at least comparable interest is the opportunity to reduce turbulence in the firm's environment by eliminating some competition through horizontal combination and by enabling greater control to be exercised over suppliers (backward combination) and outlets (forward combination). The sheer increase in market share by these means has often been observed to be a major aim especially in industries where the growth of the market has slowed down or even ceased and is therefore a characteristic of mature products and industries. It is equally characteristic of markets that have become oligopolistic in which market share has emerged as a major concern of the firms engaged.

The economic arguments concerning economies of scale and integration have therefore to be set alongside those of market control, particularly where there is increased preoccupation with competition on a wider scale, for example international and overseas competition. Here the argument about a 'secure home market' on a scale sufficient to support 'international effectiveness' may lead to the tolerence by governments of monopolistic and restrictive practices. Equally, government measures to restrain such practices by collusion among firms may encourage mergers among them so that as a single large firm they can retain the same degree of control over the market.

But these arguments have to be set against those where the combination is lateral, that is exploring a new development which springs from processes but is quite distinct from the markets in which a firm has hitherto operated. One of the features of more recent new developments has been the extent to which they have appeared to spring from existing larger firms, perhaps in fields closely related to that now explored by them for the first time. In part this is due to a realisation that their special skill or knowledge is not so much in the final product as in the processes leading to it, while their investment may lie more heavily in processes capable of a wider range of uses than in the products they have hitherto relied upon. In part this is due to the growth of 'strategic' planning and raises the fundamental question, what industry is a firm really in? This could provoke a search as to trends in the market which might trigger off interests in new activities which could best be attained in the short term by buying in to the sectors concerned.

From here it is only a comparatively short step to the remaining form of combination, the conglomerate, in which the stress is on diversification to produce a portfolio of activities in a comparable manner to the private investor with his portfolio of securities. Indeed, the analogy is even more pertinent because what we are now seeing is a company viewing its activities as an investor would view his holdings, but doing so by reinvestment of funds that might otherwise have passed to that investor. In the extreme, one could postulate a situation in which the private investor was reduced to holding a portfolio of conglomerates each having a portfolio of activities!

Clearly, at this point the whole rationale of the acquisition strategy comes closer to that offered to investors when they are invited to agree to a merger. It also has implications for the theory of the direction of professionally 'merged' quoted companies developed earlier. In this argument there are two key features of direct relevance at this stage. There is the emphasis on retaining the firm as an independent entity, with its implications for the rewards and influence of the decision-takers concerned, which demands that a strategy be followed which reduces the risk of a successful take-over raid. There is also the implication that this will be facilitated by growth and a spreading of risks through diversification even to the point of making the firm 'indigestible' to raiders. The two arguments come together if it can be shown that greater size brings greater security from take-over raids.

Before looking at the evidence from a number of studies of UK manufacturing industry over recent decades there is one further set of ideas to be taken into account. Much of the argument on take-overs views investment in another firm as if it were the same type of investment as one in plant or stocks of materials. The situation is surely very different, as there is going to be a managerial problem of merger or absorption, and this may prove much more prolonged than expected. Studies of the managerial and social problems of mergers and take-overs not only demonstrate the difficulties in reconciling the styles and methods of previously independent firms, but also the amount of managerial time and energy that have to be put into the task. This can have devastating effects on the effectiveness of the combined organisation, especially where the units are large, well-established and backed up by different systems. Indeed, these problems may be so great as to deter more than a coordinating link in the early stages. This must emphasise both the cost of seeking to complete a merger, and of the failure to achieve anticipated rationalisation after its completion. Knowledge of this may lead to hesitation to make the move, though this can be overwhelmed where a 'merger wave' appears to have started. Fear of unsolicited raids may induce firms to seek new alliances in mutual self-defence, and this may be accentuated if there is a general mood of uncertainty, either in a given industry or more widely in the economy. These points are among a number of pertinent observations that emerge from studies such as those of Singh[15], Newbould[14], Hindley[13], Kuehn[16] and Samuels and Chesher[17].

The first point about these studies relates to the question of motive for merger or take-over, in particular the significance of the profitability of the parties involved. Singh studied the period 1948-60 and especially the years 1954-60. By comparing firms that were acquired with those not acquired in each of a number of manufacturing industries, he concluded that those acquired, taken together, showed a lower average rate of return on capital, a lower growth rate and a lower valuation ratio than those not acquired when also taken together. But there was a significant minority in most industries where the performance of those acquired was above average for their particular industry. Those acquired tended to be smaller and to have retained a higher proportion of profits than those not acquired. While the evidence supports the view that lower than average performance increases the risk of a successful raid being made, better performance is no complete insurance against a raid being brought off. Therefore, within wide ranges of profitability, probability of acquisition does not decline as profit increases. If, however, size of firm is taken into account then, while smaller firms appeared to have little choice but to improve performance if they wished to stay independent, larger firms — defined as £4 M book value of equity in 1960 — could reduce this risk by further increasing their size even though, as the study by Singh and Whittington over the same period had already shown, greater size meant lower rather than higher average profitability[18].

The emphasis on greater size as a form of security comes out in Newbould's study of mergers in 1967 and 1968. Among them there is no conclusive evidence that poor performance was a reason for a firm being taken over. While the average share price of victims was lower than that of their raiders up to four weeks before a bid, the effect of the bid was to raise the share prices of the victim by from an average of 33% where there was no contest to an average of 77% where the directors contested it, compared to 9% for shares in bidding firms. Newbould analysed the performance that would have to be obtained after take-over to justify a rate of return of 10% net tax on the acquisition, this rate being chosen as comparable to that on other classes of investment. On this basis he concluded that the overwhelming majority of the companies studied would have to more then double their previous performance for at least four years ahead where the bid is contested! Even where it was not contested a marked improvement in performance was needed even to hold the present rate of performance on the enhanced value of the acquisition.

Managements, therefore, set themselves very demanding tasks if take-overs are to be justified in these terms. The higher the price paid the greater becomes the pressure for economies, many of which may be of a short-term nature, and the temptation to resort to what is known as capital stripping is clearly present. Capital stripping is selling off all possible assets, or assets not fully utilised, for short-term capital profit and expenditure savings. The danger to the successful bidder is that its performance may deteriorate, especially where there is a dilution of its profit/earnings ratio in favour of the shareholders in its victim. An outstanding example of this was in the early years of the Cadbury/Schweppes merger where the position of the Schweppes shareholders was, for a time, sacrificed to those of the Cadbury interests until such time as the operational benefits of the merger could be realised.

Why then merge? The answer coming from part of Newbould's study is the fear of being taken over in a period of increased economic and political uncertainty. This fear is seen as provoking firms into steps to reduce their vulnerability, one of which is to move into the attack themselves in an effort to achieve greater size and security. He found that seeking market dominance was the most frequent argument cited followed closely by defence and reinforcement of present position. On the other hand, economies of scale were bottom of the list behind diversification.

This low emphasis on economies of scale is supported by the follow-up evidence, and a number of studies indicate that there is an equal expectation that no action will follow as that significant action will result. The reason lies, as already indicated, in the problems of management in the new situation. What therefore has the bidding management gained?

To some extent it has gained in prestige; it has also gained in job security, though this is not universal as the shake-out following the GEC/AEI battle showed. What they hope to have gained is greater control over their environment. It is this notion that underlies the suggestion that government policy towards competition and restrictive practices may have a bearing on the situation. If the government takes a less tolerant line on collusion, as for example from 1956 through to the repeal of resale price maintenance in 1964, then this could stimulate the merger process.

Hindley[13] compared the situation in the USA pointing out the similarity in terms of the power performance shown by acquiring firms over those that have not participated in the process. His most interesting points relate to the extent to which conglomerate mergers have come to outnumber conventional mergers in the US. This is in contrast to Newbould's finding that by far the largest number of his study were horizontal mergers. Once again greater control within an industry appears to have been an important factor.

The stress on control of the environment, greater size and security from take-over must therefore lend some support to the arguments of those who are concerned at the extent to which the capital market can and does act as a market for corporate control in the interests of the most efficient use of resources. Clearly, it would be very limited if confined to contested bids which represent a small minority. What influence, other than as a price mechanism for share valuation, does the market have in agreed mergers? The answer lies in the process of financing mergers and take-overs, and in the methods of payment used for firms acquired.

For the amalgamation to give the resulting company full control over all aspects of the combined resources there should not be any minority interest in the acquired firm which would preclude full absorption. The rules covering mergers and bids therefore provide that once the bid has been accepted by a large majority, usually 85% as measured by number of shares, then it becomes binding on the rest at the price at which it was finally accepted. The offer will usually involve an issue of stock in the bidding company, with possibly a cash element as an inducement, but with the option of cash for the whole price. To be able to offer this the bidder needs backing not only from his normal bankers but from merchant banks and an issuing house. Their part in the process may stem from their existing commitments to one of the companies concerned both as financiers and financial advisers.

Therefore, financial institutions have an important role as 'marriage brokers' as well as their more obvious functions. Their backing plays an important part in effecting the merger. If the bid is being brought about by a cash offer only, then this may be being financed by borrowing, in meeting which they have a key role. This does, however, raise the question of the nature of their interest. Clearly, they may be said to gain at several stages in a successful merger or bid, and their self-interest in promoting successful amalgamation cannot go unnoticed. Furthermore, the nature and extent of their prior knowledge of what is likely to follow is one aspect of the issue of inside dealings to which so much attention has recently been given by the City Take-Over Panel.

This takes us into the remaining aspect of the merger/take-over process to which we have to give particular attention. This is the process itself and the whole basis of the debate in a particular proposition.

As for the process, what we are concerned with first is the role of the directors in the companies concerned, in particular in respect of the terms proposed both as they affect the offers being made to investors and the specific interests of the directors themselves. As already demonstrated in the British Aluminium case, there is the price that they are prepared to recommend be accepted and the wider deal which may affect their own positions as directors. There may be a question of conflict of interest as in cases where a director is involved in both companies. There is the whole question of advance inside knowledge and its use for self-advantage.

Then there is the concern of the Stock Exchange that all shareholders in a particular share class be treated on the same most favourable terms. If a firm is embarking on a bid then it should come out into the open and remain there as long as it is actively bidding. The case of Philips, the Dutch electrical group, that appeared to withdraw from Pye Ltd of Cambridge only to buy through a nominee with the connivance of a merchant bank, thereby gaining control at a lower share price, was an obvious example of this point.

But the greatest source of difficulty concerns the statements advanced in support of deals. To recall just a few outstanding examples, let us take first the abortive bid of ICI for Courtaulds. Following a series of cautious predictions from the Courtaulds Group board, ICI judged the firm to be undervalued and capable of better performance on the strength of which they put in a bid. Led by Lord Kearton, the Courtaulds reaction was a drastic reappraisal and new forecast which not only reversed the earlier ones but challenged the ICI claims with sufficient ammunition when argued before institutional investors that the ICI bid failed.

Then in the battle between GEC and AEI there was a profit forecast of £10 millions which turned out to be a loss of £4½ millions. In the Pergamon-Leasco affair not only were there very great difficulties in finding agreed bases for valuations, but once again what was claimed to be a profit, this time of £2.1 millions, was eventually found to be only £140,000.

The sheer complexity of some of the more speculative deals associated with the property boom and the suspicion of 'capital stripping' in some of the related acquisitions has created pressures for at least a code of conduct for such transactions, for fuller disclosure of interests, and for some check on whether larger mergers are in the public interest. This last demand is supported by the evidence already put forward that control over markets and industries by a greater share in present activity has become a major means of company growth instead of increased production and sales, whether at home or abroad. There is therefore a link to policies on competition and restrictive practices.

Yet, at the same time the essentially pragmatic nature of UK monopolies policy has meant that the so-called 'gateways' of the Monopolies and Restrictive Practices Act 1956, such as research and development, or international competition, have become important arguments for state-backed mergers, notably in the nuclear power, aero-space and motor industries, even to the point of intervention by a government creation, the Industrial Reorganisation Corporation and now the National Enterprise Board, to promote mergers where these might not have followed if left to the market.

Particularly in the last phase we see another powerful force at work, the pressure from organised labour for mergers and nationalisation in the interest of job protection and in the belief — not necessarily correct — that larger organisations and especially nationalised ones are in some way naturally safer in this respect. Concern at the 'shake-out' implications of mergers has led to demands for a wider accountability and even consent for mergers to at least take account of the interests of employees, notably managers themselves.

5.4 Company behaviour reconsidered

The behaviour of quoted companies has been criticised not just by their ideological opponents, but by many supporters of a free enterprise system on four main counts:

    (i)   the level of disclosure and the question of accountability as seen in take-over situations, which pose wider issues of objectives (further explored in Chapter 9);

(ii)   the effectiveness of the systems just discussed, given the poor performance in profit terms of manufacturing industry, if not business generally, by the standards of other Western countries;

(iii)   the ability and willingness of the capital markets to provide finance on the scale required to raise the level of industrial investment in the UK;

(iv)   the implications of the role of government both as a source of funds and through bodies set up to monitor this sector.

Our starting point is the level of disclosure and accountability evident in present mechanisms for evaluating performance. Clearly the corporate sector, its professional members and advisers, are concerned with both their image and the effectiveness of the present arrangements.

In two reports the CBI has examined the future role of the public company and its relationships with government.[19] These were responses to the White Paper on Company Law of Mr Heath's administration[20] and the early drafts of the European Commission on the European company. There is a welcome for the emergence of more joint action by the Institutional Shareholders Committee and for a closer interest on the part of the institutions, as key shareholders, in the effective working of the system. The take-over or merger is seen as a key element in sustaining the effectiveness of industry in an internationally competitive environment and such a step is justified on grounds of:

(a)   economies of scale

(b)   the creation of a more effective marketing unit in international competition.

(c)   rationalisation to meet changing or contrasting demand, rapid and drastic technical change, or exceptionally severe international competition

(d)   need for a strong unit to exploit new products and/or markets

(e)   complementarity, creating a more efficient combination

(f)   management deficiencies

(g)   giving opportunity for a management to realise its full potential

(h)   optimal utilisation on redeployment of assets and labour force

Clearly, this is a case for horizontal and vertical combinations but there is hesitation on conglomerates. This arises from a concern that optimal use of resources be distinguished from 'asset stripping'. It is not inconsistent with, though it perhaps puts a gloss on, the motive examined in the previous section.

But there is a clear need for much fuller disclosure of information including that on the social consequences, the personnel and the accountancy policies that are proposed and on the long-term commercial justification of the proposal. With this goes a plea in the second report for much better consultation between government and industry particularly in the light of experience in West Germany as well as elsewhere in Western Europe.

The Catherwood report on Company Affairs[21], while much more concerned with the internal organisation of firms, does come out even more firmly in favour of a code of corporate conduct at company level and supports the earlier CBI report in recommending the formal recognition of wider obligations by companies when new company legislation is brought forward. Perhaps the most immediately interesting observation is that on the separation of the chairman and the chief executive, the report also supports the greater involvement, if only through comment and advice, of the financial institutions with, however, an important reservation. While conceding the value of financial comment, the Catherwood Committee commends the institutions 'to support directors when they require support and encourage them when they had to take decisions which were desirable in the long run, but which might have adverse short-term effects on financial performance'. They then add 'If directors do not receive such support the "unacceptable face of capitalism" is bound to become more evident and the free market economy be thought to be run counter to social needs and the public interest'.

To these have now to be added the recommendations on disclosure of the Accounting Standards Steering Committee[11]. This starts from the recognition that present reporting to the 'owners' is out-dated and proposes a much wider form of reference covering government, creditors, share and investment analysts and, in particular, employees. Similarly, the matters reported are greatly extended especially in the field of employment, though it wisely rejects any attempt at human asset accounting on the basic principle that employees are not owned by the firm. Of particular interest at this juncture is the recommendation on performance data which would take UK practice at least as far as that in any other country including USA.

All this adds up to a general admission that the present framework is due for amendment, whatever government is in office, and that this will extend the well-established principle of providing information with which to judge performance and recognise accountability. How far then does this general climate reflect concern aroused by the conduct of the merger/take-over process and how has that been evolving in the light of such concern?

As we have seen, there has been an unprecedented wave of mergers and take-overs. We have also seen doubts cast not only on the precise motives of those involved but on the effectiveness of the movement in terms of subsequent company performance. To some extent this last observation should be in no way surprising if one takes account of the wholly inadequate preparation and deliberation that still attend major business decisions. Newbould concluded that in half the companies that he surveyed the whole process of negotiation and assessment took under eight weeks. What triggered off concern at the course of events was, first, the evidence that in battles fought with almost total ruthlessness shareholders could be sacrificed as much as anyone else and, second, concern at the outcome of terms of market domination.

The Aluminium case already cited was a turning point in that it led the Governor of the Bank of England to convene a working party to produce guide-lines which reminded directors that they had to bear in mind the interests of all classes of shareholder and loan capital investor according to their respective rights. A series of events, including the Philips-Pye deal already referred to, led to the establishment of a Code on Take-Overs and Mergers in 1968 as a means of self-discipline on the part of the City backed by the Panel, a supervisory and consultative body.

The Code[22] seeks to provide shareholders with the information and the opportunity to decide the issue. To this end, once an offer is made or an indication is given that one is to be made, the parties have to declare themselves. The directors of the company being bid for may not take any steps which prejudice either the right to decide on the assets or resources under consideration. Throughout, the whole emphasis is on disclosure and equality of treatment of the shareholders who have to make the decision. But the real problems remain those of what is a 'true and fair view', of what is acceptable conduct, and what moral or other sanction exists to deal with those who continue to operate as if no code existed. Events such as the *News of the World* and Pergamon battles led to the demand for sanctions over and above those of the constituent professional bodies and associations of institutions that collectively seek to protect the reputation of the City. This has forced on the argument that there should be a British equivalent of the American Security Exchanges Commission (SEC).

The case for such a body is that the existing statutory machinery, the power to appoint inspectors under the Companies Acts' is ineffectual in practice as only a handful of companies are investigated. The Panel only deals with one aspect, albeit a very important one, and lacks sanctions with which to enforce any code of practice. The power of the Stock Exchange Council to suspend dealings and even quotations is one that it is loath to use. Above all, the requirements on disclosure, until the recent report of the Accounting Standards Steering Committee, are far behind those in the USA, the nearest comparable system.

Against this it is argued that one market in a concentrated area having a closely-knit community is best served by self-discipline backed by a vigilant financial press and the powers of the Panel and the Council of the Stock Exchange. The one point upon which both sides appear to agree is the need to strengthen the requirements for disclosure to at least the American standard if not beyond. This has important implications, not least for the accounting profession.

The stress reported earlier on the control over markets therefore raises the question of governmental controls over mergers as such. This involves two stages. In the first, the Department of Trade under the Monopolies and Restrictive Practices Act 1965 has to be notified of any proposed merger where a monopoly — defined as one third or more of a market — would result or where the assets to be acquired exceed £5 M. If the Department decides to refer the matter to the Monopolies Commission then, in effect, a delay of up to six months is imposed while the Commission decides whether the proposed merger is contrary to the public interest. Effectively this may lead the parties to abandon the project as in the Boots/Glaxo and Boots/House of Fraser proposals.

But while the Department has this power to intervene, it is working within the guide lines established under the 1956 and 1965 Acts which correspond very closely to the situations already described under the first report of the CBI earlier in this section. Clearly, it has therefore not objected to a number of mergers and indeed government policy has been to encourage selected ones through such bodies as the IRC between 1967 and 1971 and more recently under the aegis of the Industry Act 1972.

Yet the real challenge associated with that Act and its successor in 1975 arises from the capacity and willingness of the market to invest in industry on a sufficient scale, relative to other directions for investment. This has arisen in part from the poor profit record of so much of industry compared to the opportunities that appeared to be open in property and other fields. But there is also the combined challenge of inflation and corporate taxation to the ability of companies to sustain an adequate level of investment out of retained profits, even with a greater willingness to face the implications of a much higher gearing ratio — where retained funds are supplemented by borrowing. The extent of the change in the source of funds is shown in table 5.1 and has been commented upon by the Diamond Commission[23]. It also lends support to the thesis advanced by Bacon and Eltis[24] that faced with a massive increase in 'communal consumption' the combined effects of inflation, fiscal and incomes policies and trades union pressure has been to put the main burden of the switch in resources, not on consumers and wage-earners but on companies and therefore on the rate of investment.

Table 5.1 *Sources of funds, industrial and commercial companies (£M)*

Year	Total	Retentions	Bank borrowing	New issues	Fixed capital formation
1965	4376	2812	497	408	2449
1970	6194	2145	1126	193	3378
1972	9920	3458	2988	606	3818
1974	14175	2668	4411	-19	5942

Annual Abstract of Statistics

The sharp rise in bank borrowing, the virtual cessation of new issues as a source in 1974-5, and the reduced level of retentions combine to produce high gearing and a shortage of funds, as the cost of meeting all requirements by borrowing is a crippling burden. The difficulty has been accentuated by the reluctance of the institutions to invest at least on a falling stock market such as in 1974. The combined effect of inflation, tight price controls with restrictions of profit margins and taxation has been to cut internal funds at a time when replacements, particularly of equipment, have been at prices far in excess of anything covered by conventional historical cost depreciation. Book profits on stocks during a period of rapid inflation became a target for tax liability, although there have now been some relaxations here. The outcome is a challenge to the continued survival of the whole system.

In so far as it has forced more companies into a greater dependence on the banking system, it can be argued that we are seeing no more than a shift of power from the stock market to the banks, such as has long been a feature of other European economies, notably that of West Germany. Critics of British performance have therefore found some consolation in their hope that the kind of pressure that the banks would exercise would have the same stimulating effect that is ascribed to banks in the German system. But as liquidity problems of individual companies have got worse, the banks have been reluctant to continue to extend credit, except where government guarantees have been forthcoming and the result has been to drive some firms into the search for state aid in the absence of private funds.

Understandably, the insurance companies and pensions funds, being mindful of their responsibilities to policy holders as well as members have not seen their function as being that of a rescue service and have sought to invest to the best advantage, which with the government financing a rapidly rising deficit by increased borrowing, has meant that it is here rather than to industry that funds have been going. Suggestions that their funds should be directed into purposes determined by the National Enterprise Board have receded but there is a real problem of what basis can be found to make their funds available over a sufficiently long term to industries that have a future on commercial criteria and not just an extended past as part of some massive piece of job protection.

The outcome is Equity Capital for Industry Ltd. This is to have a nominal capital of £50M of which £30M is taken up. It is backed directly by insurance companies, pension funds and other institutional investors and is to invest in medium and smaller companies both public and private. The controversy attending its launching has had two main elements. On the one hand, there was the concept of a 'support' role for a company, possibly over a period of years. Many of the institutions have argued that it is no part of their duty to their shareholders or depositors, etc., to underwrite other firms; their duty is plainly to invest funds to the best advantage and no more. On the other hand there is the relationship of the new agency to the existing Institutional Shareholders Committee, a joint body which seeks to act as a 'ginger group' by identifying companies with poor managements and then using their shares as the basis of votes to bring about changes.

The first role is seen as meeting a need to supplement existing machinery in such a way as to increase the amount of equity capital available 'where circumstances and prospects justify it'. It arose from concern in 'responsible quarters' such as the CBI and government departments as to the willingness of the insurance companies and pension funds to give continuing support to the private sector, especially the equity market. Precisely because of the sources of such comments there has been concern that any such new agency should be free of political influence while perhaps acting as a first line of defence to firms that might otherwise have been forced to seek the assistance of the National Enterprise Board with all the implications for future government control that it has carried since its inception.

The second is even more closely concerned with that body and other aspects of government support which are discussed in Chapter 8. The fears for the future of the capitalist system have been reinforced by the combined effects of a very high rate of inflation, high personal and corporate taxation and tight price and profit control.

The close connection between inflation, the system of accounting and the application then of corporate taxation and price control has been widely argued. The acceptance by the government of the artificial nature of the profits arising from the appreciation in the value of inventories under high inflation has gone some way to meet part of the problem of the attack on liquidity, but the CBI has continued to argue for some relaxation, if not the total removal of price controls which have been applied as part of the counter-inflationary policy. The need for an adequate level of profits as a condition for future investment is recognised in the strategic papers put out by the National Economic Development Office but have yet to be translated into action. In the longer term, the reform of company accounts recommended in the Sandilands report offers a more realistic basis for the assessment of performance even though the recommendations are likely to be implemented in the first instance by only a handful of firms.

The reform of the Companies Act to take account of many of the more controversial features such as nominee shareholding, insider dealing and the whole question of the future basis of accountability remains overdue. But not all issues are either manageable within one country or appropriate for such a form of regulation and it is to some of these that we now turn.

Notes and references

1   J. K. Galbraith, *The New Industrial State,* Hamish Hamilton 1967.
2   G. C. Allen, *Economic Fact and Fantasy,* Institute of Economic Affairs, Occasional Paper 14, Tonbridge 1967.
     J. E. Meade, 'Is the new industrial state inevitable?', *Economic Journal 1968, p. 372.*
3   R. Marris, *Economic Theory of Managerial Capitalism,* Macmillan 1964.
4   G. Whittington, 'Changes in the top 100 quoted manufacturing companies in UK 1948-68, *Journal of Industrial Economics,* November 1972.
5   M. A. King, 'The United Kingdom profits crisis; myth or reality', *Economic Journal* 1975, p.33.
6   H. Withers, *Stocks and Shares,* Murray 1910, p. 287.
7   J. M. Keynes, *General Theory of Employment, Interest and Money,* Macmillan 1963, p. 152.
8   A. G. Raynor and I. Little, *Higgledy Piggledy Growth Again,* Basil Blackwell 1966.
9   M. J. Farrell, 'On the structure of the capital market', *Economic Journal,* 1962, p. 830.
10   G. R. Fisher, 'Some factors affecting share prices', *Economic Journal* 1961, p. 120.
11   Accounting Standards Committee, *The Corporate Report,* Institute of Chartered Accountants 1975.
12   R. Spiegelberg, *The City,* Quartet Press 1973, p. 38.
13   P. Hindley, 'Recent theory and evidence on corporate merger', in K. Cowling (ed.), *Market Structure and Corporate Behaviour,* Gray-Mills, London 1972.
14   G. Newbould, *Management and Merger Activity,* Guthstead 1970.
15   A. Singh, *Take-Overs,* Department of Applied Economics, Cambridge 1971.
16   D. A. Kuehn, *Take-Overs and the Theory of the Firm,* Macmillan 1975. and 'Stock market and valuation and acquisitions', *Journal of Industrial Economics,* April 1969.
17   J. M. Samuels and A. D. Chesher, 'Growth, survival and size of

companies 1960-69', in K. Cowling *op. cit.*

18   A. Singh and G. Whittington, *Growth Profitability and Valuation,* Occasional Paper 7, Department of Applied Economics, Cambridge 1968.

19   CBI, *The Responsibilities of the British Public Company* (Watkinson Report), September 1973 and *Industry and Government,* July 1974.

20   *Company Law Reform,* Cmd 5391, HMSO 1973.

21   *The Responsible Company,* British Institute of Management 1974.

22   Reproduced in *Mergers. A Guide to Board of Trade Practice,* HMSO 1969.

23   Royal Commission on the Distribution of Income and Wealth, Report No. 2, Cmd 6175, HMSO 1975. Background Paper No. 1, Meeks and Whittington, *The Financing of Quoted Companies in the United Kingdom,* HMSO 1976.

24   R. Bacon and W. Eltis, *Britain's Economic Problem: Too Few Producers,* Macmillan 1976.

Study Questions

1   Discuss the contention that the take-over bid is so vital a check on the direction of quoted companies that no attempt should be made to interfere with its free operation.

2   Consider the possible effects of further increases in the share-holdings in industry and commerce of the institutional investors.

3   What factors may affect the attitude of a board to movements in the price of the shares in their company?

4   Outline the issues posed by the adoption of the merger/take-over code.

6

INTERNATIONAL AND MULTINATIONAL OPERATIONS

6.1 International Operations

While a large number of firms engage in international transactions, whether as importers, exporters or providers of services internationally, there is only a minority that actually goes so far as to acquire a firm abroad. It is with this aspect of international activities that this section is concerned. We have to see first why, and in what ways, firms engage in the acquisition and control of firms abroad. We have then to consider the effect of this process in both directions, acquisitions abroad by UK firms and acquisition of UK firms by foreign companies. Lastly, we have to examine some of the questions posed where multinational operations emerge on a significant scale. These are of such importance as to warrant a separate section.

Firms engaged in overseas transactions may seek to acquire an interest as part of the normal processes of vertical combination. Where they are particularly concerned at sources of raw materials or components they may try to develop their own source of supply by direct investment. Equally, where they are concerned with marketing a product abroad then they may elect to establish their own sales and distribution organisation rather than rely on agents who are serving several manufacturers, possibly in different countries of origin. Indeed, the first step is often the acquisition of an agent. Where capital goods are supplied it may well be that the agent is already a manufacturer in a related field. In such cases the manufacturer in the country of origin may acquire a stake in the firm in the export market so as to be able to offer a wide range of products or more likely to be able to circumvent protectionist policies by being in a position to include locally made parts and materials. Nowadays this is a frequent requirement of countries anxious to develop an industrial base.

The outcome is a very different type of foreign investment to that which was at its peak before 1914 and which has taken second place since 1939, namely direct investment in securities and bonds of companies and public bodies in a foreign country. Not only has rising economic nationalism in the wake of a new nationhood made such investment politically less accceptable to the receiving country as well as politically more risky for the investor, but the controls on foreign exchange movements of many countries have tended to favour other types of investment. Whereas there are still substantial foreign holdings in UK registered companies such as Shell or ICI and, equally, UK and other European holdings in US companies for example, the main interest now lies in the extent of direct investment by companies from one country in companies in another.

Despite the enforced sale or loss of much of that investment in the 1939/45 war period and subsequently, controlled UK investment has been sufficient to completely offset, in value, that of foreign companies in this country. Even at the peak period of American penetration the total US investment in the UK was far less than that in reverse, though as a percentage of the total investment in each country the US investment in the UK appears much more influential than that of the UK in the US. Political and economic changes have limited the countries in which opportunities for British capital have been available with the result that UK investment has had to be concentrated in fewer countries. It has also had to take a different form, partly because of controls on capital movements. Accordingly, there has been much more use of local capital and borrowing facilities. UK firms investing in the US have sought control with the minimum direct transfer of funds and heavy use of US banks as sources of loans. Operations of firms such as Rio Tinto Zinc (RTZ) have involved heavy use of local funds. Above all, there has been the ploughing back of earnings in the country concerned, a feature often forced upon firms in some countries because of the balance of payments problems that they face.

One study by Manser[1] shows how in the period 1964-8 affiliates of UK multinational companies obtained their funds in developed and developing countries. This is summarised in figure 6.1.

The main conclusion, that it is retained profits plus local borrowing that dominate over any contribution from the parent company, is equally true of US firms. The greater emphasis on investment, especially fixed investment in developed countries

DEVELOPED COUNTRIES   **DEVELOPING COUNTRIES**

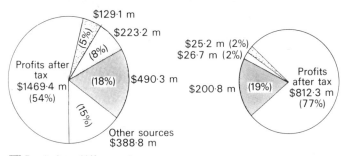

$129·1 m

$223·2 m

(5%)

(8%)

Profits after
tax
$1469·4 m   (18%) $490·3 m
(54%)

(15%)

Other sources
$388·8 m

$25·2 m (2%)
$26·7 m (2%)

Profits
after tax
$812·3 m
(77%)

$200·8 m   (19%)

☐ Funds from U.K. parent
☐ Long term liabilities
☐ Current liabilities

Source: Manser ; *Financial Role of Multi-National Enterprises*, Cassell 1973,

FIGURE 6.1 Sources of funds of UK multinationals' affiliates – annual
average 1964 – 68

is also true of both UK and US firms.

The penetration of the UK by foreign firms has been spectacular in a few industries but it has to be seen in perspective. In 1968 in manufacturing industries UK companies represented 98% of all enterprises but only 90% of all employment and only 85% of the value of net output. The foreign penetration was significantly in industries with a high added value where research and development played a very important role. A study of American ownership of UK industry shows that the US firms were in industries where the research and development in the US was on a scale comparable to that of all industries in the UK[2].

This penetration, like that of UK firms abroad, can take one of four forms: (i) outright acquisition; (ii) the establishment of a wholly owned unquoted subsidiary; (iii) an interest in a 'local' firm; or (iv) a joint venture with either a local firm or another UK firm working in a related field.

(i) Acquisition gives full access to the knowledge, experience and facilities of the 'local' firm while avoiding any minority interest which might present a problem where future switching of resources from one company and country to another becomes desirable. The main difficulty may lie in controls exercised by governments to restrict such acquisitions. Thus in the UK the Industry Act 1975 provides that the National Enterprise Board may intervene at each additional 10% of foreign ownership starting at 30%, thereby providing the opportunity to veto a loss of control to a foreign company at each point.

(ii) The second method, the establishment of a wholly owned unquoted company, is a widespread practice as long as no local capital is required. This company in turn may then be used to bid for, or to acquire shares in, companies in the country concerned so long as the laws on mergers and take-overs so permit.

(iii) Taking a minority interest in an existing concern is often preferable as it minimises the capital investment required, ensures continuity of management and goodwill, while sustaining the interest of the local firm in the products of the foreign investing firm. It may be used where significant technical knowledge has to be transferred as a part of the transaction and it may give greater commercial flexibility. Equally, the government policies of a country may rule out either of the previous forms of operation. Where this is the case, then there may even be an insistence that the local interest must be the majority one or even that the government be the majority stakeholder.

(iv) The joint venture with a local interest, be it a private person or firm on the one hand or the state, may be a suitable means of gaining entry through the special knowledge and/or personal commitment of the partner, thereby relieving the foreign backer of management responsibility in much the same way as with the minority shareholding. The alternative is a joint venture with a complementary company in a particular market or even for a specific contract. Thus, in selling mining equipment in the US, Dowty Mining, a member of the Dowty Group, also acts for Anderson, Mavor, the Scottish coal-cutting equipment manufacturers, with whom it also shares agents in other important markets. Joint actions of this type are becoming increasingly common in large capital projects in developing countries. Not all the links are as close and complementary as the one cited.

However, the desire to reduce turbulence and regulate markets is no less strong in international operations than within a country. One consequence has been the attempt to rationalise production and marketing on an international if not even a global scale. At one earlier period this led to the development of cartels but these have been subject to some internal strains where competing national self interests have proved too strong to pursue joint action. This has therefore led to the development of international mergers, though these have proved much more difficult to carry through to the point of real integration, and acquisition of a European as opposed to a national outlook.

Another consequence is strategic expansion abroad where this offers greater opportunities for profit and growth than either adhering to a home market or exporting from it. It is but a short step to acquiring a portfolio of investments on an international as opposed to, or as well as, a trading basis. This was certainly a factor for US firms between 1955 and 1967, and has been a factor for European firms, notably West German companies, with the slowing down in the rate of growth of that economy since 1970.

To these factors must be added for some countries and companies a political approach to international operations where there is a deliberate policy of penetration as part of a wider national economic and political strategy. This is evident in French activities and in industries of global strategic interest, such as oil.

Lastly, international operations have new opportunities as well as risks that arise from being in a position to switch resources from one country to another, possibly playing one off against another, and certainly implying a new relationship with, if not independence of, national governments. This is the mark of the true multinational in which a supranational view, based on the interests of the organisation as a whole, replaces the single national interest of the national enterprise operating internationally.

This phrase 'national enterprise operating internationally' also brings to our attention an important aspect of control in such firms, namely the degree of national autonomy that they accord to any one of their subsidiaries. As with delegation to subsidiaries within the parent country, there is a range of degrees of delegation from, at one extreme, the highly centralised firm in which all key decisions are reserved to the parent, with standard practices based upon its code carried to the maximum extent, to, at the other extreme, the highly decentralised operation where the subsidiaries enjoy a high degree of autonomy and where centralisation and standardisation are kept to the minimum necessary for common ownership and overall control.

International operations pose three questions. First, there is the question of to what extent the parent insists on its values — which are probably also strong national values — being observed at least by the chief executives in a national subsidiary, if not elsewhere. This may mean an insistence on key posts being filled by its nationals, subject only to local employment controls.

Second, there is the extent to which national values, law and customs compel a firm to operate on a different basis and to deviate from some aspects of company policy. Third, and often most important, is the continued strength of national feeling reinforcing practices, standards, etc. to the point of compelling the corporate body to be more tolerant of diversity. There may, however, be a point where this pressure for diversity becomes too much and may even lead to retraction from a country where control can no longer be maintained at an acceptable common level.

6.2 Multinationals

Few aspects of international operations have attracted more publicity in recent years than those of the 'multinational' corporations, particularly in the emotive circumstances of the rapid penetration of the European scene by American-based corporations and the suspicion of their involvement in high politics in Latin America. In the present study we are concerned with operations in and from the United Kingdom as a guide to the wider implications of such concerns. They represent an extension of international operations such as have been described in the previous section to the point where the interests of the organisation transcend those of any country in which it operates, including that from which it originated. As Weinshall has put it, a multinational is an 'organisation . . . in which all considerations related to its growth processes and its survival are based wholly on the interests of the organisation itself, national pressures having no influence except in so far as constraints are imposed on it by the country in which it functions'.[3]

As we have seen, a range of motives may induce a company to undertake operations in a foreign country through a subsidiary which will be largely, if not entirely manned by the citizens of that country. This may be the main opportunity for growth and/or the exploitation of its technical innovations. In this it may be encouraged by the government of its country of origin for national economic reasons, such as the balance of payments or for political reasons. Equally, it may be seeking to penetrate foreign markets to gain technical and market intelligence, or as part of a wider national strategy to secure sources of supplies, as with recent Japanese overseas operations. In the early stages a national interest and style may be very evident, but with few or no minority interests to consider, the corporation is able to look at all its operations with a much wider perspective and to consider how to switch resources and activities from one country to another.

This can be illustrated by the American investment in Western Europe though it must be emphasised that this is a two-way process in which there is substantial West European investment in the US. While the scale of the latter is not that much smaller in absolute terms than the American investment in Europe, as a percentage of the total market or of total investment in the two areas, the far greater scale of the American market means that American penetration of Europe has relatively greater significance than European investment in the US. This is accentuated when we take into account the concentration of US investment in a few firms having access to high technology and a dominant position in selected new industries, such as computers.

American firms operating in Europe were first attracted by access to the otherwise protected markets of individual countries, of preference systems such as the British Commonwealth, and then of the two customs unions that emerged, the European Economic Community and the European Free Trade Area. The combination of the UK market and industrial capacity, UK industrial investment incentives, and the Commonwealth preference area attracted much American investment in the 1950's, notably to Scotland. This was encouraged by the US government in the hope that it would both lessen the need for economic aid and offer new opportunities for American business and overseas income. When the UK failed to gain admission to the original EEC there was a switch of new investment to countries within the Community, such as Belgium, in order to avoid tariff penalties and to get access to what proved to be a rapidly expanding market. Indeed, American and Japanese firms were among the most significant beneficiaries from that expansion. Subsequently, lack of confidence in the ability of the UK to either maintain the value of sterling or to achieve improved industrial performance has led to the switch, not just of newcomers and new investment from the US, but of resources and activities from the UK to other countries in Europe. This has had profound consequences on the movement of foreign exchanges, the transfer of employment and product innovation from one country to another, and here not only from the UK to, say, West Germany, but from other countries, sometimes to UK. The multinational, because it operates in many countries, is able to switch resources to determine which export markets will be supplied from its factories in say the UK and West Germany, and equally to select its sources of supplies on a wider basis, though this is only slowly developing.

There is, therefore, a threat of a clash of interests between such a company and a particular nation-state. The latter may seek to regulate the movements of funds and the employment of expatriates, but it still does not control the centre of power and innovation even when it is the apparent country of origin. The scope for non-disclosure of financial and other information is enhanced where, as in Europe, there is far less disclosure even than in the UK, let alone the US. If we then take into account the fact that some multinationals are truly international in having two main bases, as with the Anglo-Dutch pair, Royal Dutch Shell and Unilever, or through the development of a largely international management team embracing many nationalities, then the tendency for such a corporation to act on a wider frame of reference than that of specific national interest is enhanced. Two further factors have to be taken into account.

The first is the sheer size of the larger multinationals. A few such as General Motors, Unilever or Shell are handling larger resources than some of the governments with which they deal, even in Northern Europe, let alone those of developing countries. The resources that these could move across exchanges is therefore a considerable factor in the balance of payments of individual countries.

The second is the extent to which the policies of government influence the outcome. This can be seen, on the one hand, in the effect on operations of both American and European companies of American anti-trust legislation and its enforcement, which has led American firms to seek overseas opportunities and at the same time has limited the ability of European companies to penetrate the US except by direct take-over. Furthermore, its effects are felt in arrangements between American and non-American firms elsewhere if there is any possibility of American imports being affected. On the other hand, there is the emergence of a policy in the European Economic Community when faced with transnational mergers and associations of companies. Here we have the beginnings of an international approach to the regulation of such corporations, but it occurs against a background of greater tolerance of such arrangements and, indeed, of a deliberate encouragement of appropriate 'marriages' between companies based in Community countries. To overcome the problems presented by existing national company legislation the Commission has, therefore, proposed the establishment of a European Company to operate alongside those registered under national statutes. This has, however, raised the whole question of structure and representation as is indicated in the next section.

To counteract the extent of international operations, and especially those of the multinationals, there has been a marked growth in international action on the part of organised labour, and this has come into prominence in 1975 with the attempts of a number of multinationals to rationalise production in the face of recession by closures and redundancies in particular countries.

While there is a realisation that there is a strong case for international supervision, even if only on a limited scale, of multinationals, this is extremely difficult to achieve for three reasons. The first is the extent to which their operations can be effectively controlled by any group of countries when their activities and resources are spread over a far wider range of countries. The second is the practical one of information and secrecy both within companies and between countries. The third lies in the continued nationalism at three levels: the operating company in a given country, the multinational corporation itself, and the country from which it stems or in which it is most susceptable to government pressure.

6.3 The European Company

Faced with the range of impediments to the free movement of factors of production, some of which have just been highlighted in respect of multinationals, the founders of the European Economic Community have rightly regarded the removal of such traditional obstacles as tariffs and quotas as the first but not the only step required. One of the most important features of the Community is its stress on harmonisation of policies, not for bureaucratic tidiness but because specifications, procedures and institutions can be more effective means of frustrating the whole aim of the wider market represented by the Community. Company law is one such feature and here the Commission has had a special interest, as already stated, in facilitating mergers on an international basis in order to achieve economies of scale and greater effectiveness in dealing with world competition. The concern at the *Defi Americain* as portrayed by Jacques Servan-Schreiber, finds practical expression in the attempt to create offsetting European groupings which, backed by the now larger potential market of the Community as compared to the US, offer a better basis for world competition. While some of the earlier enthusiasm for such mergers as a basis for a technological revolution has abated, the difficulty of bringing about close associations such as the Dunlop-Pirelli alignment, has led to the development of the concept of a European Company, and this has now been formulated in a revised draft fifth directive.

As in some countries merger with a company registered in another country necessitates the creation of a new company and the extinction of the previous ones, not to mention the tax problems posed by trans-frontier mergers, the need for a distinct European Company simultaneously registered with the Community and in each member state has come to be regarded as an important element in promoting cross-frontier mergers. The difficulty that has arisen has derived from the wide differences in the extent to which company law and practice have reflected the pressure for some form of worker participation or representation and the level at which this has so far been agreed. While the full discussion of this issue is deferred to Chapter 9, the core of the debate on the fifth directive is the proposal for a two-tier structure as in West Germany and the Netherlands.

The proposal is that there should be a Supervisory Board, representative of shareholders and employees having ultimate responsibility for the direction of the enterprise but with a second board of management largely or entirely made up of full-time executives. The latter reflects current practice not only in some European countries but also in the USA. There are therefore two main questions.

The first is whether there should be two bodies or one. The UK tradition is the single-tier board having both full-time executive and ordinary non-executive members.

The second concerns the form of worker representation, and at what level it should occur. The proposal is for employee representatives to form part of the Supervisory Board.

At the time of writing the proposal has been put forward for discussion by the nine member governments through the Council of Ministers and by the European Parliament. If the various national differences can be reconciled sufficiently to approve the fifth directive it would now only apply to European Companies which could be formed as joint controlling companies by two or more existing national companies. All other existing companies would continue according to their various national laws and practices. However, it is clear that in political terms the adoption of such a type of company would be bound to have an effect on the future national laws and practices.

Notes and references

1   J. F. Manser, *Financial Role of Multi-National Enterprises,* Cassell 1973.
2   T. G. Parry, 'The international firm and national economic policy', *Economic Journal,* December 1973.
     C. Layton, *Transatlantic Investments,* The Atlantic Institute 1966.
3   T. Weinshall, *The Multinational Enterprise,* Management International 1975.

Study Questions

1   Outline the principal issues posed by the greater involvement of governments in international trade for the operations of firms engaging in overseas operations.

2   Examine the basis of the fear and suspicion with which multinational corporations are often regarded.

3   International operations involve differences in national cultures and attitudes. Discuss this in relation to the evolution of the European Company.

4   Consider the impact of foreign and multinational companies on the United Kingdom and the possible reactions of government to them.

7

THE PUBLIC SECTOR

7.1 Scope and Range of State Owned Enterprises

At the outset let us say that we are only concerned with 'business'; therefore we are not directly concerned with the agencies through which government provides a whole range of services — e.g. health, education, training — even though the boundaries are often obscured. Furthermore, we are only concerned in this chapter with those enterprises in which, on whatever foundation, government exercises control over the key aspects of policy, as with any private firm. In practice this means control over the raising of new capital, the use of profits, the general strategy of the concern and the appointment of its chief officers.

For our purposes we can distinguish three situations. In the first, the enterprise is wholly the property of the state. The four key aspects of policy are controlled by, or are subject to the approval of, a Minister. These are what we conventionally regard as the nationalised industries.

In the second, the state is the largest, possibly the dominant shareholder, and may have a built-in veto on the decisions of the company. Outwardly it remains a public company, the balance of its shares being quoted on the Stock Exchange in the normal way. This would cover British Petroleum and now British Leyland.

In the third, the state has become a significant shareholder, for one of many reasons, but the firm operates in the same way as any other public — or private — company. The state may have advanced funds as part of regional policy or as a rescue operation in the face of a liquidity crisis which threatened employment.

Given these three categories it is then possible to explore the distinctive issues that arise in each. The advent of the Industry

Act 1975 in the wake of earlier legislation in 1967, 1968 and 1972 in no way invalidates this approach. What is new is the role of the National Enterprise Board which extends beyond the existing public sector. In this chapter we concentrate on the wholly owned sector where the financing, the policy criteria and the ultimate control are on a different basis to that of the private sector. Then in Chapter 8 we examine the ways in which government seeks to influence the direction of firms in which it does not have this degree of control.

In examining the wholly owned sector we come face to face with issues that will have to be thought through as any further evolution of the mixed economy takes place. In the rest of this section we review the main elements of the 'nationalised industries' and indicate the less well-known agencies as well as the important companies in which the state has a controlling interest. In the second section we concentrate on the nationalised industries as such, beginning with their objectives. The third section looks at accountability and control and the fourth is concerned with finance. In the light of this review all the enterprises in which the government has a controlling interest can be brought together with the nationalised industries so that we may identify some of the key questions that carry over into the following chapter.

One way of resolving the question of the scope of the 'nationalised industry' sector is to separate all those organisations engaged wholly or partly in activities of a commercial or trading nature, financed otherwise than through the Estimates, in which the government has a controlling interest. The Select Committee on the Nationalised Industries in its report on ministerial control did recommend that all these bodies should fall within the scope of its review.[1]

On this basis, the sector comprises first the well-known nationalised industries brought into public ownership by specific Acts of Parliament. These embrace the entire coal mining industry, the main iron and steel industry, electricity generation and distribution, gas manufacture and distribution, railways, the National Bus Company, the largest road haulage network, the principal national airline, atomic energy and a stake in the exploitation of North Sea oil. To these has been added what was previously a government department, the Post Office, and a group of bodies in which the government is the sole shareholder such as the Bank of England and Cable and Wireless Ltd.

Also in the wholly state-owned sector are a number of

companies that have been acquired at various times as part of a rescue operation to retain their facilities and output as with Short Brothers and Harland or the Beagle Aircraft Company, at an earlier period, and now Rolls Royce (1971) and the ship-building interests of Court Line. Clearly, there are two further distinctions becoming evident here. The first is between the state's acquisition of an industry and the taking into public ownership of a single firm in what remains a private sector industry. The second — and directly related — distinction is between situations that call for a public corporation and those where the public company format suffices.

These two overlap in so far as public corporations often operate through companies which they own or at least control, or through companies that they have established for a specific purpose. Thus, British Rail has a host of joint companies with other railway administrations or with other transport bodies through which international and other facilities are then provided. Joint ventures may be undertaken with public companies, as for example the National Coal Board and Powell Duffryn when engaged in coal mining consultancy services. A further distinction is now to be made between those enterprises and industries that are the responsibility of specific public corporations established by special statutes, and those enterprises that are henceforth to be transferred to control through the National Enterprise Board (NEB). The NEB is itself a striking extension of the public corporation principle.

Already the public corporation has been used as the vehicle for the organisation and management of entire industries, often on a scale far beyond that of any previous private sector body in those industries or indeed any industry. Now it is to be extended to what is essentially a national holding company, thereby raising again two questions: first, the suitability of the public corporation as a means of public sector business management and, second, the desirability of further separating the individual corporations from the 'sponsoring' departments through the use of some much wider holding corporation as has been done in Italy.

To tackle the first one only at this stage, it is valuable to recall the evolution of forms of organisation of business and other activities in the public sector. The idea of a public service could imply that a department of state or a local authority should be directly responsible. However, the scale and complexity of managing generally accepted public services such as health and education are such that delegated powers have been inevitable.

Initially, these have usually been exercised by local authorities which act as agents of central government over a wide range of their present functions. Even here, however, delegation to 'professionally managed' or representative bodies has become widespread. When the first large public undertakings under public ownership and control came into being, special trusts and statutory companies were used, but when they were at national level there was a conscious decision, first with the BBC and then with London Transport, to entrust management to an independent corporation, appointed by and answerable to government but free from interference in day-to-day management. The idea that they should be 'professionally managed' by a board with management structure modelled on that in comparably large public companies was firmly established in the London Transport case. With it was a clear rejection of notions of syndicalism or workers control. The only change, which came with later creations, was a statutory obligation to establish formal negotiating and consultative machinery in respect of the employees of such concerns.

The aim was to enable the board of each such Corporation, wherever its revenue was dependent on its sales of a product or service, to manage its affairs on the same broad commercial principles as a concern in the private sector. At the same time there was a presumption that it would be a monopoly in most cases, and therefore any safeguards which had previously applied where monopoly had been in private hands were initially continued, albeit in a modified form.

Initially, there was great concern that there should be no suspicion of ministerial patronage in the appointment of members of the BBC and the LPTB (London Passenger Transport Board). Indeed, these two organisations set a precedent for a highly independent style of management and a standard for the operation of such bodies. It is hardly surprising that when a major extension of public ownership was launched by the Labour Government 1945-50 the pattern adopted followed closely on the earlier models.

However, there was a fundamental difference in aim. The two cases quoted were both special problems calling for new solutions, based on the ideas — and fears — at the time of their establishment. The measures from 1945 onwards had both ideological and pragmatic objectives. On the one hand there was the commitment in Clause Four of the Labour Party constitution to the public ownership of the means of production, exchange and distribution, and the specific programme to nationalise the mines, electricity, gas, transport, steel and the Bank of England. On the other hand, there was the argument that only by state investment and planning on a much wider base than present ownership permitted would these industries be made more efficient. In the specific case of coal there was a blueprint available — the Reid report on the need for reorganisation and investment in the industry. In others, some plans for reorganisation existed, as for transport, but elsewhere no such plan had yet been formulated.

The subsequent evolution of the entire public sector of industry has been strongly affected by the decisions taken at this time or made possible as a result of the choices made. A significant number of the differences between industries and boards is a consequence of the personalities and power relationships that existed at the outset. Whereas the coal mining industry found itself in the centre of an acute fuel crisis and an initially very adverse financial position in which it was very much subject to political pressure and ministerial control, electricity and gas were able to enjoy a far higher degree of independence. While railways were to become the centre of attention from successive governments, buses and indeed road haulage were to enjoy a high level of independence. Both situations were to be fruitful sources of future friction.

Each public corporation is set up by a specific Act of Parliament which lays down the scope of the undertakings that it is to acquire, its aims and powers, and the main features of its relationship to the relevant Minister and to Parliament. There may be provision for special controls on aspects of its activities, especially where extensions are concerned, and there is invariably provision for negotiating and consultative arrangements with employees. As a body corporate, a corporation can then set up or acquire an interest in companies lying within the broad scope of its permitted activities. The critical issues are, therefore, the nature of its objectives, and its relationship to the community, and it is to the first of these that we now turn.

7.2 Nationalised Industries and their Objectives

While there are specific objectives relating to the industries or undertakings for which particular corporations are responsible, three main objectives have been common to all of them. These are the duty to provide a product or service in a defined industry and/or area, the obligation to break even taking one year with another, and the requirement to have regard to the interests of employees and of the community.

At first it appears that each board has a duty to supply a product or service in the industry for which it is made responsible, but this is not an unqualified obligation. On the contrary, even where the board is by law the only supplier of a service for which there is no permitted competition — the Post Office, for example — it is open to the board not only to so adjust its prices that it may break even on the service concerned even at the additional cost to the community of a serious deterioration in service, but it may refuse to provide certain services altogether. In practice there are very few products or services for which there are no alternatives or even close substitutes and most boards are faced with competition from substitutes. These substitutes may be provided by the private sector or by other public corporations between which the consumer is free to choose. Thus, in fuel and power there are nationalised coal, electricity and gas industries competing with each other and with the mainly private oil industry. In transport, the nationalised railways have to compete with the National Bus Company, private bus and haulage operations, and customers using their own cars and commercial vehicles.

A problem with such public enterprises is, therefore, the element of choice that is retained by the consumer and the extent of substitutes that are available. While in this the public enterprise is not in a different position from a private one, there are important constraints on its freedom of action. Thus the extent to which it can fix its prices in order to compete may be limited, first, by direct controls on its pricing policy, whether or not these are strictly authorised by law, second by the requirement to provide services which may involve it in extensive cross-subsidy between parts of its undertaking, and third in terms of the initiatives it is free to take, for example by entering into the supply of competing products which would entail entry into another industry. Thus the National Coal Board has participated in oil exploration in the North Sea but this is now to be transferred to the British National Oil Corporation. In effect, the objects may prove more difficult to amend if only because of the political controversy as to the extent of the public sector.

But the duty to supply has come into increasing conflict with the second obligation — to break even — and successive governments have agreed that commercial considerations should apply, with the result that there has been an increased willingness to allow boards to abandon products and services even where no direct substitute is readily available where it could be shown that usage was small in relation to the cost of supply. This is seen most forcibly in the case of public transport, first rail and now bus. The public corporations concerned can seek to withdraw services unless there is a subsidy offered either by central government or local authorities.

The obligation to break even, therefore, appears to take precedence, despite the monetary losses of recent years which the boards ascribe to governmental insistence on nil or inadequate price increases. When first introduced, this obligation to break even was taken to mean that each board would have to balance its accounts by ensuring that revenue was sufficient to cover costs and these were to include interest on capital, both that representing the compensation to former owners, and that arising from new borrowing to finance investment. The assumption was that such funds would be raised on similar terms to other government borrowing, that is at rates comparable to Treasury borrowing and, indeed, all stocks issued both at the time of take-over and subsequently had Treasury guarantees of interest. If a corporation failed to break even in one year the Treasury financed the deficit in the expectation that in subsequent years when profits rose it would take back the sums advanced in this way.

In the event, four changes have occurred. The most significant was the move away from a zero-profit policy to one where corporations were both expected to earn a target rate of return on capital employed and to finance investment out of retained profits. The second was the encouragement of other forms of borrowing, both from the Treasury as such and from abroad. The third was the persistent failure of certain corporations to break even leading to widespread intervention and frequent policy changes. The fourth was the use of the public sector as a whole in short-term economic policy so that criteria might be set aside in favour of price stability at the expense of monetary deficits.

The change from zero-profit to a target rate of return was introduced in 1961 by a Conservative Government and extended in scope by a Labour Government. The target rate was to be agreed between the Treasury and the board and applied to a definition of capital employed. This was triggered off by the need, in particular, of the electricity supply industry for capital to enable it to meet the demand which it was stimulating by its price policy. Each industry emerged with its own rate and this was a factor to be taken into account when capital investment projects came up for approval as part of the government's control on public sector spending.

There were, however, two exceptions to this, each representing an extreme case. On the one hand there were undertakings that could not break even, let alone make a target profit, notably the railways. Here, a series of financial settlements has led to the transfer to the taxpayer of all interest on capital invested up to 1968, the grant of subsidies, originally for specified services but not as an aggregate, and the acknowledgement in 1973 that such subsidies are inevitable. At the other extreme are undertakings that had hitherto been profitable, such as the National Freight Corporation which has a conventional enough target, to make as much profit as possible.

The 1961 White Paper[2] had been introduced against the background of the failure to attain even the limited obligation to break even, in the long run, bearing in mind the need for replacement of assets. The rate of return on capital in the public sector was very low when compared to the private sector, and while it was conceded that a gap was to be expected its size was regarded as excessive. The phrase 'taking one year with another' was to be defined as five years and this was to be the period of investment planning.

The three elements, prices, investment and rate of return were recognised as interdependent and the interest of Ministers in pricing, even where they had no powers to intervene, was recognised. The stress on rate of return posed the question of why regulate all three or alternatively why not set price criteria and/or investment criteria leaving profits as the residual as is in fact the case in the private sector?

In 1967 a further White Paper[3] made just this change of emphasis. Prices were henceforward to be related to the marginal costs of supply, the use of revenue in the industry and the tests to be applied to new investment projects. These were now to be subject to discounted cash flow as if each project were a low risk commercial proposition.

But while this remains the stated basis of policy, in practice the requirement that prices be kept down as part of a counter-inflationary policy has at least temporarily destroyed the whole framework and placed those operating the industries in an incredible situation, where pricing and investment decisions are subordinated to current wider economic and political purposes. The decision to return to the break-even situation has been taken, and partly implemented, but the nightmare has been intensified by the rate of inflation. Measures to restore solvency are proving difficult to carry through as the continuation of economic recession and consumer resistance has brought about a sharp fall in demand. There are therefore very serious unresolved questions.

The second change, in the use made by public bodies of the capital market, is linked to the fourth, control over public sector spending as an instrument of overall economic policy. It has meant that while the obligations are unchanged the ability of each corporation to meet them may be dependent on the investment that can be made, and even the working capital requirements that may arise from time to time. The effect has been to restore to the relevant departments a means of control over the investment and operations of each corporation. This has meant delay and intervention in forward planning in which the whole question of political control is involved. This is discussed in section 7.3.

The third problem, that of persistent failure to break even has led to successive reorganisations and policy changes. In the case already cited, the railways, major changes in policy have been associated with changes in governments but have not been confined to that cause. The extension of the public corporation concept to the Post Office has been followed by a series of problems as the Post Office Board has sought to break even on its postal services. This has highlighted a problem which goes back to some of the earliest extensions of public ownership, namely what is the unit which has to be judged on a break even or notional return basis.

This leaves the third obligation to be considered, that of social responsibility. In part this arises from the monopoly position of most boards, their exemption from Monopolies legislation, and the removal of some of the monitoring bodies that previously operated where there had been private monopolies. The main issue is, however, the absence of any definition or criterion as laid down by statute or ordained by any minister. In large measure each corporation has to make its own assessment of what is in the public interest and it is only when a proposal is made to stop a product or service that a procedure for hearing objections and judging the issues is invoked. In practice it means that social objectives are a matter of political judgement both nationally and locally, and once again we have a situation where there is a tendency to assume that a public enterprise can be 'leaned on' to a greater extent than a private concern. Basically this poses the question of where the dividing line

between government, local government and operating enterprise should fall. Public expectations of public corporations are
different from those of private firms, partly because some of
these services were once provided by local authorities, e.g.
electricity, gas.

Equally important is the role of the public corporation as an
employer and of public expectation of its duties in this respect. It
is here perhaps that some of the most serious misunder-
standings have arisen, especially as several of the corporations
have been faced with the need for severe pruning of manpower.

Thus the National Coal Board, British Railways and now the
British Steel Corporation have had to reduce manpower on a
scale unknown in private industry because no single
organisation has had the task of running an entire industry, and
one that was as labour intensive as well. The social obligation
developed by these corporations has provided a measure of
easement of the conduct of the changes concerned, but the
extent of political intervention in the implementation of the
modernisation plans of the British Steel Corporation has shown
how blurred is the division of responsibility between
governments and corporations. Given the widespread myth that
nationalisation is a palliative to unemployment this presents yet
another reason why there has to be clarification of objectives
and criteria of performance throughout this sector.

7.3 Accountability and Control

Given the aim of encouraging professional management on a
day-to-day basis free from political intervention while retaining
overall accountability to the community, the relationship of each
board to Parliament and the community has evolved in a manner
that might not have been anticipated when the great extension
of the public corporation model was launched. Ultimately, a
board can only act within the powers and scope of activities
provided for in the statute which set it up and within the
resources at its disposal. This distinction is important. On the
one hand there is provision for a system of accountability and
control based on statute and precedents; on the other there has
emerged a greater degree of control over investment, prices
and, at times, wages and salaries than either the specific
nationalisation statutes or any other legislation authorise. In
this section we are concerned with the former. This is the
theory, whereas the practice is somewhat different and

occupies part of section 7.4.

At the outset the Act authorising the establishment of a corporation specifies the undertakings to be acquired, the powers and objectives of the corporation, and the statutory boards and other bodies that are to be set up. In most cases the policy of government has been to establish a single national corporation having a monopoly of a section of an industry or service, if not the entire industry. Two issues arise here.

The first concerns the range of activities involved since acquisition of companies engaged in one industry could take a corporation into other industries. Thus the acquisition of the railway companies took the then BTC into docks, shipping, and the travel agency field — Thomas Cook & Sons Ltd. The nationalisation of steel, being based on a definition of a minimum size of iron or steel plant, required the exemption of the Ford Motor Company in the UK on account of its Dagenham plant and the 'hiving-off' of many of the ancillary operations of companies such as United Steel. The proposed nationalisation of aircraft manufacture is to exclude helicopters and be confined to the airframe activities of Hawker-Siddeley. In part this is a political question as to the scope of public ownership; there are those who, on ideological grounds, would wish to see the maximum extension of the public sector but equally there are those who wish to limit its field of operations as far as possible. In part it is a question of policy as to the future freedom and continuity of the body being set up. A firm in the private sector which found itself faced with a long-term decline in demand for its products would seek to move into another field. It would diversify and seek new alliances. Should a public corporation have the same freedom to evolve or must it be confined to its designated industry and such ancillaries as are directly relevant to its operations? Given the association of public corporations with declining industries this is an unresolved question. By no means all public corporations are in such a situation; in fact the majority are in industries with much potential for growth. Nevertheless it is an important difference between public and private sector organisations.

The second issue is whether there should be some regional or functional organisation with a board structure. Originally the National Coal Board was provided with eight regional divisions covering over forty areas. Each division had a board appointed by the Minister and was an accounting unit as was each area, the main level of operational management. In electricity, separate generating and distributing boards were established in

England and Wales with a system of regional supply boards, whereas in Scotland separate regional boards were set up each of which undertook both generation and distribution. To coordinate the various boards an Electricity Council was set up, whereas in the gas industry, until the onset of natural gas, a regional organisation handled generation and supply through area boards with the Gas Council as a coordinating body. The development of the natural gas grid has led to a change to a British Gas Corporation having as subordinates the regional organisations. Only in electricity do we continue to find this regional supply board as a separate entity.

In other situations different approaches have been tried. The first steel nationalisation created a holding company leaving the companies as wholly owned subsidiaries. When they were bought back a second time the British Steel Corporation emerged as a single entity having a regional/product organisation internally. As already indicated, inland transport has seen a succession of organisations beginning with the BTC with its executives for each industry or activity passing on through the device of a holding company for all non-railway undertakings and now taking the form of an interlocking group of corporations with a network of subsidiary companies.

When we refer to a board or corporation we normally mean one for an industry or section of industry, but in a few cases we also mean what is a regional body. Such a board is appointed by the relevant Minister and is made up of a chairman, usually full-time, and full and part-time members. The full-time members are usually appointed from among senior managers in the industry. So far only in the case of the Steel Corporation is there an employee-director. Part-time members reflect a wide range of business and trades union experience. Where the chairman is not full-time then there is a chief executive who is usually deputy-chairman. All board members are appointed for a fixed term of years and their appointments are renewable.

Whereas the board of a company has almost complete control of its membership in the absence of a specific financial or share interest, that of a public corporation is in the hands of a Minister with influence from within the department concerned and — except where chairmanship is concerned — the chairman himself. This can place a very large number of appointments at least nominally in the hands of a single Minister, e.g. Energy.

While the membership, apart possibly from a more frequent use of trade union officers at least in part-time roles, closely resembles that of a large public company so far as their

relationships within the board are concerned, the key relationships are not with financial institutions as groups of
shareholders; they are with the 'sponsoring' department.
Immediate relationships are with the Minister concerned but as
he is likely to change within the lifetime of a single parliament,
let alone with changes of government, a crucial relationship is
with the senior civil servants in that department. This in turn
poses a two-tier system. The department while operating within
the context of the legislation relevant to the particular board is
also subject to Treasury influence, if not control, notably on the
criteria that have to be applied when assessing proposals from a
board. The Treasury — like the department — is, in turn,
dependent on decisions in cabinet on major policy issues. The
importance of political relationships that such a system implies
is reflected in the pattern of appointments to the key role of
chairman. Here three main features should be noted. The first is
the extent to which the chairman is also in effect the chief
executive, and this is reflected in the variation in practice
between those who hold full-time appointments, and those who
combine part-time appointments in both the public and private
corporate sectors. The second feature is the appointment of
politicians to key posts alongside professional managers from
within nationalised industries and what might almost be termed
'professional chairmen', those who move between large
corporations in the public and private corporate sectors. The
third is the controversy as to their remuneration, with the
tendency to a compromise between the salary levels in
government and those in private corporate bodies of
comparable scale.

Whatever his background a chairman is going to be involved
in complex political relationships as long as corporations remain
directly subject to sponsoring departments and their Ministers.
These relationships are thus simplified or complicated
according to the degree of continuity of policy or its lack as
between successive ministries of opposing political outlooks, in
which the whole question of the scale of the public sector is in
conflict. It is not only a question of policies but also of roles and
their perception by ministers and chairmen alike. Some
Ministers have clearly sought to exercise much closer control,
for whatever reason, than others. Equally, the tactics if not the
policies of chairmen have varied in the degree of independence
they have sought to sustain for the operations of their
corporations.

This relationship of the chairman, and indeed of the whole

board, to a sponsoring Minister raises the question of accountability and parliamentary control. Where an industry has been brought under public ownership as a result of a specific statute there is a largely standard relationship of such a board to government and to Parliament. In the first place, Parliament must approve all forms of legislation, such as amending statutes, and matters requiring an order that has to be laid before or financially voted by Parliament, including any authorisation of additional or amended finance where this is to be provided through the Treasury. There may also be private bills put forward in order to facilitate aspects of a board's operations where special powers are required. Clearly, there is opportunity for debate on a wide range of issues of policy when such an occasion arises. Secondly, each board presents an annual report that is laid before Parliament and there is again an opportunity for a wide debate when it is received. But in both situations it is the Minister who speaks for the industry concerned. The question therefore arises as to the extent of more direct control over the affairs of public corporations.

One possibility is the traditional device of the parliamentary question but this is dependent on the admissibility of the question. Ministers have long sought to establish that they cannot be made to answer questions of day-to-day management. Originally they argued, and the Speaker upheld this view, that they would only be questioned on the exercise of their own duties in relation to the nationalised industries. If and when they formally exercised, or subsequently accepted responsibility for doing so informally, a control over a corporation on, for example, an investment decision or a pricing matter, then they could be questioned. When, however, they relied on informal contacts with chairmen and boards then it was less easy to question them, even when they came to exercise far wider control over performance criteria, investment decisions and prices. In particular, price control was exercised long before prices and income policies were made statutory and in the absence of any authorisation in the relevant nationalising statutes. The changes in criteria brought about with the White Papers of 1961 and 1967 undoubtedly contributed to a wider interpretation of what a Minister could be questioned upon, but general experience of the working relationships of Ministers and boards has also facilitated this approach. However, the decision as to whether a matter is one that a Minister will answer, where it has not been established by precedent, ultimately rests with him. The alternative is for the member to put the question direct

to the chairman in writing but any such communication — and
its reply — is not covered by parliamentary privilege.

There remains one very important method of parliamentary
control, the Select Committee on Nationalised Industries, which
undertakes a review of the policy and decisions of each industry
at intervals of not more than seven years. The Select Committee
takes evidence from and cross-examines the senior civil
servants in the sponsoring department and the chairmen and
members of the board(s) concerned. One of the issues that has
surrounded the work of this committee has been the extent of its
review in respect of the institutions to be examined. In its own
report on this matter in 1969 it proposed that any body not
financed by estimates but wholly or mainly owned by the state,
or in which the state had a right of veto on decisions of the board,
as in British Petroleum, should be brought within its purview.
One institution which the Treasury argued should not be
included, was the Bank of England itself.

The reviews carried out by the Select Committee are
penetrating and wide ranging, and have exposed many of the
pitfalls and uncertainties that have been present in the
relationships of Ministers, departments and boards. Primarily a
policy review, it provides a basis for a wider debate on the issues
involved, over and above that which arises with government
proposals or as a result of special review committees such as
the Morris Committee which advised the then Minister of
Transport before the Transport Act 1968.

One matter which emerges from reports of the Select
Committee is the likelihood of distinct views on future policy on
the part of a board and the sponsoring department. An industry
in which this has been very obvious is transport, where the
department has responsibility for several boards that are
operating in competition both with one another and with the
private user and operator.

In addition, like industries in the private sector, but with the
difference that a corporation may be the only 'firm' in an
industry, there is the type of comment and control that is
exercised by statutory bodies as part of a prices and income
policy. The original Prices and Incomes Board, and the present
Prices Board, have both exercised control over price increases.
In its reviews of price increase applications the National Board
for Prices and Incomes carried out an appraisal of policies and
operational effectiveness, and although this is less explicit in
present reviews, the same considerations have to be taken into
account. The one review body from which nationalised bodies

are exempt is the Monopolies Commission.

Faced with this range of review bodies in contrast to the analysts of the City or the financial press, the chairman and senior managers of public corporations are in a more public and exposed position than their opposite numbers have been hitherto in the private corporate sector. Given the emphasis on public accountability, and on taking public interest considerations into account, this is to be expected. The difficulty lies in the criteria that have been evolved for the assessment of their performance and the definition of what is the public interest.

As for the first, there has been a steady move away from the earlier concept of merely breaking even to doing so over a five-year period at an agreed rate of profit on capital employed, reinforced since 1967 by additional checks on investment proposals and new criteria on price policy. The investment check, requiring the application of discounted cash flow analysis on the lines of a commercial profit rate for a low risk project, is subject not only to Treasury control as to the rate to be applied but also as to the amount to be spent. This is part of a wider control over national economic policy. Here short-term policy considerations have presented problems even to the extent of making long-term investment and strategic planning difficult for boards.

The degree of political intervention as part of wider economic policies has been greatest under the successive Conservative and Labour governments since 1970, so much so that in 1975 the chairmen made a collective approach to the Prime Minister as to their concern at their own roles. To offset this it has been argued that there should either be a single ministry to deal with all such industries or the interposition of a holding company or state investment bank which would then relate to individual boards in a manner similar to that envisaged for the National Enterprise Board and the companies in which it will hold a controlling interest for government.

Another aspect of this problem is that the only level at which a board can be made accountable is a national one. Yet some boards deal only with matters in Scotland or Wales while others were set up in Northern Ireland accountable to the Stormont parliament when it existed. With devolution proposals under consideration there is the possibility that in these three countries or provinces, an opportunity might arise for accountability at that level. However, the regional bodies in England remain, and these have no regional elected body to which they might relate.

The remaining external check, if it can be regarded in the same light, is the Consumers Consultative Council which is a feature of many boards. This is to enable consumers to have a means of making their views known to boards though they are clearly not regarded by the boards or their members as means of handling individual complaints. Essentially consultative, their one claim to attention has been their reaction to proposals for price increases but even this has now been overtaken by national review boards.

The original aim of separating political and policy issues on the one hand from those of everyday management on the other was bound to be a difficult one to achieve. In the event the combination of wider policy implications and greater departmental vetting of all investment plans has produced a situation where boards propose but Ministers and departments dispose. One factor has been the degree of dependence on investment or other financial decisions by the sponsoring departments. Any board which had modest investment requirements but a good profit record might enjoy a high degree of autonomy. But wherever financial support was involved, or a major change in either employment offered or services provided, then even a financially attractive prospect would not exempt a Board from very much greater supervision and delay in decision from the department concerned. Inflation and the attempt to check it by curbs on public sector price increases have been blamed for the loss of financial discipline and the subsequent loss of independence. But at least as damaging have been two other factors.

The first is the intervention to slow down or delay the rate of reduction in employment in those undertakings that are clearly overmanned, especially during the recession from 1973 onwards. This has led to the review and partial postponement of the plans of the steel industry and to a complex struggle within the field of fuel policy between the interests of the mining industry — and of the employment of miners — the finances and policies of the electricity supply industry, and the nature and scale of future investment in nuclear energy. The requirement to fly Concorde even at a loss cannot be avoided by British Airways, while British Rail have been caught in a cross-fire of confused arguments on transport policy. The second has been the pressure for greater accountability and open government in the public sector backed by strong trade union pressure on government. This, when coupled with the degree of intervention already noted and the effect of political decisions on the rate of remuneration of chairmen and board members, has produced a crisis in manning the boards themselves, even from within the industries concerned. It has even brought about regular meetings by chairmen to discuss their positions and in consequence to make representations to the Prime Minister.

Subject to this key relationship to government on vital issues of policy, the management of a public corporation is very similar to that of a large public company in most respects. The real influence lies with professional managers, most of whom have always served in the industry, and the more obvious differences concern the extent to which affairs have to be conducted under much greater public scrutiny from individual members of parliament, local authorities and the media, and the built-in requirement for formalised consultative and negotiating arrangements, which extend in the case of steel to employee-directors. It has to be said, however, that the outcome has been an industrial atmosphere that shows little difference from that under private ownership.

7.4 Finance and Criteria for Economic Performance

Whereas in the earlier forms of public corporation there was a close parallel to the private corporate sector, there has been a growing separation of the sectors in the ways in which they are financed. Thus the original London Passenger Transport Board had stockholders who, while they had no control over the appointment of the members of the Board, did have the right to institute a winding up if it failed to meet the interest on their stock. The post-war boards mainly took over from companies by the issue of fixed interest securities upon which the Treasury guaranteed the interest. Additional borrowing was to be on a similar basis. It was expected that profits would be earned sufficient to cover the cost of the interest. It was as if the capital was all loan-capital, with no equity on which earnings could vary from zero upwards. However, when boards failed to break even, they were, in effect, compelled to borrow from the Treasury to meet the interest payments and the deficit on current trading, thereby incurring additional interest liability on the extended borrowing. Where there was subsequently a return to profitability it was possible to end this liability but in some cases this proved impossible.

Faced with this situation two solutions have been tried. Whereas in a private sector body in such a situation there would possibly be a capital reconstruction under which the accumulated losses were written off by a writing down of the nominal value of the holdings of shareholders, in a public corporation a reconstruction means a transfer of responsibility for interest from the corporation to the general taxpayer. So far as the corporation is concerned its capital is possibly written-off and its interest liability reduced. So far as the stockholder is concerned the Treasury assumes full responsibility for meeting the interest out of taxation. This has happened twice in the case of British Rail, with a further transfer on a 'temporary' basis of responsibility for a further tranche of capital.

The second approach has been for the Treasury to advance 'equity capital' in expectation of a rate of profit which while varying from year to year gives what is agreed between the Treasury and the board concerned to be a rate of return on the sum advanced similar to that expected as a profit on capital employed in other nationalised industries. This system was first used with British Overseas Airways in 1960 and has subsequently become more general.

Faced with higher interest rates on the London market, some corporations were encouraged to finance expansion by borrowing from abroad at lower rates, thereby also reducing their demands on the London market. Then in the late 1960's came an even more important switch away from raising funds directly on any market or by direct borrowing from financial institutions, to sole reliance on advances by the Treasury. This has meant much more obvious Treasury control over the raising of funds though the fact that the Treasury was guaranteeing borrowing from the markets meant that it was always involved in control of any new borrowing under the earlier system. In any event, the overall borrowing powers — and the Treasury's powers to advance — are both subject to the formal consent of Parliament.

Whereas the earlier system left a borrowing board open to the current interest rate of the market — itself a factor subject to governmental influence — the newer system places more of the emphasis on the tests of performance and techniques of appraisal applied by the sponsoring departments under the overall guidance of the Treasury.

The change of emphasis began with the 1961 White Paper[2] in which the notion of an agreed rate of return for each industry was introduced in place of the zero-profit approach to break even. One factor in this change was concern for the scale of new investment that appeared to spring, at least in part, from pricing policies which stimulated new consumption, notably in electricity. At least prices would henceforth have to provide a profit margin out of which capital could be found for at least part of the expansion.

The changes in 1967-8 amounted to the imposition of an alternative set of criteria. Capital projects were to require departmental approval using discounted cash flow analysis at the rate judged by the Treasury to be for a low commercial risk, initially 8% but later raised to 10%. This has meant that capital programmes have been subject to detailed appraisal, often leading to considerable delays in decisions, and involving the application to a wide range of proposals of techniques that are most appropriate for plant investment decisions. There is reason to submit that the criteria have often been applied too narrowly when one considers the wider responsibilities for expenditure decisions of the departments concerned.

The price criteria as presented from 1967 placed an emphasis on marginal cost pricing but with the requirement that specific projects or activities should be fully self-financing. This has presented problems in cases of what is really joint supply as well as in the narrow base that has sometimes been used, e.g. in transport decisions. Although set aside as part of prices and incomes policy from 1973 onwards, the subsequent return towards a situation in which nationalised industries are largely self-financing raises once again the appropriateness of the criteria as such, and of the particular ways in which they have been applied. We return to these questions at the close of this chapter.

But there is one other criterion that we have to bear in mind, and that is the nature of the choice that is left to the consumer. While he or she may only buy electricity or gas from state corporations there is still freedom to choose between them, quite apart from the alternatives based on nationalised coal and largely privately supplied oil. In both the power and transport industries this element of choice is important in a study of criteria.

It makes for an element of competition between corporations and raises further policy issues for governments. Thus the nationalised gas industry has been free to abandon town gas production from coal in favour of natural gas and reformed gas derived from oil. But the nationalised electricity industry has found itself subject to strong pressure to burn coal as it is now the principal outlet for the National Coal Board. While successive reports have commented on the economic aspects of

using different fuels for different purposes, the choice has been
left very largely with the consumer. The one restriction has been
that on private electricity generation in industry.

The situation in transport is even more striking. Not only do
we find competing nationalised rail, bus, road haulage and civil
aviation undertakings but there is a private sector in road
haulage, aviation and coastal shipping. All these 'providers' of
public transport are thus in competition with the private car and
commercial vehicle, aircraft and ship. Yet all transport requires
an infrastructure of roads, airports and ports which are almost
entirely a governmental responsibility.

The problem of balance between the public and private
sectors is seen most clearly in civil aviation. The continued
political controversy as to the role to be accorded to private
operators, both of scheduled services and on charter, is only
partly contained by the use of a route licensing body on domestic
routes.

The civil aviation industry also faces, in respect of the tourist
trade, the problems of the extension of publicly owned activities
and controls over private operators by state licensing bodies.
Nationalised industries have an initial scope in terms of the
definition of undertakings to be acquired. Where such
undertakings have subsidiaries in other fields it may be that they
are 'hived-off' or they may be retained and developed. To
supporters of the free enterprise system it may seem logical to
'hive-off' activities that are regarded as ancillary and for which
buyers can be found. Thus Thomas Cook, after a long period of
state ownership following the acquisition of the railways in
1947, was eventually sold to a consortium of the Automobile
Association and the Midland Bank.

Both to the protagonist of greater public ownership and those
concerned with the evolution of a particular corporation as a
concern, the ability to diversify, at least as a part of the total
product or service that it is trying to sell, is an equally strong
argument not only for retention but for new endeavours. Given
the extent to which undertakings in the private sector evolve
with technical and market changes, there is at least a case for
allowing public corporations to do likewise.

Two further questions are posed by this. The first concerns
the terms upon which a public corporation may seek to extend
its scope. The second relates to possible joint ventures either
with other public corporations or with private interests.

As regards the terms, the important issues are, first, the
sources of finance for acquisitions or new developments and,

second, the criteria upon which a public corporation would then trade, possibly in competition with private sector firms. Any acquisition involves Ministerial consent to the financial investment, and given the basis of financing already described, it can be argued that a public corporation has access to sources of finance on a scale and in terms that are not open to a private rival. However, the use of this power may not enable a government to transfer into public ownership undertakings by any industry in which it has an existing undertaking without having to seek parliamentary approval through a new nationalisation statute. The bid by the British Transport Docks Board, the successors of the railway-owned docks organisations, for Felixstowe Port in 1975 is a clear example of this.

Where, in consequence of such a take-over, the public corporation is in competition with other operators, an important consideration is the commercial basis of competition, especially where legislation on other counts may require preferential treatment to any public body, as occurred with Selective Employment Tax. Electricity Supply Boards, which compete with private electrical contractors, found themselves in a position to compete on more favourable terms through not being subject to that tax. They chose not to exploit it.

One test of a mixed economy is the way in which the interface of public and private bodies operates. A particular application is where a joint venture is involved. This may, of course, be a joint venture between two public corporations or between a nationalised industry and a continental counterpart as in British Railways and their shipping interests. However, there are a number of joint ventures involving, for example, the National Coal Board with, in one case, Powell Duffryn, on coal mining technical consultancy, and in another in North Sea Oil exploration. Throughout all of these normal commercial criteria are expected to be applied.

Next, and most difficult in practice, is the application of economic criteria to productivity and performance where labour manning and productivity is at the heart of the problem. As already indicated, the public sector includes at least three industries in which there is a continuing problem in this respect, despite massive reductions through redundancy and natural wastage — coal mining, railways and steel-making. There is still despite the evidence of what has happened in all three industries, a strong feeling that a nationalised concern can or should offer greater job security. There is a consequent attempt on the part of government to so regulate investment and development as to protect employment as far as possible. Although rarely specified as a criterion it is nevertheless an important factor to be weighed up by the management of a public corporation.

The nationalised industries therefore present basic policy dilemmas for government and for society. Are they to be operated on 'normal' economic criteria, albeit modified to include some measure of social costs and benefits, or are they to be instruments of social or political policies to which economic criteria are to be subordinated? What is to be the division of responsibility between the government and the enterprise and, given some such division, on what criteria are those charged with the management of such concerns to operate? Equally, there are questions as to the basis upon which sponsoring departments are to work. Should the Minister have even more power to intervene through directives as Mr Benn has argued? Given the type of decision being vetted — and effectively made — by civil servants, on what criteria and with what background of experience of such types of decision are they working? The analysis of the record of government subsidies to the private sector released by the Department of Industry must pose fundamental doubts as to the whole approach adopted hitherto, let alone the extensions of this form of influence and choice under current policies.[4]

Notes and references

1 *Report of the Select Committee on Nationalised Industries 1967-8* House of Commons Papers 298, 371.

2 *Financial and Economic Objectives of the Nationalised Industries* Cmd 1937, HMSO 1961.

3 *Nationalised Industries; a review of economic and financial objectives* Cmd 3437, HMSO 1967.

4 Department of Industry, *The Economics of Industrial Subsidies,* HMSO 1976.

Study Questions

1 Taking any one nationalised industry trace the evolution of its policies and try to identify the role of governments in their evolution.

2 Why should nationalised industries be required to make a profit?

3 What problems are posed by the introduction of social criteria into the objectives of nationalised industries?

4   Compare and contrast the type of surveillance to which the board of a nationalised industry and a large quoted company are subject.

5   Discuss the questions posed where the 'sponsoring departments' virtually determine the investment strategy of a nationalised industry.

8

GOVERNMENT INTERVENTION AND INDUSTRY PLANNING

8.1 The Framework of Intervention

Government is inevitably a major party in a 'negotiated environment'. Even the most fervent adherents of the market economy have to concede that (i) its performance can be improved as well as hampered by some forms of government action, and (ii) there are social costs and benefits that have to be taken into account. An advanced industrial society demands an infrastructure, much of which takes the form of 'communal' provision and consumption. Indeed, as such countries have moved towards what some writers have termed the 'post-industrial phase' the pace of growth of 'communal consumption' has come to pose new problems. The United Kingdom, with government determining the use of 60% of GNP in 1976, is clearly in such a situation.

Even if there was no conscious industrial strategy on the part of government the sheer scale of its demands for resources creates a threat to the future viability of its productive industries and services when massive transfers have to be made to sustain both consumption and investment in the public sector. The taxation and borrowing implications of such huge demands underlie the White Paper on future public expenditure issued in February 1976.[1] The way in which such funds are raised must have effects on not only the general level of consumption but on the fate of individual products and therefore the firms that produce them. The fact that government has to take account of such elements as the country's balance of payments and the external purchasing power of its currency adds to the likelihood that government will seek to regulate the level of economic activity by continual adjustments — the so-called 'instant tuning' of the economy. The government then becomes the immediate source of uncertainty and turbulence unless it is able to sustain some continuity in its policies as they affect business enterprises.

Equally, the investment demands of the public sector plus the spending of those it employs and those whom it supports through social security constitute demands which businesses are seeking to meet. There is consequently a need for economic-cum-political forecasting on the part of individual firms. If they are to be able to do more than merely react to events then they have to seek to influence those events when they are the results of decisions of governments. Therefore there is a need not only for vigilance but for attempts to influence the way in which policies may move and this calls into play not only the methods of consultation described in Chapter 2 (section 2.4) but also the extent to which interventions by government are negotiable. Such negotiation takes place at two levels, The first is what is usually described as economic planning in this country; the second is in the process of advice in the execution of particular policies of an interventionist type. In both, the participants may have little sympathy with either the systems they are seeking to sustain — as with many trades unionists — or the concept of interventionism, as with many managers, but both acknowledge that for political reasons they have to engage in these processes if only to negotiate with the other parties — including government — to safeguard their respective interests.

Taking the national level first, the position before 1962 was that there were periodic dialogues between the CBI and the TUC on the one hand and the Treasury on the other, usually based on the then annual budget cycle of government. Subsequently, not only have budgets become more frequent and the process of comment therefore almost continuous, but the emphasis on such issues as prices and incomes policy has brought about new institutions through which dialogue can occur and from which it may be stimulated by informed comment from time to time. The National Economic Development Council has been the principal such forum. Successive governments have varied their use of this approach just as they have varied their enthusiasms for government intervention, thereby producing another cycle in the approach of government to industrial planning. Thus Conservative governments have sought to move away from a strongly interventionist line towards greater reliance on the market and on indirect control through monetary and fiscal policies; they have then found themselves drawn into particular problems — as on their attitude to 'lame ducks' — and ended with a restoration of interventionism which is then taken up by their Labour successors. Starting with enthusiasm for planning they extend interventionism until forced by the pressure of events to check the process and even restore greater reliance on the very market forces that their opponents uphold. But whichever political party is in power there is the need to reconcile the demands of the public sector with the resources and external balance of the economy.

The paper presented by the Chancellor of the Exchequer and the Secretary of State for Industry to the November 1975 conference convened through NEDC entitled 'An approach to industrial strategy' is the most recent attempt to encompass both public spending and industrial strategy. Earlier attempts at National Economic Plans were little more than statements of aspirations; the earlier NEDC reports concentrated on what were the main constraints on faster growth.[2] Two features in the November 1975 paper are therefore of particular interest.

The first is the emphasis on more effective industrial planning with a far greater emphasis on the need for consultation and a realisation that this is going to be a complex matter. While there is reference to 'powerful new instruments . . . . in particular planning agreements and the National Enterprise Board',[3] the subsequent emphasis is on 'a more flexible approach'[4] based on sector studies which lead to discussions with both sides of industry and call for reconciliation of government forecasts and intentions with those of the main sectors. A timetable for such discussions is suggested involving an annual cycle.

The second is the analysis of the relevant factors in the present poor performance of manufacturing industry and the inclusion of those for which government is responsible, viz:[5]

(vii)   sharp and frequent changes of economic regulators to meet the conflicting needs of economic and social priorities, which make it difficult for companies to plan ahead.

(viii) pre-emption of resources by the public sector and by personal consumption to the detriment of industry's investment and export performance.

(ix)   government intervention in the pricing, investment and employment policies of the nationalised industries.

The subsequent White Paper on public expenditure in which the growth of public expenditure is to be slowed down so as to reduce its share of GNP from 60% to 53% in 1979-80 is an important sequel. On closer study the White Paper appears to indicate a net increase in public spending on 'trade, industry and employment' averaging £500M per annum from 1976-7. However, while there is to be increased support through the

Industry Act, including such operations as the recent Chrysler UK agreement, other forms of support are stabilised or reduced.

It is therefore appropriate that we turn our attention to these other forms of support as they constitute the inherited framework into which the National Enterprise Board and planning agreements have now to be introduced. Immediately a distinction has to be drawn between two broad groups of activities:

(a) services provided free or at a charge in support of business activities;

(b) subsidies and grants.

(a) Services in support of business activities: These have two main justifications. First they seek to improve the efficient working of the economy as in the example of the Manpower Services Commission and its Employment and Training Services Agencies. Second they may provide services abroad where both commercial intelligence and political support may be called for. There are the Overseas Trade Board and the Export Credit Guarantee Department. These all represent services that are open to all who care to use them either free of charge or at a price for the service — as with the Executive and Scientific Register of the Employment Services Agency, and the ECGD.

While such agencies are all financed against the Votes for particular departments they each tend to be directed by a board or commission representative of business and the trades unions together with other interested parties e.g. education. The members both of the boards and of the various advisory panels and committees that are then set up are able to reflect the interests of their organisations and to participate in yet another set of networks through which both the formation and the implementation of policy may be influenced. However, the disposition of resources, especially regionally, may reflect political decisions related to regional policy.

(b) Subsidies and Grants: These comprise investment allowances and grants, subsidies, support for research, development and product launching, and regional policy measures which tend to overlap nearly all the others. They represent an important if controversial aspect of public policy in that there is a clear intention to influence the decisions of those directing enterprises both generally and in specific categories as well as direct support for, and intervention in, the affairs of specific firms. Indeed, the first distinction to be made is between

aid that is generally available and that which has a condition attached to its availability. The second distinction is then as to the breadth or narrowness of the categories eligible for aid culminating in the provision for help to specific firms.[6]

Prominent in the first group are investment allowances and grants. In part the distinction between them is one of form rather than intent or even scope. Allowances designed to promote investment by bringing forward tax allowances on new investment so that they fell most heavily in the first year of the life of an asset were the practice to 1966 and from 1970. Grants were used 1966-70 and then added in 1972 in respect of firms in Assisted Areas only.

Originally provided under the Industrial Development Act 1966, grants were provided to stimulate investment with particular emphasis on selected industries — computers, hovercraft, and mining. The change in 1972 under Section 7 of the Industry Act enabled grants to be made for removals to and buildings in Development Areas as well as allowing subsidies to support employment including aid with the cost of private borrowing. It was under the legislation that the arrangements emerged for specific help to individual firms, the second main category already identified.

Thus the assistance given to Govan Shipbuilders followed the collapse of Upper Clyde Shipbuilders — itself a government inspired merger — in 1971. Funds were made available partly by the government taking up £10M in equity holdings and partly by advancing working capital. In the case of Cammell Laird some £20M was to be advanced, partly through acquisition of 50% of the equity and partly by an interest free loan secured by a floating charge. In a third case, International Computers, no less than £40M was to be made available as grants for research and development, to be repaid as a levy on pre-tax profits.[7]

Given the scale of support two types of question arise. The first concerns the criteria and the process of sanctioning such aid. The second is the effectiveness of such measures in relation to the stated aims of government policy. On the first, general assistance should satisfy the four criteria set out by Field and Hills in their paper on 'The administration of industrial subsidies'[8] namely:

(ia) The scheme should be readily understandable . . . . . .
(ib) It must be possible to secure the Parliament's and Ministers' intentions are carried out, by ensuring that subsidy goes only to those industries and for those purposes for which the scheme

was intended.

(ic)   Public money must be safeguarded as far as possible against the possibilities of fraud, of legal abuse, of failure to observe the conditions of the assistance, and of losses arising from the collapse of companies . . . . . .

(id)   The need to secure equity in the treatment of applicants.

Of these the last cannot apply to cases of specific rescues of firms where in desperate situations they come to government and politicians may decide to trade 'policies for votes' as was so clearly demonstrated in the later case of Chrysler UK at the end of 1975. Once criteria of normal commercial prospects of viability are subordinated to rescues in which either employment in particular localities or experiments in industrial democracy take precedence then not only is the review system overridden but a much more contentious set of criteria take over. Thus the Industry Act 1972 provided for an Industrial Development Advisory Board both centrally and in each region qualifying for assistance. Drawn from industry and finance these bodies have examined each case for assistance and made recommendations to the Secretary of State. It was well known that Mr Benn when in that office overturned the advice offered in a number of controversial cases — Scottish Daily Express, the Meriden Motor Cycle Cooperative and the West Kirkby Cooperative. In the first of these his successor was obliged to bring support to an end.

The main outcome of the subsidies and grants outlined above can be seen in three ways. First there is the extent to which investment allowances and grants may have influenced the level of investment. The second is in terms of their contribution to such success as has attended regional policy. The third is the legacy of problem firms now to be inherited by either the National Enterprise Board or the new public corporations for the aricraft and shipbuilding industries.

Turning to the second type of subsidy/grant situation, that concerned with research, development and launching aid, government assistance occurs at three stages. The first, covering what is conducted at universities and government research establishments, is funded partly by direct grant without preliminary assessment of the nature of the work to be undertaken and partly through the Research Councils and departmental contracts working increasingly on the lines recommended by the Rothschild report. The second is that directly sponsored by the Department of Industry through launching aid and similar grants. Here much larger sums may be involved but they still represent barely 20% of such spending. The main review mechanism is the relevant Research Requirement Board. Eight of these came into existence in 1973 to help identify the area which will most benefit from research and development support and to determine the objectives and balance of programmes in support of departmental policies. They exclude the two largest users of resources, aero-space which in 1971 accounted for 51% of civil R & D aid, and nuclear energy which accounted for 27%.[9] Lastly there are the Industrial Research Associations to which government makes a contribution but which are mainly funded, and their policies therefore determined, by the contributing firms in the industries concerned.

The support for regional policy has already appeared in looking at investment allowances and grants, but it has wider aspects, notably the Regional Employment Premium. Given the range not only of incentives but also of negative pressures against new developments that involve construction or extension of plants in the Midlands and the South East their total impact might be expected to be much greater than appears at first sight. Clearly, they represent a major effort to divert the larger units of growth and to secure some transfer of smaller concerns but the persistence of problems of overmanning and redundancy in the traditional industries of the Development Areas has partially obscured the success that the policies have attained. Even so the main factor making for higher levels of employment in the areas concerned, as well as for conditions favourable to transfer of sources of new employment, appear to lie in the general level of profitable performance and in improvements such as communications and infrastructure that increase the attractiveness of particular regions for new investment.

At regional level the processes of consultation are more extensive. They begin against the background of Regional Economic Planning Councils for each of the eight English regions and with direct Ministerial involvement in the case of Scotland and Wales. Here the existing machinery is now to be supplemented by the Scottish and Welsh Development Agencies set up in 1975 to undertake a wide range of projects in terms of infrastructure and support, including the administration of some of the subsidies and grants already referred to. In each case the Agency has an existing counterpart, the Scottish Council (Development and Industry) and the Welsh Development Corporation, with similar aspirations to those of certain

English regional development bodies. Both the CBI and the respective Scottish and Welsh TUC's are represented and able to exercise influence. While the bodies in both countries and that in Northern Ireland have direct access to a Secretary of State, the eight English regions have to rely on their Regional Economic Planning Councils, the local advisory boards set up to handle regional aid where it applies, and the regional organisations of CBI and TUC.

With the pressure for devolution the extent to which economic policy can be delegated is clearly one of the principle issues but it is beyond our present task to speculate as to its implications.

Looking at this whole framework the evidence of a largely pragmatic evolutionary approach is clear for all the ideological support for greater emphasis on economic planning. This contrast becomes even more striking when we turn to the principal new instruments of the Industry Act 1975.

8.2 Industry Act 1975 — New Interventionism

The ideological approach has proclaimed this statute to be the basis for nothing less than the regeneration of industry by means of a marked extension of public ownership and supervision across the whole of the previous private sector. Indeed, in the heady enthusiasm of the initial launch of the bill, the financial crisis facing so much of industry was seen as the collapse of capitalism which was an opportunity to be exploited to achieve an irreversible change to socialism. In the event the final form and context of the legislation, while resting more firmly on the basis of a mixed economy, does nevertheless mark a significant change in the role of government in relation both to the private sector as a whole and to that part which receives government financial support in particular. One of the tenets of the policy now adopted is that such assistance, whatever its rationale, is to be conditional upon a permanent stake in the company concerned, involving a share in control, not only for the state but for the employees and their trade unions.

Pragmatic views have led to suggestions that there should be a new approach to both the interventions of government and the handling of the greatly extended group of companies that are now wholly or partly state owned and controlled. The experience of the Industry Act 1972 whereby the Department of Industry could advance funds subject to receiving — though not necessarily accepting — the advice of an industrial advisory panel, while not ended, is at least more likely to be entrusted to the National Enterprise Board. This is the new mechanism for handling the various forms of aid as well as for deploying an initial borrowing power of £1,100M in assistance, restructuring of firms and industries, and investment in new projects. The Board becomes a giant holding company to which may be entrusted the government's shares in companies, as well as acting as a form of industrial banker. The scale and scope are substantially greater than with the former Industrial Reconstruction Corporation.

Economic planning is to be supported by the requirement upon firms to disclose a much wider range of information as to their plans and intentions, and there is provision for voluntary planning agreements between departments and key companies, with the opportunity for greater financial assistance and exchanges of information on economic forecasts between such companies and government. There is a provision to require disclosure to employees or their representatives which the House of Lords extended to include shareholders. Lastly there is provision for intervention through the National Enterprise Board to prevent control of important firms or undertakings passing out of British ownership.

The National Enterprise Board has as its objects, as prescribed in Clause 2 (1):

(a) the development or assistance of the economy of the United Kingdom or any part of the United Kingdom;

(b) the promotion in any part of the United Kingdom of industrial efficiency and international effectiveness; and

(c) the provision, maintenance or safeguarding of productive employment in any part of the United Kingdom.

To achieve this very broad and massive aim the Board is empowered to maintain, develop, promote or assist any industrial undertaking, promote or assist the reorganisation or development of any industry or industrial undertaking, take over and manage publicly owned securities and property. It is required to promote good industrial relations and the involvement of employees in the affairs of undertakings which it controls. It is then given full powers to acquire, hold and sell securities, to form corporate bodies either on its own or jointly with others, to lend, guarantee funds, acquire, hold, sell or make available to others assets such as land, premises, or plant. Lastly it is empowered to provide services in respect of finance and management of industry.

Given such wide powers it appears to be able to support not only existing or reconstituted firms but workers' cooperatives of the type that have already appeared at Meriden and elsewhere. Clearly, the key issues posed by such powers relate to the objectives and criteria that the National Enterprise Board is encouraged to set. The statute does specify the promotion of international effectiveness alongside the safeguarding of employment, which is also the subject of additional legislation, notably the Employment Protection Act.

The principal aims, more investment to produce a more competitive industrial economy and providing or safeguarding employment, are to be achieved by six main means:

(i)   The provision of investment capital to both existing and new companies either by loan or share acquisition.

(ii)   The restructuring of industry by mergers and its own involvement in the ownership and control of firms.

(iii)   The extension of public ownership into profitable industry through agreed mergers or take-overs — which are, however, subject to the take-over code — in two main circumstances, to prevent a firm passing into foreign control, and 'to stimulate competition in a sector where it is weak'.[10]

(iv)   The promotion of industrial democracy in those companies that it controls.

(v)   The taking over of existing government shareholdings except where these are to be transferred to other corporations or their operations are largely overseas. The firms so acquired include Rolls Royce (1971) Ltd, International Computers (Holdings) Ltd, British Leyland Motor Corporation Ltd, George Kent Ltd, Alfred Herbert Ltd, Nuclear Enterprises Ltd, Dunford and Elliott Ltd, Kearney Trecker Martin Ltd, and Norton Villiers Triumph Ltd.[11]

(vi)   The provision of financial assistance delegated by the Secretary of Industry including that under the 1972 Act.

In addition it may be used to provide technical assistance to Third World countries where the Minister for Overseas Development agrees. Because of the extensive powers proposed for the Scottish and Welsh Development Agencies the main thrust is in England.

If the emphasis is on support for projects with a reasonable chance of commercial viability rather than on indiscriminate propping up of 'lame ducks', then the Board may be able to meet one of the criticisms of earlier interventionism, namely its prolongation of the inevitable rationalisation of undertakings so as to release resources for expanding industries and undertakings. It starts with some massive problems before it, not least of which is the 95% stake in British Leyland.

But the magnitude of the task for a single corporation must compel it to delegate to company boards as has been the case in some successful undertakings in the existing nationalised industries. The board comes between the company boards and the department, let alone the Minister, and much will therefore depend on the relationship of the Board and its Chairman to government, not only the Secretary of State for Industry. The links with the Minister are very extensive in view of the powers he may elect to delegate and the issues upon which his consent, or that of Parliament through an order, are involved. The main issues that may be delegated concern financial assistance under the 1972 Act and activities in connection with overseas aid that arise through the Department of Overseas Development. The consent of the Minister is required where the Board would acquire control of 30% or more of the voting rights or where the assets and the consideration involved exceed £10M. There are special restrictions designed to ensure that the Board disposes of a controlling interest in a newspaper publishing business or a radio or television contracting company. The approval of Parliament is required for any Prohibition Order, aimed at preventing a sale of shares which would give control of a 'qualifying' percentage of votes to persons or a company outside the United Kingdom, and to a Vesting Order which transfers the shares in question to the National Enterprise Board. These powers can be exercised at each of the three 'qualifying percentages' of 30%, 40% and 50% respectively. The Secretary of State is the judge of where there is a 'serious and immediate probability' of a change of control and that such a change would be 'contrary to the interests of the United Kingdom' or of any substantial part of same.

While the Secretary of State retains substantially similar control over the Board as would be exercised over any nationalised industry there are important changes. Although he appoints the Board, all appointments in companies controlled or partly owned by the Board are its responsibility. Technically these are directors of companies in the normal way and in many cases they will be working with directors who are still elected by the shareholders, though the size of the NEB shareholding may give it control over all appointments if only by way of veto. The question therefore arises as to what difference this is likely to make in the selection of directors and therefore the style of management of such firms.

Clearly, this depends on the relationships established at the outset. Is the Board to operate as a conventional holding company with very close control on the budgets and decisions of its subsidiaries? If so, given the range of companies within its orbit already, is this a feasible proposition or does it depend on the development of some form of divisionalised structure based on industrial or other groupings such as existing large firms have found to be an essential condition of their own strategic capability?[12] In any case, what is to be the relationship of each company to the Department which would normally have dealt with it previously and which must presumably be the one concerned where planning agreements are involved? If, as in the case of Rolls Royce (1971), there is a traditional set of contacts with a number of government departments as customers and sponsors, how do these contacts stand if the NEB seeks closer control over the companies which are transferred to it? Does the NEB seek a common pattern of control and style of management in those companies? Clearly, the answers to these questions may influence the ability of the Board to recruit chairmen and chief executives for such companies.

The main sources of recruits are private sector firms including those concerned professional firms such as accountants and consultants, and financial institutions. In much the same way, the main providers of services and advice are likely to come from established accountancy and consultancy organisations. The appointment of part-time 'watch-dog' directors has a long-established practice of drawing upon top managers in other public and private firms. Indeed, the spread of a 'professional' management outlook through such appointments has been favoured for the private sector as a whole in such reports as the Catherwood Committee appointed by the British Institute of Management.[13]

Looked at in another way this represents an immense field of patronage in the gift of the Board, if not of the Secretary of State, in organisations which may be almost wholly owned by the state. Overall control by Parliament is even more remote than in ordinary nationalised industries even though the financial support may be wholly or mainly in furtherance of a political policy objective, such as the development of particular areas or the protection of employment in a specific industry.

The fundamental questions posed by the new machinery remain much as before. First, what is the basis of the argument that massive restructuring in one or a few large organisations is still necessary to produce greater international effectiveness? Second, if this restructuring and, indeed, the pattern of the injection of new capital is to be on a different basis to that which would have occurred if left to private sector institutions including the capital market, in what ways is it to be different and with what rationale? Third, in view of the poor performance and rate of return on capital in existing public enterprises, coupled to the background of job protection at almost any cost at the onset of the new policy, what reason is there to expect a better performance in future?

Crucial to all these questions are three more. There is the matter of how far overall economic policy is going to further accentuate or ease the dependence of the private sector on the state as a source of equity finance, and with this, the question of the future role of the financial institutions both on their own account and as part of some coordinated policy with the NEB. Then, there is the question of how strongly will government lean on the Board for political reasons. These questions are only partly answered in the guidelines published by the government in March 1976.

At the outset, these provide for the preparation of both a corporate plan and an annual investment and financing programme which is to be the basis for determining its borrowing requirements. These programmes are to be set in the context of the industrial strategy developed in the National Economic Council. But it is recognised that, unlike the operations of other nationalised industries, the activities of the NEB cannot be planned to the same degree if it is to be free to respond to opportunities for investment or intervention. This applies particularly to acquisitions.

Here two situations are envisaged: in agreed acquisitions the NEB would be free to proceed but in the absence of agreement there are to be safeguards. The NEB itself may only seek to acquire more than 10% of the shares in a company *or* incur a cost in excess of £10M *or* thereby acquire 30% or more of the shares in a company where the Secretary of State for Industry has given his consent. There is provision for subsidiaries of the NEB to acquire more than 30% of the shares in firms acquired where this is not opposed and where the cost does not exceed £0.5M. Throughout, the intention is that the City Code on Take-overs and Mergers is to apply and the requirements for stock exchange quotation where these are relevant. Similarly, the NEB and all its subsidiaries are subject to the Fair Trading legislation, e.g. where a monopoly situation might arise from a bid. As for its lending powers, these are limited to a maximum of £25M to any one project except where the Secretary of State approves a higher sum. Normally there is to be an interest rate charged above that at which the NEB borrows from government through the National Loans Fund and projects are to be appraised using discounted rates of return that are to be determined by the Secretary of State in conjunction with the Treasury. Here as elsewhere the emphasis is on operating 'primarily within the profitable sectors of manufacturing industry and its financial objectives will be consistent with its duty of securing the efficient management of the companies in which it has an interest'.[14]

However, the very next paragraph refers to the wider purposes such as safeguarding employment notably in assisted areas. Where assistance is to be given under the direction of the Secretary of State, first the Industrial Development Advisory Board, which came into being under the 1972 Act, must review the application and advise him, and second the funds then provided are to be separated for accounting purposes so as not to undermine the financial discipline of the NEB.

Already it is clear that the largest companies in its portfolio may have a range of separate contact with government, first through their normal trading relationships where they are suppliers to government, second where they receive financial assistance under other arrangements, as for example launching aid for new aero-space projects, and even to the extent that they may be among the first to have planning agreements. The arrangements announced in the case of Rolls-Royce (1971) Ltd indicate that these other contacts are to continue though the NEB will have to be brought into the main negotiatons with the companies concerned.

These restraints coupled to the requirement to comply with the main rules and practices of the City, and then taken alongside the resources at the disposal of the NEB greatly reduce the significance of its operations when set against the total resources and the investment needs at stake. Indeed, the guidelines have been described by one of the authors of the interventionist policy, Dr Holland, as a 'sell-out'.[15]

8.3 Planning Agreements and Economic Planning

While it was originally intended to make planning agreements compulsory where the Minister saw fit, Clause 21(2) expressly defines a planning agreement as '. . . a voluntary agreement as to the strategic plans of a body corporate for the future development in the United Kingdom over a specified period of the body corporate or of one or more of that body's subsidiaries, or a joint undertaking . . .' where the Minister concerned is of the opinion that the agreement 'is likely over the specified period to contribute significantly to national needs and objectives.'

Although one factor leading to the introduction of this feature in economic planning is the concern at the concentration of control through mergers in a small number of key companies, and in particular the presence among them of powerful multi-nationals, the case for some form of understanding can be made on the practical grounds of the infrastructure implications of the intentions of such firms. A modern society involves a high degree of interdependence of industry and a whole range of public services, from sewerage and water to higher education and environmental control. The impact of the North Sea and other oil developments on the economic structure and physical environments of the areas from which oil exploration and extraction is serviced is a clear example. Given the aceptance of policies on regional development, governments may need to know what sort of projects are likely to be emerging and with what employment implications. It is known that the relevant departments have long maintained a close look at the operations and likely expansion plans of larger firms if only to anticipate what expansion might be steered into areas of higher unemployment.

However, the scope of projected planning agreements goes considerably further to judge from a consultative paper prepared by the Department of Industry and gives a much clearer idea of the scope of matters upon which the government is intended to have an interest, if not some form of involvement. Furthermore the duty is now imposed on the government to make available information and forecasts based on the Treasury model of the economy, both at a general national level and in respect of the possible prospects for an industry in which a firm entering into a planning agreement is involved. This emphasis on the exchange of information is one of the two inducements to participate in such agreements, the other being the additional financial assistance that can be made available to firms doing so.

The matters to be covered and their relation to government policies can now be reviewed.

1   Economic Prospects: Here the government is to contribute
the assessment of trade and economic prospects derived from
the Treasury model with some estimates of the possible effects
of changes in economic policy on the prospects for the
industries concerned and therefore for the company. There has
long been criticism of the secrecy surrounding the Treasury
model, including suggestions that its insulation from open
debate with economists may have lessened its validity. As part
of the wider disclosure now required under the Act, the
assumptions upon which the model is built are now to be
revealed though the Treasury still retains some discretion as to
how much it can be compelled to disclose. In view of the
unhappy record of UK performance greater openess here is to be
welcomed but the real test is how far politicians and their
advisers adapt to the realities as revealed by the joint disclosure
of forecasts and intentions.

2   Broad Strategy and Long-term Objectives: This focuses on
the implications of company strategy and objectives on
investment, productivity, employment, exports, product and
process development. The concern is with the broad lines of
development, not the details, and there is a specific exclusion of
any disclosure of the technical details of new products or
projects. Clearly this heading provides the basis for the development of agreements covering important sectors of the economy,
and the intention is to move, over a period of years, to a situation
where the principal sectors are so covered. Obviously, the
extent to which companies straddle industries is important here
and may lead, as has already been suggested, to the need for
separate corporate and governmental planning activities on the
part of large companies having wide interests. The scope of
subjects anticipates the more detailed headings which follow. It
implies a concern for, if not an intention to seek to influence,
most key areas of managerial responsibility.

3   UK Sales: This is to cover products, market share, and the
comparison of company forecasts with those available from
government sources such as NEDO. The effects of government
policies are to be considered and attention is to be paid to
possible import-savings. Clearly, several interests are covered
here. There is competition/monopoly policy and with it the role
of foreign competition which, with increased concentration of
ownership, may now be the main or only source. There is the
balance between home sales and exports, a matter upon which

the British Overseas Trade Board is particularly concerned with its interest in strategic decisions to switch more emphasis on to exports. Corresponding to this is the concern for import-saving partly triggered off by the growing evidence of the effects of recovery in the UK economy on its demand for imports of finished manufactures.[16] Full employment in UK industry has been accompanied by inability to expand output to meet home demand leading to an exceptional dependence on foreign consumer goods compared to other leading manufacturing companies.

4 *Exports:* What is sought here is a three-year forecast of exports as part of an indication of company strategy. The balance of payments situation coupled to past deficiencies in relative UK export performance underlies the concern for the future level of exports, especially if any future recovery is to be export-led. Again, forecasts available to government may be of assistance and there is the growing range of promotional assistance to exporters through the British Overseas Trade Board.

5 *Investment:* There is an overall concern at the level of resources available and the need to increase investment as a precondition of higher productivity. At the same time there is almost a preoccupation with the position of 'assisted areas'. Information is sought on the level of investment in major projects, the proportion that is envisaged in assisted areas, the expected contribution to exports or to import-saving, and to the amount of investment per employee. Constraints on investment are to be included. The Act provides a framework within which funds can be made available directly or through the National Enterprise Board, but it has also to be seen in the wider context of ideas which have led to the launching of Equity Capital for Industry Ltd.[17]

6 *Employment and Training:* Here the agreements are intended to cover prospective changes, in particular, redundancies and the scope for more employment in assisted areas. The Department of Employment and the Employment and Training Services Agencies are to be brought in to discuss recruitment, wastage and special problems upon which they might be able to assist, notably plans for changes which involve training, the handling of major redundancies, and the implementation of undertakings entered into concerning

assisted areas. Given the scale of changes still required in some industries this is an inevitable concern of governments.

7   Productivity: The levels of performance of labour, capital, and management are to be reviewed, in particular to identify constraints on higher performance. Given the problem of investment and its justification through higher productivity this is a sensitive field.

8   Finance: So far the implications are much less clear than with some of the earlier items, the main concern being with the availability of finance to secure investment, the consequence of inflation, and the combined effect of both in terms of future levels of employment. The concern here is for the recent phenomenon of threats to continual solvency and therefore to employment that have driven so many firms not only to the financial institutions but to government itself.

9   Prices Policy: Given present prices and incomes policies and the operation of price controls, this could be regarded as a legacy from the earlier price freeze of the CBI and a continuation of government leverage on business to maintain price stability. But it is also concerned with the implications of the government's own pricing policy in the nationalised industries.

10   Industrial Relations: Given the extent of other concurrent legislation it is difficult to see what additional scope there is here except in respect of the communication of the contents of agreements and other related matters to employees.

11   Interests of Consumers and the Community: Here we see an extension of an outlook based on present nationalised industry practice to a wider range of topics and to firms in the private sector. Companies are to be asked to indicate in what ways they are organised to deal with problems with customers, local communities where they operate and environmental issues generally arising in their industry. They are to be invited to indicate in what way they report to the community where they operate and as a whole, on the effects of their activities, and how they handle customer complaints. At two levels this is a significant item. First, it brings into review a whole range of environmental and community issues, many of which are covered in the recent study of the 'Corporate Report' by the accountancy profession. Second, it emphasises 'bureaucratic procedures', not just the market, as part of the growing concern for consumer protection.

12 Product and Process Development: Here the interest is in the main lines of development, and the extent to which government research facilities and financial support might be of assistance. The whole emphasis of state research financing has undergone a change since the acceptance by the previous government of the Rothschild report with its emphasis on 'contract' and 'mission-oriented research'. The Science and Technology Act permits financial assistance to research projects having industrial applications.

The scope of such agreements is of interest on two counts. First, while the number negotiated is expected to be small — a figure of 25 over three years has been canvassed — their impact through key companies including major multinationals is likely to be substantial in terms of providing a basis for planning the likely growth of key industries in the private sector. The inducement of government financial support and — for what it may be worth — of data derived from the Treasury model of the economy, may attract a small number of large firms that would have had the contacts with government in any event. If this were to produce greater mutual understanding and provide a basis for stability in government policies then it could be advantageous to the economy as a whole. However, there is the perennial danger that such plans might be interpreted too rigidly and that unless they satisfy that well-known adage about government pronouncements — 'definite but vague' — they could restrict adaptability to changing circumstances.

The second reason for interest is that this list of topics provides an indication of the possible scope for disclosure of information to government as required under Part IV of the Industry Act. Clause 28 provides that where a Minister is of the opinion that information is needed for the purposes of forming or furthering national economic policies or to enable government to consult with employers or workers on the future of a sector of industry, he can require a company or group operating wholly or mainly in the UK and having a significant contribution to a sector of industry or a part of the UK, to provide government and employee representatives with information. The requirement is initially to disclose to government but this information, subject to certain safeguards, may then be made available to employee representatives and to shareholders.

The headings under which such information may be required are set out in Clause 29(2) as follows:

(a) the persons employed (not specifically as to individuals);
(b) capital expenditure;
(c) fixed capital assets employed;
(d) disposal or intended disposal of such assets;
(e) acquisition or intended acquisition of fixed capital assets for use in the undertaking;
(f) productive capacity and its utilisation;
(g) output and productivity;
(h) sales;
(i) exports;
(j) sales of industrial or intellectual property owned or used in connection with the undertaking, grants and contracts for sales or grants of such property;
(k) research and development expenditure.

Where a Minister requires that this information be provided, it may cover the last complete financial year and any future specified period.

The safeguards concerning disclosure to trade unions and shareholders in Clause 30 provide that information may be witheld if the Minister considers that it would be contrary to the national interest, if it is contrary to any other statute, or for what is termed a 'special reason'. This covers information disclosed in confidence, and information the disclosure of which would cause injury to the undertaking or a substantial number of its employees.

An Appeal Committee is to be set up to hear appeals by a company against being required to disclose information to trades unions, etc., and by a trade union against a witholding of disclosure. Information that is witheld from publication is, however, to be available to any department for the exercise of its functions and to the Manpower Services Commission, the Employment Services Agency and the Training Services Agency.

The effect of this requirement of disclosure has to be seen in three aspects. First, there is the amount and range of information that will now be available to government which will provide departments with even greater opportunity to influence decisions of firms and to take industrial plans into account in formulating government policies. Second, there is the general effect on the whole basis of assessing company performance of extended disclosure of information, subject in practice to the degree to which companies succeed in getting this retained as confidential to government. Third, there is the specific effect of disclosure to trades unions on the whole process of consultation and negotiation, including the pressure that may be exercised on governments to protect employee interests. This last point is further considered in Chapter 9.

The requirements of this and concurrent legislation are such as to provide for more open discussion of business plans where these have wider effects on employment and on the community. What remains fundamental is the spirit in which the entire exercise is applied. Is it to be a means of stimulating efficiency and competitiveness as in one of its stated aims or is to be a vehicle for continued conservation of firms and industries that ought to be replaced or reshaped as a condition of future economic performance?

Notes and references

1   White Paper, *Public Expenditure to 1979-80,* Cmd 6393, HMSO 1976.
2   National Economic Development Office, *Conditions Favourable to Faster Growth,* HMSO 1963.
3   *An Approach to Industrial Strategy*, NEDO, November 1973, Para. 2.
4   *Ibid,* para. 11
5   *Ibid,* para. 5.
6   A. R. Prest, 'The economic rationale of subsidies to industry', in A. Whiting (ed.), *The Economics of Industrial Subsidies,* HMSO for Department of Industry 1976, p. 65-74.
7   G. M. Field and P. V. Hills, 'The administration of industrial subsidies', in A. Whiting (ed.), *The Economics of Industrial Subsidies,* HMSO for Department of Industry 1976, pp. 14-17.
8   *Ibid,* p. 1.
9   K. Pavitt, 'The choice of targets and instruments for government support of scientific research', in Whiting *op. cit,* pp. 113-136.
10 White Paper, *The Regeneration of British Industry,* Cmd 5710, HMSO 1974, para. 31.
11 Incomes Data Services Briefs No. 73, p. 7.
12 See D. Channon, *The Strategy and Structure of British Enterprise,* Macmillan 1973.
13 *The Responsible Company,* BIM 1974.
14 Guidelines, para. 18. *Financial Times,* 2 March 1976.
15 *Sunday Times Business News,* 7 March 1976.

16   M. Panic, 'Why the UK's propensity to import is high?, *Lloyds Bank Review,* January 1975.
17   Equity Capital for Industry Ltd, is backed by insurance companies £17M, pension funds £17M, investment trust companies £8M, unit trusts £4M and Finance for Industry Ltd £4M. See pp. 123-4.

Study Questions

1   Distinguish the principal aims of government subsidies to commerce and comment on their interaction.

2   Is it possible to have anything other than a political basis for intervention in specific firms?

3   Compare the National Enterprise Board and any other nationalised industry board. In what ways does the NEB break new ground?

4   What would you expect to be the main challenges that the NEB must face in the longer run?

5   What effect, if any, do you think that planning agreements will have on the planning and freedom of action of large companies?

9

WIDER ACCOUNTABILITY OF BUSINESS ENTERPRISES

9.1 Theory and Practice of Wider Accountability

At the heart of the debate on the future direction of business enterprises is a clash of approaches to the basis of power. To the Marxist, as to an older form of conventional capitalist, property and its ownership is the source of power. The ownership of an enterprise therefore confers power to determine its fate. The traditional owner-manager has a clear basis for his authority and an exclusive right to determine the policy of his firm. To the student of bureaucracy, Weber's idea that power derives from role not property is all-important. The directors of a firm derive their authority from the roles they perform, and these are conferred upon them by a sanctioning process that happens to be based on share ownership. The justification for their power is their ability to perform the role. While this view was initially developed in relation to those who hold office in state bureaucracies it is clearly extended into the private corporate sector once we have a managerial hierarchy stemming from a board of directors who are increasingly there as professionals and not as large shareholders.

Given this interplay of ideas based on ownership and an office held, it is but a short step to the assertion that in determining their actions a board of directors has to have regard to a much wider range of interests than those of the shareholders alone. Faced with the pressures that can be exercised by organised labour, by financial institutions and through both factor and product markets, those directing enterprises have to strike some form of balance between conflicting pressures. The most obvious of these is that of the employees of the enterprise, usually through an organised form, that of their trades union(s). But the conflict is not confined to the providers of finance, whether share capital or loans, or of labour, of whatever level; it also extends to the interests of suppliers and the demands of customers. Firms operate in localities where there are relationships with local communities. These, in turn, form part of a larger community, a nation-state, which is likely to be concerned to protect wider interests not only of employees and customers but of society as a whole that are affected by a firm's operations. The effect may be environmental or it may be strictly economic in the sense of the exercise of economic power by one firm over another.

While it is the pressure for employee representation and participation that has been most obvious in recent years, this move towards a wider basis of accountability stems from the earlier notion of a 'negotiated environment'. The very licence to set up a partnership or a company confers upon the promoters certain privileges. The law has been reinforced to protect those who trade with, and later those who participate in, companies against malpractice and improper use of power. The continued emphasis on ownership as the one source of sanction to be formally recognised in the constitution and the tests of performance of corporate bodies has become a source of confusion and contradictions.

Whereas the Marxist view is that ownership is made the basis of exploitation of the rest of the participants, and a neo-Marxist view extends this to the exploitation practised by a managerial class, the alternative view is that those in charge are tending to take a less sectional view, and are indeed moving in search of a concensus among the interests of the various stakeholders. Business enterprise is therefore to some a potentially unstable means of economic exploitation, to others an uneasy coalition of conflicting economic interests, and to yet others a potentially harmonious system.

Much of the argument in practice is about where a particular enterprise, or the system as a whole, stands in this spectrum. It is argued by those who see a clear separation of ownership from control that aims and behaviour are distinctly different in firms where this holds good than from those where owner-management prevails. Against this is set the argument that such is the cale of common membership and values across the private sector that no such significant difference can be discerned whether in attitude or in economic performance.

But whatever the connection between the source of authority and economic goals as just discussed, there is little doubt that a distinction can be drawn between enterprises, in terms of the rules to which they are working, on the following lines:

(i)   firms operating conventionally to business criteria
with emphasis on growth and profitability;
(ii) firms in transition to a different set of criteria;
(iii) firms having no clear rules whatsoever;
(iv) firms operating under a different set of criteria such as
publicly owned enterprises.

It is arguable that firms in moving from (i) to (iv) are leaving a
position where they aim to maximise rate of return on capital for
one where they maximise return to those groups in power, in
which case organised labour is *de facto* in a power-sharing
situation even though not as yet represented *de jure.* It is also
arguable, as Galbraith has done so strongly,that whatever the
society, the institutional forms that facilitate the 'technical
imperatives' of production, distribution and supporting functions, are substantially the same.[1] They require, whatever the
degree to which the market is used as an indicator, a
decentralised management with professional technical involvement in planning and decision-taking. Simultaneously, there is
a new need to recognise the change in relationships at work,
even the changes in management style, that can bring about
greater participation in the working of enterprises, negatively to
prevent the development of dysfunctional behaviour, positively
to give job satisfaction.

The outcome as represented by this 'convergence thesis' is a
new interdependence between a firm and its environment at
many levels. This interdependence is not confined to essential
public services on the one hand and job opportunities on the
other. It extends to the interplay of ideas and values not only
with local communities in the areas in which a firm operates but
among the professionals whom it employs, all of whom have a
wider frame of reference than that of the firm itself. In particular
the managers, given a more open market for their services, are
likely to be subject to influences that extend their awareness of
the influence of the firm on society and of changes in it upon the
way the firm is operated.

Among the last-mentioned, none is more important than the
challenge to the basis of managerial authority. Writing on this
as far back as 1947 Wilfred Brown (now Lord Brown of
Machrihanish) argued that a manager's authority was based on
sanctions derived partly from the suppliers of risk capital
through the legal structure of the enterprise, partly from his
representation of the interests of the customers and suppliers,
partly from his representation of the continuing interest of
management in the survival of the enterprise and partly from

the consent of those he managed. This consent he saw as being conferred through a form of joint decision-taking which he sought to formalise in a works council system.[2] Like Patterson[3] he saw the manager's immediate work role in a wider social context in which authority stemmed from several sources. Patterson argued that every manager had three potential sources of authority: his position or role, which he termed his structural authority; his professional knowledge and professional standing, which he termed sapiential authority; and his own conduct as a man in the role, namely his personal authority.

While at the level of the small firm this analysis could apply to the enterprise, at the level of the corporate concern the parallel is less easily drawn. The very conferment of corporate status has involved not only protection of third parties and even of members through the Companies Acts, but increasing concern at the power that such concerns can exercise. This has led to specific controls on specific issues whether to do with the environment, or competition or consumer protection. In addition, there has been a general increase in the sensitivity of firms to their public image, especially when the scale of their impact has been such as to arouse reactions from governments and pressure groups.

On the one hand, the power of such groups and the scope of their activities has introduced a new dimension into considerations of accountability. Thus the consumerist movement has focussed on the quality of products and the value for money of what is on offer. The growing concern for environmental pollution has forced firms and governments to adopt more stringent standards now that technology offers new opportunities for processes and materials that may have harmful side-effects. Social problems such as the disabled, minority racial or other groups, and the attempt to influence policies in other countries, e.g. South Africa, have brought new issues before firms which even the more enlightened have not had to face hitherto.

On the other hand, there has always been a wide spectrum of styles of management and of value systems emanating from the values of senior management. This has resulted in a range from those with the minimum concern for wider social responsibilities to those having a very strong sense of social duty which has led them to pioneer social policies and facilities that have subsequently become a community responsibility. But as one area of social concern has been so adopted, so others have appeared as a result of the very development of a modern industrial society. Consequently, concern for the effectiveness of the activities of an enterprise is no longer confined to profitability; it extends to a range of relationships with the society, both local and national, of which it is a part.

This is illustrated first by the notion of a social audit as presented by John Humble in which a management is recommended to study its own position in respect of employees, their working conditions, the quality of the product and its implications for customers, and the communities among whom it operates, thus covering environmental and local economic interests.[4] An extension of this approach is that carried on by specific groups such as Social Audit. Backed financially by such bodies as the Rowntree Trusts, this seeks to evaluate the conduct of companies in terms of products, working conditions and relationships, and external policies. It sometimes works by invitation, drawing upon interviews with management and employees amongst others, and at other times by using whatever published data are available. One of the problems of such approaches when compared to conventional financial auditing is the question of whose standards are being used. The aim in conventional auditing is to evolve workable standards that can come to command more general acceptance. Is this possible in the very wide fields covered by some of these 'self-appointed' social auditing bodies?

As we have seen, the scope of issues to be covered by planning agreements includes such wider subjects. The CBI has argued that 'a company should behave like a good citizen in business . . ' and '. . be responsible to the movement of informed public opinion as well as the requirements of authority.'[5] This requires the involvement of employees in public affairs and on this issue the same body has, in its evidence to the Bullock Committee, called for a statute to require all larger firms to enter into a participation agreement within four years. This is in line with their earlier view that firms should '. . . recognise duties and obligations (within the context of the objects for which the company was established) arising from the company's relationships with creditors, suppliers, customers, employees and society at large; and in so doing to exercise their best judgement to strike a balance between the interests of the aforementioned groups and between the interests of those groups and the interests of the proprietors of the company'.

Representation is one issue; another is the possibility of measuring the performance of the enterprise not only in conventional terms but also of the added value that it creates.

The first is considered in the next section; the second we return to in the subsequent discussion of social responsibilities.

9.2 Employee Representation in Theory and Practice

The pressure for greater industrial democracy coincides with the greater spread of more participative styles of management and methods of organising enterprises to create a situation in which widely divergent arguments and forces are deployed to modify if not, in extremes, to overthrow the existing order. The outcome is a wide range of approaches to greater employee involvement ranging from the normal processes of collective bargaining and consultation to profit sharing, employee directors and full workers control. To these forces and those of political parties are now added the influence of European ideas on participation as in the proposed statute on a European Company and the draft fifth directive of the Commission on the harmonisation of company law.

In part the pressure is of long standing and linked to the aim of overthrowing the capitalist system in favour of some form of self-management, ranging from the extreme of the anarcho-syndicalists, who would have individual interests asserted in all significant decisions, to the guild socialists who advocate a constitutional representation of worker interests. For all such groups some form of 'worker control' is a target. Such a change would raise questions about the future role of trades unions. Are they to be free to veto changes, if not of owner-management, as in the past, perhaps of the state where it replaces the capitalists as the coordinating institution?

While there is some support for such ideas the main aim at this stage is some measure of democracy within the enterprise through some sharing in decision-making if only to safeguard the interests of employees in the long run. Here the emphasis is on the amendment of existing institutions through representation and a right of veto such as are implicit in the policy document adopted by the Trades Union Congress in 1974. This provides for a supervisory board, equally representative of management and workers, with the former responsible to the shareholders and the latter only through the trades unions representing employees, initially in companies employing 2,000 or more but eventually 200 or more.

There are two groups of underlying assumptions. The first concerns the ideal of democracy for its own sake and has less to do with subsequent performance. The second is concerned with the reduction of conflict and the attainment of greater consensus in industry. It is argued that in management's own interest, for example, greater employee commitment can be achieved through agreement as to decisions on objectives and methods. Better communications and less alienation from current tasks are seen as essential prerequisites for improved performance. Therefore it is asserted that it is not only right in principle but sensible in practice to achieve greater involvement in decision-taking. Examples are cited of how a resumption of wider tasks, including integrating decisions previously taken by supervisory managers, can bring about improved performance and reduced conflict with its attendant costs.

Throughout both sets of arguments there is a common thread of the need to legitimise decisions of managers, or of those who, in whatever way, perform management roles. The process is, however, confined to legitimising in respect of those to be managed; it does not extend to those who may be equally concerned as customers or users of a product or facility, and there is a real problem where the body concerned is a public one, elected by the community, e.g. a local authority. The TUC report aims at 50% employee representation on all boards and consultative bodies operating publicly owned services.

The arguments against extended participation can be taken to start right at this point. If there is a wider range of interests, as indeed there must be for every undertaking, then should they not all be formally represented, and if so in what way? In Lord Brown's view this was clearly part of what he described as 'definitive' policy, that which was not open to joint decision making, in constrast to 'conditional' policy which could be. Critics of worker participation see this as a weakness in most forms of worker control that are put forward. However, it can be argued that the normal market relationships have to apply to transactions with those outside the unit, as is clearly proving to be the case in several of the worker cooperatives set up with government finance in 1974-5.

But the criticisms go much further. There are those that are fundamental, regarding consultation to the point of joint decision taking as an assault on managerial prerogatives and on the very institution of private property. They question the demand for widespread participation and the extent to which it is generated by trades unions or by groups having much wider political aims.

Yet management in its efforts to overcome problems of

communication and worker alienation has itself introduced a measure of joint decision-taking, at least at shop-floor level in industry. The whole emphasis of the 'human relations' approach in management thinking has been towards greater consultation and even joint decision-taking. Cases such as the replacement of supervision by shop steward control at one stage in Standard Motors reported by Melman[6] or of productivity agreements involving job enlargement through work allocation decisions in nylon spinning[7] can be found on an increasing scale. While the emphasis remains on joint control of what happens at the work place rather than wider issues of policy it is from such beginnings that more extended joint decision-taking is evolving. Furthermore, in anticipation of future pressures, even legislation, a number of company participation schemes have been initiated, notably in the motor industry by Chrysler (UK) and British Leyland.

Alongside are the pragmatic arguments as to its real effectiveness based on experience. That there are major difficulties there can be no doubt at all. Principal among them is the time taken to reach decisions — both as a consequence of the consultative process and the need for those newly involved to learn — both management and representatives — about working together as well as about the matters under discussion. Then there is the extent to which it calls for common interests if it is to produce more acceptable decisions for all parties and there is the question of how far, in a competitive situation, information as to intentions can be divulged and to whom. Yet there is a strong body of evidence of attempts at worker participation, both in the UK and elsewhere in Western Europe. What does this show us?

As Professor Kenneth Walker has pointed out in his review of research on participation,[8] three questions are crucial: the basis of power-sharing, the achievement of cooperation, and personal involvement. Power-sharing can be seen as existing as soon as either party has to consult the other before implementing or even reaching a decision. Thus, once a management acknowledges that it has to consult employees before carrying out a decision, power sharing has begun. The next step is negotiation and after that comes joint decision-taking.

But it is not so much the nature as the scope of the power-sharing that is of interest. The process of collective bargaining has involved both consultation and negotiation, with the boundary between these being increasingly blurred. It has also involved a gradual extension of the scope of issues for discussion from those of the immediate work place and the conditions of employment prevailing there, to the longer term prospects for employees and, therefore, the plans of the enterprise that have a bearing on those prospects.

Clearly, there are two views as to how these interests can be protected. On the one hand, there are those trades unions which argue that the normal process of collective bargaining can do so. This has the additional merit of not prejudicing their independence as involvement in joint boards might do. In part, this attitude is based on experience of the difficult role that they would assume once they became a party to a management decision. There is the inherent risk of opposition to the point of rejection by their rank and file members, quite apart from the possible presence of those who believe that the conflict of interest, at least as far as a private employer is concerned, is so basic that to do otherwise would be to compromise their principles.

On the other hand, there is the view that both routes can be followed simultaneously and that, while retaining their right to withdraw at any time into a traditional conflict role, they should as a matter of democratic right be able to influence, if not veto, management decisions at each main level in an enterprise. Furthermore, even where they are concerned only to protect the interests of their members, the adherents of this approach argue that to do so they must be able to exercise a wider influence and veto than at present. In particular, they seek to influence major policy decisions that could affect future prospects for employment, notably investment and the possibility of a take-over.

To this end, official TUC policy is to work towards 50% membership of supervisory boards, and to seek amendment of the Companies Act so as to give their members or representatives the right of access to at least the same information as shareholders, recognition in law as interested parties in the same way as shareholders and outside creditors, and the transfer of responsibility to supervisory boards for major policy decisions including the appointment of members of the management board. The supervisory board while responsible to the shareholders, so far as the management members are concerned, is seen as being responsible to the employees through the trades unions on their part, with no veto over its decisions by the shareholders. Furthermore, a similar arrangement is proposed for all public bodies.

While the main employers' organisations are in favour of a form of employee participation their view is that this should evolve through consultation and negotiation, possibly to the level of a company consultative council, and while not ruling out the type of employee directors envisaged under the proposals for a European Company, the emphasis is on participation at a pace acceptable to the employees themselves. There is concern for the position of those who are not traditionally unionised such as managers, as the BIM report indicates.[9] While the whole question has now been referred to the committee under Lord Bullock the terms of reference given to it take the TUC proposition as a starting point. It is therefore of particular interest that the Plowden Committee on the future organisation of the Electricity Supply industry has come down against the TUC proposals in a publicly owned industry.

The main arguments used by the Plowden Committee concern the accountability of members of a board. They argue that in a nationalised industry they must all be appointed by and responsible to the Secretary for Energy and not any outside body such as the trades unions. They also see the likelihood of the supervisory board being not a policy forming but a collective bargaining body.[10]

UK experience to date has been largely of consultation and negotiation without membership of boards or policy determining bodies. Furthermore, there has been a distinction, now increasingly blurred, between consultation and negotiation, the former being on a local or company basis and the latter on a district or national agreement basis. The TUC report acknowledges the need to end this distinction and to combine these activities to a greater extent. While there have been individual company experiments and one use of employee directors in a public corporation, the British Steel Corporation, the stress has been on consultation at plant level. The small number of company consultative councils range from widespread works committees and councils through the more formally defined Works Council, as in the well documented Glacier Metal case,[11] to the structure of plant and group councils as in Philips Industries. Whichever form is used, collective bargaining or a company or works council, the effect is the same, namely the establishment of a practice of consultation and negotiation. Only in the case of the British Steel Corporation is there a system of employee directors. This involves the appointment of employee directors to the divisional boards, which advise on the main product groups, and not the Corporation itself. They are appointed by the Chairman of the Corporation from a short list prepared by the TUC Steel Committee and the senior management of the Corporation. They serve in a personal capacity but are required to take an active part in joint consultative meetings. They may hold union office. There is one employee director on the main board of the Corporation.

This is still some way from the ideas incorporated in the proposals of the European Economic Commission, already outlined in Chapter 6. There would be two separate bodies, a supervisory board and a management board. The supervisory board would be made up equally of shareholders' representatives and members coopted by, but independent of, these two groups; this last category would be proposed by the general meeting, the management board and the works council. While the statute provides for such a structure it would be for the employees to decide whether or not to have representatives on the supervisory board. Similarly, at national level, the Commission in seeking harmonisation of company law, proposes a similar two-tier system except that each country could decide which of two systems of employees representation it would adopt for the supervisory board.

The first system would be the West German system which provides for one third of the membership of the supervisory board to be elected by the works council, itself a compulsory feature of all companies employing more than five persons. In the Dutch system, the supervisory board selects from candidates put forward by the shareholders and by the works council, each of which has a right to veto a particular cooption.

Only in the mining and iron and steel industries of West Germany is there a parity of representation of shareholders and employees but with one independent member agreed by the other members. However, a proposal is now before the German parliament to apply this system to all large companies.

9.3 Social Responsibilities of Enterprise Managements

The extent to which enterprises are or should be responsible for more than their own economic efficiency is itself a matter of debate. On the one hand there is a rigorous 'free enterprise' outlook which regards any departure from the pursuit of economic efficiency, as measured by the profits available for distribution to shareholders, as a negation of managerial responsibility.[12] To those who hold this view the enterprise

should do no more than it is compelled to do by the law of the
country in which it operates, that law being the application of
the responsibility that lies with the state to protect its citizens in
such ways as it sees fit. Indeed, those who adhere to this outlook
would usually argue for a minimal role of the state, arguing that
it is for the individual to safeguard himself as far as possible
without leaning on the collective support of society.

This point of view was strongly developed in this country
during the Industrial Revolution and still has its adherents. To
them it is no part of a business management's responsibilities to
be concerned with wider social considerations, still less with
any notions of patronage of the arts, education or social welfare.
These are not only distractions; they represent an undesirable
exercise of economic power in society.

However, right through that ruthless Industrial Revolution
there has been a growing concern on the part of management at
the social consequences of its own economic power, sometimes
on a religious or other ethical standpoint, sometimes on an
essentially practical basis that excessive working hours, for
example, are uneconomic because of the fall in output per hour.
The history of modern management thinking is marked by the
views and actions of men like Robert Owen and Seebohm
Rowntree who, a century apart, were concerned at the evidence
of poverty and the relationship of better management to
improved social welfare.

At the other extreme from the 'free enterprise' school are
those who see the modern business corporation having wide
social responsibilities which it seeks to fulfil by the use of its
discretionary economic power. The second and third viewpoints
outlined here overlap in large measure not only with each other
but with those of other groups in society, notably trades unions
but now extending to other pressure groups such as those
concerned with consumer protection or the control of
environmental pollution. While the main concern of trades
unions has been with the existence of employment for their
members and with working conditions, notably in respect of
health and safety, the need for countervailing powers in other
fields has brought about a much wider pressure for at least a
more responsible approach, if not for collective action to
regulate conditions.

The control over conditions at work is only partly achieved by
collective bargaining. There is a long history of regulation from
the first Factories Act 1833 to the Industrial Health and Safety
Act 1974. But whereas this has been confined to conditions

inside the place of work, problems of environmental damage and pollution have attracted growing concern and organised opposition to new projects from those where environment is expected to be affected. A railway siding accepted for over 130 years but which then had an oil fire became the subject of opposition to planning permission for renewal and building. Proposals for road schemes, especially in urban areas, and for the rail link to the Channel Tunnel have provoked widespread opposition. Events such as the Flixborough explosion or the lead contamination at Avonmouth have led to demands for new controls and protection of health.

In a sense these are inescapable consequences of the need to consider the social as well as the private costs of industrial and commercial activities. Economists, even of the more extreme free enterprise school, have long accepted the need to take social costs into account. The environmental issue has provoked some major examples of conflict of interest, notably in projects such as the Maplin airport, Concorde or the disposal of atomic waste.

To these concerns is now added the consumerist lobby. Concern at the quality of products, at the denial or reduction of the legal protection open to the customer, and the whole exercise of economic bargaining power has focussed attention on a much wider area of business operations. Earlier protection took two forms: legal protection through the Sale of Goods Act 1893 and various measures concerned with hire purchase agreements, and steps to restrain economic bargaining power through reinforcement of competition under Monopolies and Restrictive Trade Practices legislation.

Latterly this has been reinforced first by the Trade Descriptions Act and then by the creation of the Office of Fair Trading, culminating in the redesignation of a department as that of Prices and Consumer Protection. The outcome, partly also as a feature of overall prices and incomes policy, has been a two-fold pressure on firms. On the one hand, they are being pressed to revise their terms of sale so as to give consumers greater protection. This, combined with the use of the Trade Descriptions Act, takes the form of much clearer specifications of conditions of sale and of service as well as of the meaning of the terms of credit offered. *Caveat emptor*, let the buyer beware, may remain a basis of contract law, but there is far greater control over the information which is put before him or her. This is supported by the pressure of bodies such as the Consumers' Association and represented formally through a

Consumer Protection Council. The effect on firms is to make them much more sensitive to such issues. On the other hand, there is the matter of control of prices and profits that has been introduced to counteract inflation. This results in a detailed control of price increases on key commodities in the home market associated with a prescription of a permitted level of profit. This has substantial implications for the profitability of firms and for their strategies, especially as between home and export activities.

But while consumer protection, like environmental and employee protection, has a more widely accepted basis, the ethical and political issues that are also canvassed are less widely accepted. Yet in at least one instance, the compensation of thalidomide children, the ethical issue became so strongly supported even among the shareholders of the Distillers Company, that a settlement was reached without exhausting the legal processes of resisting the claims. The wages paid to the employees of British firms in both South Africa and Sri Lanka (Ceylon) have been the subject of parliamentary investigation as well as press publicity. The question of investments in South Africa is a continuing source of campaigning by opponents of apartheid.

There is a much more difficult issue posed in such cases of operations abroad as attempts are made to bring indirect pressure on foreign governments and on situations which cannot be influenced by direct action from this country. These pressures add up to a formidable list of interests to be considered in addition to those of employees, shareholders and customers. They extend to suppliers, competitors and users of products. They include not only communities where firms operate but where their products are used. They even include their right to operate and trade with other countries and communities. On several occasions attempts have been made not only to define the extent of management's responsibilities but to provide some form of social responsibility audit.

Perhaps the most striking example of the possible future scope of such assessment is the discussion paper of the Accounting Standards Steering Committee on the 'Corporate Report'.[13] While it is arguable whether accountants could or should assume responsibility for the preparation of such reports in future, this paper is of particular interest on three counts, its view of who is entitled to know, what they should be able to know about, and how this might be done. Although much of the argument overlaps the Sandilands Report on the basis of accounting statements, the significant development is the extension of reporting in a social responsibility context.

The paper identifies seven groups who have an interest in a report on a corporate body, each of whom have particular information needs. Collectively, they sustain the basic philosophy of public accountability which is seen to be '. . . . separate from and broader than the legal obligation to report and arises from the custodial role played in the community by economic entities.' Corporate bodies are '. . . . involved in the maintenance of standards of life and the creation of wealth for and on behalf of the community.'[14] The seven groups are equity investors, loan creditors, employees, analysts/advisers, business contacts, government and the public. Taking the last two, the government is seen as having an interest, like the other groups listed, in 'assessing the effectiveness of the entity in achieving objectives established previously by society.'[15] This is an interesting prescription in terms of where the objectives are specified. It recognises that enterprises work within the context of a national culture as well as an economy.

The committee then goes on to speak of 'the capacity of the entity to make future reallocations of its resources for social purposes' and the need to evaluate the social costs and benefits attributable to it. So far as the public is concerned, they have a right to know about the support given to pressure groups, political interests, and charities, and factors affecting society or the environment.[16] Most of the data are henceforward required under either the Industry Act 1975 or the Employment Protection Act 1975.

What is additional is the proposal that enterprises should attempt some form of social accounting, an assessment of costs and benefits and of net added social value, though it is recognised that this must depend upon 'the development of acceptable, objective and verifiable measurement techniques'.[17]

Similar concern and debate is proceeding in the US and in Western Europe. The significance of this is twofold. First, in response to the ideas presented at the start of this section it is clear that the narrow 'free enterprise' view is rejected in favour of a new view of corporate accountability. Second, it is equally clear that a great deal remains to be done before such wider accountability can be anything more than subjective judgements. Indeed, the debate is not ended; it is translated to a variation of the initial issue, namely the future division of responsibility between government, enterprises and individuals.

Notes and references

1 J. K. Galbraith, *The New Industrial State,* Hamish Hamilton, 1967, chs. 6 and 8.

2 W. B. D. Brown, *The Factory as a Social System,* Tavistock 1947, and *Exploration in Management,* Heinemann 1960.

3 T. T. Patterson, *Management Theory,* Business Publications 1966, chs. 7, 10, 15, 16.

4 J. Humble, *Social Audit,* Foundation for Business Responsibilities 1970.

5 CBI, *The Responsibilities of the British Public Company,* 1973.

6 S. Melman, *Dynamic Factors in Industrial Productivity,* Oxford University Press 1958.

7 Bath Conference, *Men, Machines and the Social Sciences,* Bath University 1969.

8 K. Walker, 'Worker participation in theory and practice' *International Labour Studies,* October 1974.

9 BIM, Report of the Committee on Company Affairs, 1974.

10 *The Economist,* 28 February 1976.

11 E. Jaques, *Changing Culture of a Factory,* Tavistock 1951.

12 F. A. Hayek, 'The corporation in a democratic society: in whose interest ought it and will it be run?' in M. Ashen and G. Bach, *Management and Corporation 1985,* McGraw-Hill 1960.

13 *The Corporate Report,* Institute of Chartered Accountants in England and Wales, 1975.

14 *Ibid,* para. 2.35.

15 *Ibid,* para. 2.37.

16 *Ibid,* paras. 6.46 and 6.47.

17 *Ibid,* para 6.47.

Study Questions

1 What do you understand by the 'convergence thesis' as applied to the behaviour of the boards of larger companies and what effect would you expect it to have on the decisions they might make as to future policy?

2 What do you understand by a 'social audit' and what issues might it cover?

3 Examine the contention that good participation can only be achieved through very effective management leadership.

4 Consider the effect of consumerist and environmental lobbies on expectations of future management behaviour.

10
FUTURE ENTERPRISE MANAGEMENT

10.1 Business Structure and Behaviour

In Chapter 1 the structure of business government was approached in two ways. The first involved a distinction between 'plant or establishment', 'firm' and 'industry'.[1] Most models of behaviour are based on the 'firm' as the principal level of decision-taking. Applying tests of autonomy the independent firm was then defined as that body which had the final say in the disposal of profits, the direction of investment and the appointment of top management. Furthermore, the models of firms' behaviour derived from economics treat the firm as though it was a single person — a classical entrepreneur — although behavioural theories recognise the existence of power struggles and policies. The subsequent review has shown that while in the private firm, as defined in this study, this identification with a single individual or a small integrated group still holds good, the emergence of the quoted public company has created a very different situation in which the apparent autonomy of the firm may be much reduced, at least until the company has grown to so large a size as to be independent of short-term stock market pressures and private sector take-over threats. Furthermore, a variety of governmental interventions — price control with its associated profit control, information disclosure and planning agreements — have the effect of limiting the freedom of action of individual firms and superimposing both an industry level and a national level in decision-taking where these were previously absent.

At the same time the effect of greater emphasis on industrial democracy discussed in Chapter 9 has been to stress decision-taking at plant level. The outcome of the two-stage process of wage negotiation, at national and then at plant levels has been a similar stress on decision-taking at levels other than the individual firm.

The three levels all show changes in the context of managerial action. At plant and shop-floor level there are movements towards a greater involvement of employees in decisions governing their immediate tasks and work allocation. These spring at least as much from managerial innovations as from employee or trades union pressure. At firm level, the pressures of employees and their representatives, of consumer protection agencies, of financial interests and of government all interact but with a changed emphasis. Just as employees and trades unions exercise more open pressure in their own defence so the greater dependence on borrowed funds enhances the power of banks and financial institutions. The outcome is less room to manoeuvre on the part of boards of directors, or at least a need to consider a wider array of factors. The general concern for environmental and community interests imposes new constraints for most firms as well as opportunities for others.

The need for some form of national economic strategy in the wider context of public financial support and investment adds to the movement towards greater industry-level planning and to the need for a means of relating proposals of government to their possible implications for business as a whole. This therefore suggests yet another level at least, of consultation, that of overall policy in the business sector in both private and public ownership.

While the original three levels continue to be the principal ones there has to be added the national level. This may call for new institutions such as the suggested Council for Industry in which employers, managers and trades unions would be represented.[2]

The second addition to the three levels arises from the development of diversified groups, some of which warrant the designation 'conglomerate'. There is a clear distinction between the independent firm using the definition adopted here, which can only mean the holding company in charge of investment decisions, and the operating company which may be sold by one group to another. An effect of the merger wave described in Chapters 5 and 6 has been the extension of this type of structure to a wider sector of industry and commerce.

The initial grouping might therefore be restated as 'plant or establishment', 'operating firm', 'independent owning firm', 'individual industry' and 'industrial sector'. At present, we have little to go on in terms of predictive models for the last two except in terms of 'planned economies' in which the role of the market is greatly reduced if not largely eliminated. As for the levels of 'operating firm' and 'independent owning firms', the study of business policy based on the extension of portfolio analysis to the range of products and even industries in which a firm is engaged provides a springboard.[3] What is needed, however, is further study of the strategies of those groups that are essentially industrial in origin in contrast to those that are financial, the latter including at least some of the so-called 'institutional investors', e.g. insurance companies.

The alternative classification, introduced in Chapter 1, was that based on the type of ownership, notably the 'private firm', 'the private corporate sector' and 'the publicly owned sector'.[4] While the boundaries of the publicly owned sector have become increasingly blurred, the broad classification still stands but the issues developing in each sector are such that further subdivision is appropriate in each case.

Taking the private firm sector the principal issue is upon what basis it is to survive under the combined pressures of inflation, price and profit control, taxation and the imposition and recovery of social costs whether for environmental reasons or administrative purposes. The independence of the private company, in particular, may be the key to the continued contribution of the traditional entrepreneur and the capitalist market economy of which he is the prototype. The onset of capital transfer tax and the threat of a wealth tax may mean that the basis of financing this sector will change, resulting in much greater dependence on borrowing, or direct investment in private companies by investment consortia such as the Industrial and Commercial Finance Corporation or by subsidiaries of merchant banks or other groups such as Small Business Finance, Venture Capital, and Development Capital.

Although the Bolton Committee was concerned at the supply of future small business proprietors, the extent to which they can come forward from new sources, such as men leaving much larger concerns to develop their own idea or to sub-contract an activity which such a firm might hive off, remains important. What is vital to such enterprises is the ability to raise cash, and here the problem lies in the difficulty of accumulating capital, itself the consequence of the taxation system and the resulting system of managerial remuneration.

As Chapter 3 shows, the private firm remains of substantial significance both nationally and regionally. Not only does it dominate some activities but the grouping of small firms in mature industrial centres is a major source of flexibility and new innovations. This is especially true in questions of regional development where the balance of local and national initiatives is concerned. The key questions for such firms appear to be first, their ability to find a role in the current economic structure; second, their management knowledge and skill, particularly if they seek to grow; third, their approach to risk and therefore their ability to attract funds; and lastly, the ways in which government can ease or harden the circumstances in which they have to work.

In Chapter 3 it was argued that the very growth of larger concerns and the extension of integration by administration may help to ensure the survival of a flexible small firm sector. But the ability of such firms to exploit that situation depends upon their attitude to change, their ability to probe opportunities and to learn from experience. Studies of attitudes of firms to change, notably those that identify firms as 'parochial'[5] or 'sleepers'[6] as opposed to 'progressive' or 'thrusters', do stress the dangers of small firms, especially in the second and subsequent generations.[7] It may well be, therefore, that the new context of financing may help to select more quickly those firms that have the best chances of survival rather than leaving things to a slow decline to ultimate insolvency.

Of importance to this more rapid selection is the range of advisory services available, their direct relevance to the special features of the smaller firm, and the confidence that can be developed between small firms and those whose task is to assist them on a sound economic base, not as a form of social security. To this end, government and public bodies need to look to their own specialised and dispersed activities which all too often present the small firm with a need to cater for the demands, in time, data and costs of a seemingly endless procession of bureaucrats, inspectors and advisers. It is certainly no argument for government to accept the plea of those bureaucrats who assert that small businesses have no place if they cannot provide the professional response to their demands upon such firms! The Bolton Committee argued very strongly on these lines and secured some improvements as well as the creation of the Small Firms Division of the Department of Trade and Industry.

Turning to the second group, the quoted public companies, while there is no general threat to their survival in quite the way there is to the private firm, there are three major pressures at work which change the context of policy-making. These are the changed relationship with financial institutions, the effect of governmental interventions and the move towards employee participation.

In Chapter 4 the relationship of the financial institutions is first explained in terms of their increasing dominance of equity shareholding and therefore their potential voting power in the affairs of companies. This poses problems for the institutions in two distinct respects. As already argued, there is the question of their perception of their own role and therefore of the nature of their strategies both as operating organisations and as investors. There is also the issue of their possible joint action both as investors through various consortia and as custodians of economic assets. To apply the custodial concepts of the 'corporate report'[8] to them is to raise a major question as to the future balance of power between government and the City.

To this there has to be added the wider assembly of banking and financial interests now that there has been such a sharp increase in the average gearing ratio. This is discussed in Chapter 4. The overall effect is to move the UK situation much closer to that of other members of EEC by strengthening the influence of the banks. Once again questions are posed for all concerned. Overall, is it prudent to rely so much less on equity capital? The Diamond Commission[9] has challenged this and pointed to the need to redress the balance. For the banking institutions it represents a new challenge given their traditional role as short-term bankers and for all concerned it resurrects questions as to the adequacy of the financial system that go back to the Macmillan Report of 1930.

If the pressures of the City have become so much greater what is the effect of their recent impact in the sixties and early seventies? The departure of Mr Jim Slater from Slater Walker in October 1975 provoked a spate of reappraisals of the take-over wave, the switch of resources that it released from industry into property and fringe banking, and the nature of the psychological impact that it had on a whole array of companies. With the end of this phase of external threat to secure better use of resources, albeit on a short-term basis, comes the start of a new phase of governmental intervention through the National Enterprise Board and related financial support of government to protect employment.

This represents the second main innovation affecting public companies. As already argued, it involves industry-level and national-level decision-taking, and may therefore have interesting effects on the two parts of the corporate or quoted company sector that we can now proceed to distinguish. What has been described hitherto is largely that of the small to medium public company, where stock market and institutional appraisal are very imminent in the minds of directors. But there is a smaller group of large public companies, including many of the so-called multinationals, which, for one of two reasons, enjoy greater independence. The first reason is that they may be so large as to be virtually impregnable to take-over and of such national importance that the provisions of the Industry Act would almost certainly be invoked to prevent them passing into foreign control. The second reason is, of course, that they are foreign firms operating on a world wide basis. They may straddle both categories as in the case of British Petroleum. For such companies the extent of their control of markets and output is such that they can expect to be invited to enter into planning agreements, and certainly their liability to be 'leaned upon' by government is already well established, not only here but even on a world-wide basis.

The dilemma that they face is, therefore, as to how free they may be to pursue a particular company strategy. This is especially the case if planning agreements were ever to become the rigid detailed agreements envisaged, for example, by the Association of Technical, Managerial and Supervisory Staffs (ASTMS).

For both groups of public companies, those that are very large and the general body, there is then a third pressure, that for employee participation. This poses important questions not only as to its constitutional form and the basis of representation, but the future policies and freedom to act of the management board. Conceivably it could see, if not the end of the take-over pressure, then a material check to its operation where the consent of those employed had to be sought. But in the context of the external economic pressures, not least those of the financial institutions and government, it poses the question of whether the real strategic decisions will continue to be taken only in the firm or be at least shared with, if not taken by, the financing bodies, as has already happened in West Germany.

The autonomy of the larger company is therefore likely to be reduced except to the extent that management is able to anticipate and influence the new sources of influence through its political skill, whether internally through consultation and participation, or externally through communication with financial institutions and government. Subject only to ability to sustain a firm financially — in terms of both solvency and profitability — this is a feasible task and one that might well leave top management with as much influence as before.

Indeed, the very complexity of the situation, of its learning and influence processes, and the key leadership and information-holding roles of top management are likely to enhance this. But as will be argued later in this chapter, this does call for a new approach by management to its dialogues with government, employees and the community.

Such a dialogue is nowhere more needed than in the third sector identified, that of the publicly owned enterprise. Here two distinct situations are emerging. First there are the so-called nationalised industries operated by public corporations established by specific statutes. Second there are the companies, whether controlled through NEB or not, in which the state has a shareholding, especially where this represents overall control. The problems in the first situation are mainly for government. As indicated in Chapter 7, there is a central issue of on what basis and to what extent they are to be treated as commercial undertakings and to what degree social objectives are to be pursued and at whose expense. But the issues are not confined to government. They concern both management and the consuming public as well. The extent to which public corporations should be used as instruments of social policy, e.g. price restraint, when they are also required to break-even may produce further distortions in the prices charged to industry and therefore in the costs that have then to be recovered elsewhere. Perhaps the most difficult questions are those presented where a nationalised concern has to operate on alternative criteria as in some aspects of public transport.

Finally there is the growing sector of companies in public ownership in which government has intervened as a banker of last resort. As indicated in Chapter 8 these present a new set of challenges to government, to the agencies set up by government, such as NEB and to those entrusted with the management of such diverse companies as British Leyland, Ferranti, Alfred Herbert and Rolls-Royce. The issues of strategic survival and adaptability have a special significance here. These in turn depend on the overall strategy of government.

10.2 A Re-negotiated Environment?

On past performance the most crucial could be the extent to which any continuity of public policy is attainable. Whatever the degree of agreement as to the nature of the problems facing the UK, it is clear that there is no such agreement as to the methods to be used to resolve them. Each main political party approaches the business scene with its own interpretation — or misunderstanding — of the working of the economic system and its own predilection as to how to resolve it, whether by more central planning or by less intervention. Added to this is the degree of understanding — or lack of it — on the part of the administrators of policy, and the dilemma of those who are advisers in terms of the balance between what appears to be justified by the facts available and what is politically acceptable to a particular government. Indeed, fears that this gap might be narrowed by experience in office have led to both the use of political advisers and the increasing pressure on governments through their party machines.

The price of the security and abruptness, let alone the confusion, of governmental intervention is high. A particular financing and pricing policy for the Post Office has had a traumatic effect on the market for telecommunications equipment. Successive interventions in particular industries have produced new forms of uncertainty.

But fundamental to the chance of any continuity is the approach to the central issue of national planning versus the use of the economy as currently organised. Thus the document submitted to the NEDC 'strategy' meeting in November 1975 appears to adopt an industry level basis of planning despite the fact that firms, which often straddle several industries and which may be very different in character, are the present units of decision-taking. The suggestion that issues be explored on an industrial sector basis may provide an indication of how the government may seek to apply its interventionist powers. But would such a form of planning (a) be compatible with the present ownership and therefore decision-taking structure of business, and (b) be likely to continue if there were a change of government?

The nature of the inflow and outflow of resources in the British economy leaves no option but to operate in the context of world trade, and therefore the vagaries of markets and governments of every hue. The complexity of the trading relationships of business firms with both firms and governments abroad, coupled to the basic necessity to export goods and services to pay for imports of food, raw materials and fuel would mean subordination to world economic trends even if the country were not a member of a wider economic community. Membership of the EEC therefore entails acceptance of the broad principles of what is often called a 'social market economy'. This means a degree of governmental intervention at both national and community levels alongside measures to achieve a free market in goods and services including factors of production. Such a market will be achieved in one sense by the nine present members in 1978 when all tariff and customs duties of a protectionist nature will have been abolished on industrial goods. Gradually another form of concealed protectionism, differing national specifications, standards and tendering restrictions are to be eliminated through 'harmonisation'. The overall effect is a centrally regulated market economy in which the terms of competition are more clearly defined and where an important element is international competition with freedom of movement of factors of production.

The starting point, as described in Chapter 1, is therefore a predominantly market economy having not only a substantial public sector as discussed in Chapters 7 and 8 but a wide range of interventions in the conduct of the private sector. These interventions range from legislation requiring minimum standards and practices in relations with employees and customers through increasingly detailed requirements as to the conduct of corporate bodies to measures to influence the direction and location of activities. For some forty years governments have sought to influence the choice of location of manufacturing industry and latterly of a wider range of forms of employment. At particular periods there have been controls on investment and on the use of particular materials in short supply.

But of most import is the range of controls and pressures that have resulted from attempts to combat inflation through some form of prices and incomes policy. It was in 1947 that the first White Paper on this theme was put out by government and in each major attempt at a pay pause, 1948-9, 1966-9 and 1973 onwards, there has been an increasing element of price control.

By the much closer prescription of the basis of such controls, notably in relation to what are termed 'reference levels' of profits and costs, not only is a very close control maintained but it has significant effects on the emphasis that companies may place on home versus export business, on investment here or abroad, and on the allocation of costs between customers where particular products or types of customer are protected against some price increase through cross-subsidy by other customers.

Similarly, the very attempt to define the basis of competition in the EEC or of product specifications in any country places a much greater emphasis on detailed knowledge of the rules of the game. In effect both nationally and internationally the closer specification of standards, safety requirements or rules of conduct, being largely on a national basis, presents a growing problem for businesses that seek to trade across frontiers. Those who are heavily concerned with exports are all too familiar with this problem. What is increasingly obvious to the smallest business is the extent to which this has been carried in domestic UK legislation in recent years.

The sheer weight and complexity of this is seen as being enough of an imposition on the costs of firms without the continuing vagaries of government policy, especially with the polarisation of attitudes on interventionism that characterises recent UK policies. The role of firms as tax collectors and other administrators of public policy is only one element; there is a cost in ensuring conformity to an ever-widening range of requirements and of being informed as to one's obligations and freedom of action in each. But the most common complaint concerns the continual change, often creating serious uncertainty on major issues of expenditure, as in the pensions controversy.

The argument in Chapters 8 and 9 has shown how the wider responsibilities of firms also exposes them to increasing pressure by governments as part of national economic and social policies. The emphasis in planning agreements on import-saving and export contribution is matched by the range of pressures not only to maintain high levels of employment but to protect the interests of minority groups, the disabled and the mentally handicapped as well as to end discrimination on the basis of race or sex.

The interplay of social objectives and economic survival has become a major issue as governments have used taxation and inflation to effect major redistributions not only of income but of savings and investment away from the business community into the public sector, notably the non-industrial sector. The rate of growth in non-industrial non-marketable activities has been especially marked in recent years.[10] There is consequently a need for both a review of priorities at national level and a new basis of continuing dialogue between government and business in view of their interdependence.

While the review of priorities is ultimately a government responsibility after consultation with the CBI and the TUC through such agencies as the National Economic Development Council, the need for a better level of communication exists not only at national but at regional levels. Already there are a number of regional development bodies notably those in Scotland, the North East and Wales, often having a long record of development activity. To these are now added the two special government-financed Development Agencies for Scotland and Wales. Since 1965 there have been Regional Economic Planning Councils for the main English economic planning regions. These have provided a means of consultation and the initiation of policy proposals related to the priorities of their regions. But the key question of economic policy remains highly centralised and, so far, there is no evidence that proposals on devolution will change this. Yet the dialogue is needed at both national and regional levels.

Within the UK the need for fuller consultation at all levels reflects the political and industrial power of organised groups, notably the trades unions. The emergence of new forms of industrial action such as the 'sit-in' has been symptomatic of the changed balance of power. The stress on group action places both independent proprietors and the self-employed in a real difficulty which is shared by most managers in private industry and commerce. Their whole ethic is individualist yet they find themselves 'squeezed' by particular organised groups, not only the large powerful trades unions but small groups of key workers able to shut down an industry or service at a critical point. Furthermore, this ability to exercise power is not confined to manual workers; a shut-down in computer operation could paralyse managerial and governmental systems.

The outcome is a need for a reappraisal of the many ways in a pluralistic society that are open to exercise influence and to put the point of view of the modern successors of the entrepreneur of earlier economic theory, be he the proprietor, manager, professional man or public servant. But the interaction is needed not only at national, regional and local levels but also at international level, notably within the European Community.

What is needed is a new test of fit for our institutions in the government of business. Not how can they be so centralised that huge enterprises are run as if they were still small firms, but how can the diverse groups that still make up the mass of business enterprises be made more responsible and respon-sive, and bureaucratic centralism, that perennial problem of Eastern European economies, be kept in check.

That test of fit is their strategic capability. How wide-ranging is their awareness of the forces at work in the environment within which they work? How do they learn about new developments and how far ahead are they able to even attempt to anticipate forces, economic, political, technical or social that could affect both their ability to do what they do now and the opportunities open to them? How adaptable internally are they in terms of structure, systems and above all the attitudes they encourage among the members of the enterprise? How well do they relate to their communities and their aspirations? How effective are they not just at identifying good prospects but abandoning poor ones?

Business is not just administration of the present but the anticipation and exploration of the future. This must be the basis of its government.

Notes and references

1   Chapter 1, section 1.1.
2   P. Parker, 'A council for industry', *BIM Management Abstracts,* Autumn 1975 Viscount Watkinson, *Blueprint for Industrial Survival,* Allen & Unwin 1976.
3   I. Ansoff, *Corporate Strategy,* Penguin 1968.
4   Chapter 1, section 2.1.
5   C. F. Carter and B. R. Williams, *Industry and Technical Progress,* Oxford University Press 1956.
6   PEP, *Attitudes in British Industry,* Penguin 1964.
7   J. Boswell, *The Rise and Decline of Small Firms,* Allen & Unwin 1972.
8   *The Corporate Report,* Institute of Chartered Accountants in England and Wales 1975.
9   Royal Commission on the Distribution of Income & Wealth, *Report No. 2,* Cmd 6172, HMSO 1975.
10 R. Bacon and W. Eltis, 'What's wrong with Britain?', *Sunday Times,* 2 Nov. 1975.

Study Questions

1   What government policies would be most conducive to the revival and continued development of the private sector?
2   Given that some form of corporate state has emerged with government interventions on so large a scale how can it be made more effective?
3   Compare and contrast the possible future roles of the National Enterprise Board and the main institutional investors.

RECOMMENDATIONS FOR FURTHER READING

Chapter 1
D. Channon, *The Strategy and Structure of British Industry,* Macmillan 1973.
J. Child, *The Business Enterprise in Modern Industrial Society,* Collier Macmillan 1969.
P. J. Devine, R. M. Jones, N. Lee and W. J. Tyson, *Introduction to Industrial Economics,* Allen & Unwin 1974.
K. George, *Industrial Organisation,* Allen & Unwin 1971.
M. Gilbert (ed.), *The Modern Business Enterprise,* Penguin 1972
H. Liebenstein, *Economic Theory and Organisational Analysis* Harper 1965.
D. Needham, *Economic Analysis and Industrial Structure,* Holt, Reinhart & Winston 1969.
E. Penrose, *Theory of the Growth of the Firm,* Basil Blackwell, 1959.

Chapter 2
P. Sargant Florence, *The Economics and Sociology of Industry,* Watts 1964.
A. Knight, *Private Enterprise and Public Intervention,* Allen & Unwin 1974.
J. M. Livingstone, *The British Economy in Theory and Practice,* Macmillan 1974.

Chapter 3
J. Boswell, *The Rise and Decline of Small Firms,* Allen & Unwin 1972.
Committee of Inquiry into Small Firms (Bolton Committee), Report and Research Reports, HMSO.
P. Clarke, *Small Businesses: How They Succeed and Survive,* David & Charles 1972.
Royal Commission on the Distribution of Income and Wealth, Report No. 2 and Research Report No. 1 (Meeks and Whittington), HMSO 1975-6.

Chapter 4
P. Sargant Florence, *Economics and Sociology of Industry,* and *Logic of British and American Industry,* Routledge & Kegan Paul 1952.
L. C. B. Gower, *The Principles of Modern Company Law,* Stevens 1969.

Chapter 5
D. Kuehn, *Takeovers and the Theory of the Firm,* Macmillan 1975.
R. Marris and A. Wood, *The Corporate Economy,* Macmillan 1971.
D. Newbould, *Management and Merger Activity,* Guthstead 1970.
A. Singh, *Takeovers,* Department of Applied Economics, University of Cambridge, Monograph 19, 1971.
A. Singh and G. Whittington, *Growth Profitability and Valuation,* Department of Applied Economics, University of Cambridge, Occasional Paper No. 7, 1968.

Chapter 6
D. Channon, *Strategy and Structure of British Industry,* Macmillan 1973.
J. Jewkes, D. Sawyer and R. Stillerman, *The Sources of Invention,* Macmillan 1958.
J. M. Livingstone, *The International Enterprise,* Associated Business Programmes 1975.

Chapter 7
A. Nove, *Efficiency Criteria for Nationalised Industries,* Allen & Unwin 1973.
A. Thomson and L. C. Hunter, *The Nationalised Transport Industries,* Heinemann 1973.
G. Reid, K. Allen and D. Harris, *The Nationalised Fuel Industries,* Macmillan 1974.

Chapter 8
N. Abraham, *Big Business and Government: The New Disorder,* Macmillan 1974.
S. Young with A. Lowe, *Intervention in the Mixed Economy,* Croom Helm 1974.

Chapter 9
J. Child, *The Business Enterprise in Modern Industrial Society,* Collier Macmillan 1969.
J. Kelly, *Is Scientific Management Possible?* Faber & Faber 1968.
W. B. D. Brown, *Exploration in Management,* Heinemann.

INDEX